Stumbling Toward Truth

Stumbling Toward Truth

Anthropologists at Work

Philip R. DeVita

State University of New York at Plattsburgh

WAVELAND
PRESS, INC.
Prospect Heights, Illinois

For information about this book, contact:
Waveland Press, Inc.
P.O. Box 400
Prospect Heights, Illinois 60070
(847) 634-0081
www.waveland.com

 Contents

How many people know what cultural anthropologists really do? Don't most people equate anthropology with those things found in museums or on "digs"? An anthropologist is asked to write a travel article about his years of work in Vanuatu and, unlike the experiences of some others (especially Ali Pomponio, Mac Marshall, and the Rodmans), his fieldwork has been essentially a pleasant interlude in a South Seas paradise.

I. UNEXPECTED WELCOMES TO OTHER WORLDS

Professor Raybeck's initial contact in his first field research in Malaysia is with the village half-wit. This is but one of the many problems encountered in his extremely insightful portrayal of ethnographic research—accidental lessons, which ultimately and admittedly transformed the researcher into a trusted and more sensitive and perceptive observer of people who were to become his friends.

From the very beginning, Professor Gmelch received overt indicators that he was not welcome by either the Tlingit Indians or the white salmon fishermen in Alaska. Initially they thought him to be an IRS investigator. Two significant events turned his reluctant hosts' view of him as an "eastern egghead" into that of an acceptable researcher. That he had once played professional baseball for the Detroit Tigers was unexpectedly to his advantage.

A young anthropologist is sent to a remote island in Polynesia and, before-hand, establishes a set of rules that he intends to follow to successfully com-plete his first fieldwork. By total accident, while in transit to the island field site, he meets a maintenance worker at a resort who turns out to be the highest ranking member of the society he intends to study. The pre-established rules go by the wayside and the education of the ethnographer begins.

"If you can survive a stint in Nigeria, you can survive anywhere." Professor Eames survived but not without frustrating, uncommon, and unexpected tribu-lations in a bureaucratic system filled with cumbersome mysteries. These mys-teries are succinctly analyzed, not that it made her two and a half years of Nigerian research any easier.

In his welcome to the field, Mac Marshall encounters two unexpected situa-tions of violence. In the second instance he becomes personally involved in a local dispute that, once reconciled, will lead to important ethnographic studies that become the primary focus of his professional career.

Fieldwork entails personal involvement with the people whom we are trying to understand. What happens when the ethnographer is admittedly shy? This eth-nographer finds, by accident, that she has gained acceptance in the Microne-sian community she is studying.

After making precise arrangements for preliminary summer research among a group of Acadien speaking lobsterfolk in Atlantic Canada, Professor DeVita is greeted with the news that he is not welcome on the island. As we've discov-ered from Dr. Gmelch's essay, nonacademic attributes contribute to acceptance as a fieldworker. However, during his five years of intermittent research, Dr. DeVita's perceived identity was hardly that of a professional anthropologist.

NINE
Of Teamwork, Faith, and Trust in Western Sumatra   74
Carol J. Colfer

Gaining trust and acceptance can too often be tedious and filled with complex cultural maneuvering. The intentions of the ethnographer are interpreted with suspicions based upon past experiences with outsiders. And, we are generally unknown outsiders. In this instance, Professor Colfer, in the face of cross-cultural complexities, gained acceptance through a simple, kind act that provided the unending trust desired.

TEN
Some Consequences of a Fieldworker's Gender for Cross-cultural Research   84
Susan Dwyer-Shick

How does a female gain entry into the rigidly male dominated sector of a sexually segregated Turkish society? And, how did Professor Dwyer-Shick handle truths about herself when honest responses would not satisfy the gender expectations of her Turkish female friends?

ELEVEN
Fieldwork That Failed   95
Linda L. Kent

On two different occasions, Professor Kent's fieldwork into the world of gypsies failed. In the first attempt, she couldn't even find members of her intended research population—the "elusive laughing vagabonds" of New Orleans. Because of an innocent mistake and the barriers of her own personal identity, her second efforts also were unsuccessful. Yet, in spite of failure, significant lessons were learned.

II. OTHER WORLDS, OTHER CULTURAL LOGICS AND REALITIES

TWELVE
Not a Real Fish: The Ethnographer as Inside Outsider   107
Roger M. Keesing

How much, if ever, do we completely understand the beliefs and values of the Others? How do our own unquestioned values compare? The late Dr. Keesing learned a lesson from his Kwaio hosts in the Solomon Islands that provides a lesson for all ethnography. It strikes to the heart of the ethnographic enterprise: we will always be outsiders who have learned something of what it is to be an insider.

THIRTEEN

The Abelam people of Papua New Guinea teach the young anthropologist much about themselves. But, especially in this case, Professor Scaglion learns so much more about himself. Expecting to participate in men's communal hunting activities, he is made to work alongside the women. And, in attempting to explain physical phenomena to his hosts, he learns that their traditional folk explanations might satisfactorily serve as logical explanations.

FOURTEEN

Participating in a treacherous communal duck hunt with the Alaskan Yupik, Professor Morrow learns that the apparent lack of leadership provides significant indicators for other Inuit cultural patterns, especially, in this case, for better understanding the logic of performance in the classroom.

FIFTEEN

What does the anthropologist do when a major earthquake hits a small island in New Guinea? In a letter to friends informing them that she is well, we get a vivid description of fieldwork in time of physical disaster, community sorrow, and personal suffering.

SIXTEEN

Was it totally by accident that a female anthropologist was thrust into the job of a male to record and preserve the profound ancient traditions and ritual and religious knowledge of the Mescalero Apaches? Professor Farrer's experiences appear to be only accidents, but they can be viewed from a different standpoint in understanding the Apache's constructs and universal implications of centering.

SEVENTEEN

Like all scientists, we search for facts, for truths, for the confirming pieces by which we can complete the puzzle. Not heeding the repeated warnings by his Native American friends, Professor Clifton persisted in searching for an old, supposedly sacred Potowatomi drum in the possession of an aged shaman. What the researcher experienced defies explanation based upon Western scientific principles.

EIGHTEEN
A Very Bad Disease of the Arms   166
Michael Kearney

Professor Kearney discovered that the belief system of his research population in southern Mexico was saturated with harmful forces perpetrated by witches able to use black magic to harm or kill. In helping to cure one acknowledged witch, he was advised to leave the field to escape the wrath of a competing witch. He refused the advice and became victim to an event that defies rational explanation.

NINETEEN
Too Many Bananas, Not Enough Pineapples, and No Watermelons at All   177
David Counts

What do we do when we know that someone is taking advantage of us? A more complex question would be, what *can* we do when, as guests conducting field-work in a remote Melanesian village, we discover that we are being taken advantage of? Can we be taught to prepare ourselves for such situations or do we have to devise novel and uncertain strategies in the course of conducting our fieldwork?

TWENTY
Lessons in Introductory Anthropology from the Bakairi Indians   184
Debra S. Picchi

Learning the indigenous language makes you human in the eyes of the people studied. As Professor Picchi discovered, involvement in the everyday humanity of the people we study may be more meaningful than the data we collect in our professional capacity.

TWENTY-ONE
Arranging a Marriage in India   196
Serena Nanda

During her first visit to India, Professor Nanda discovered the common practices of arranged marriages to be both objectionable and oppressive. The extensive and complex cultural contrasts became evident as the researcher soon learned that her own expectations in matchmaking were unacceptable in India. Dr. Nanda did eventually find a wife for her close friend's son, but not until she learned how to search in other ways.

TWENTY-TWO
'Pigs of the Forest' and Other Unwritten Papers   205
Terence E. Hays

The anthropologist accidentally discovers something about sorcery and curing in the New Guinea Highlands that has never been documented by an outsider. Furthermore, this discovery, if proven true, has anthropological implications which will certainly shake the academic world. However, upon further investigation, we're made to question the absolute or shared quality of cultural beliefs.

TWENTY-THREE
Lesson from the Field: Gullibility and the Hazards of Money Lending   213
Cindy Hull

Despite explicit warnings beforehand, Professor Hull becomes innocently involved in money lending during her fieldwork in a Yucatan village. She and her husband soon learn that they are being grossly taken advantage of and find a way to extricate themselves from a difficult situation. How does one sever conflicting interpersonal ties in the fieldwork setting and, in the end, what important lessons are learned?

TWENTY-FOUR
To Die on Ambae: On the Possibility of Doing Fieldwork Forever   220
William L. Rodman and Margaret C. Rodman

Most often, the anthropologist is adopted into a society, as was the case with this husband and wife team. One becomes a son, or a daughter, and is treated as such by the host parent. What happens when, in a life-threatening situation, the children reject the advice of the father and, in this instance, seek the care and treatment of Western "scientific" medicine instead of trusting local cures and sorcery?

TWENTY-FIVE
A Letter from the Field   240
Marty Zelenietz

This anthropologist went to Melanesia to study sorcery but had little luck and began to suspect that sorcery had either disappeared or that the villagers simply refused to talk about it. But an accusation of sorcery surfaces and not only does the ethnographer learn of sorcery, but a renowned sorcerer from a different village offers to teach him the techniques of sorcery. What does one do, especially when the host villagers don't want one with special powers living among them?

TWENTY-SIX
Turning Tears into Nothing   248
Miles Richardson

Who has not traveled to witness abject poverty on many continents? And who has not felt the sense of sadness and injustice that still pervades this world? Professor Richardson describes a situation in Mexico City, a situation wherein a young teenage girl will never know the joys of youth. Most upsetting is the question that we all must face: "What can we really do about it that will make a difference?"

TWENTY-SEVEN
"Did You?"   253
Ward H. Goodenough

Fieldwork often has many inconveniences, especially on remote Pacific islands. However, these may be inconveniences only to us and not to the residents. There is much that we take for granted and, even in the most personal of matters, we may have trouble adjusting to the habits of our hosts. Our hosts, however, often find it easier to accommodate the personal necessities of the ethnographer.

TWENTY-EIGHT
Munju   257
Trecie Melnick

A Peace Corps volunteer finds a caring sense of family and sanctuary from racism with a black Muslim family in Central Africa. Trecie Melnick, a Jewish girl from Texas, heartwarmingly shares her experiences that may serve as a metaphor for a more tolerate, kind, and understanding world.

TWENTY-NINE
**The Inseparability of Reason and Emotion in the Anthropological Perspective:
Perceptions upon Leaving "The Field."**   264
Kris Heggenhougen

"What is fieldwork? Why do it?" These are queries that Professor Heggenhougen thoroughly addresses after spending a year among a mountain people of Guatemala. Through profoundly personal insight, the scholar comes to grips with the realization that fieldwork "is all about being touched by a different reality."

 Preface

> One of my professors, when asked what to do in the field,
> responded that I should go find myself. If this was to be the
> goal, pity the poor community of my choice.
>
> George N. Appell (1989:48)

In August of 1983, Ed Cook and I sat talking on a porch overlooking
Lake Champlain. There I proposed the idea for a collection of articles
by Pacific anthropologists, which was originally to be edited by both
of us. For the remaining three days of his visit we retreated to my
farmhouse in the Adirondack Mountains where we formulated strategies and developed scenarios for the completion of what we believed
was to be a unique set of essays by anthropologists—essays that
focused on unexpected encounters in Oceanic fieldwork written in a
style comprehensible to a general audience and, hopefully, of some
interest to the specialist.

I had developed the idea for a single Oceanic volume. Ed enthusiastically argued that we develop two volumes, one on the Pacific
Islands and a second to focus on ethnographic problems throughout
the world. That was vintage Ed Cook. For him, there was always something reachable beyond what was readily imagined. He was always the
kid in the intellectual candy shop who wouldn't settle for the jelly
beans. He'd set his sights on the jars beyond ordinary vision . . . those
undiscovered, extraordinary goodies on the topmost shelves. Both
volumes, dedicated to the memory of my friend, were eventually published: *The Humbled Anthropologist: Tales from the Pacific* in 1990,
and two years later, *The Naked Anthropologist: Tales from Around the
World*. This volume, an edited collection of articles from both of the
original collections, is also dedicated in Ed's memory.

The original idea for the first volume germinated from my fourteen years of friendship with Ed Cook. Four important issues
appeared to coalesce during Ed's last visit—a pilgrimage to visit old
friends, which Ivan Brady and I suspected was, more honestly, Ed's
farewell journey. First, Ed's great success in the classroom, especially
at the undergraduate level, was due to his genuine concern for his
students as participants in the anthropological experience. As a grad-

uate student with minimal undergraduate training in anthropology, I sat in on many of his undergraduate classes. Whether teaching an introductory cultural course, a course on the Pacific, on kinship, or on language and culture, he had a rare, engaging habit of emphasizing a critical intellectual issue by referring to a particular personal event wherein he, a most rigorous and dedicated social scientist, had either misunderstood the situation or had screwed up in his fieldwork. Unknowingly, I stole this practice from him and employed similar practices in my own teaching. I have found this method of accenting an issue by displaying oneself with "egg on one's face" to be most successful—not as a strategy for students' amusement, but as a means of providing a personalized account to complement, and often confound, a particular anthropological point.

Second, from attending national anthropological meetings for the primary purpose of spending time with Ed, I discovered another fact. During our extended social hours many of *his* friends, colleagues, and former students would join us, and I listened to humorous tales of how they had screwed up in their fieldwork. However, as with Ed's classroom stories, these anthropologists were telling more than humorous stories. There were, in most cases, important lessons embedded in the content of their experiences. If one listened closely and paid attention to not only what was said, but what was left unsaid, there were lessons to be learned—lessons about the anthropologist, about the people being studied, and about the human experience in a cross-cultural context. I stole these stories also and, where applicable, used them with success in my lectures.

Third, especially in teaching the introductory course in cultural anthropology, I decided not to make the mistake that I'd found evident during my undergraduate training in engineering, mathematics, and philosophy. Whether valid or not, I remain convinced that the problem that many educators have is with their approaches to the teaching of the particular subjects in their particular disciplines. I'd publicly argued in guest lectures, especially to students and professors of mathematics and computer science, that they might seriously reconsider their pedagogical approaches to the general classroom audience. If they are, as seems the case, teaching to train students to become mathematicians or computer scientists—to become *like them*—they might be severely missing the boat. A more practical and successful approach might be to teach students—who, at the undergraduate level, are more generally enrolled in these classes simply to satisfy some college-wide requirement—"what" mathematics or philosophy can inform about such issues as problem solving, decision making, or universal social issues, and how the subject matter might further contribute to the excitement of logical thinking and a sensitivity to the vast complexities of the human situation.

Whether or not this approach has been as successful as I intended, it was how I approached my lower-division classes. I did not teach to convert students to the discipline of anthropology. I made every deliberate effort to introduce the introductory audience to "what" anthropology can teach us about others and ourselves—to help us to better understand the complex nature of the human condition, ours and others', especially in this rapidly shrinking world. In the introductory course, the less traditional, more personal, literate and humanistic writings of Bohannan (1966), Chagnon (1983), Hayano (1990), Lee (1969), Turnbull (1962), Ward (1989), and a few others have measurably tendered more productive seeds to the initiates to this discipline. These writings had been the honey that made the vinegar more palatable, the humanistic interlude that breathed life into the otherwise sterile, theoretical, and methodological concepts in anthropology. Where, in anthropology beyond the classroom, do our students discover the social scientist to be a true humanist—*someone* so much more than a reference in a text or an author in a collection of readings?

The fourth feature behind the form and substance of these projects has a direct relationship to the enterprise of ethnographic fieldwork. I had spent approximately fifteen years living outside of the United States—not as an anthropologist, but in various capacities on sailing and motor vessels. I'd prefer to forget many of the personally embarrassing encounters in foreign places but cannot. Too many times, especially when younger, I discovered myself screwing up on someone else's turf—naively doing something that I believed proper in my own country, but later learning that the behavior was quite inappropriate in my hosts' arena. As the years passed and as I grew (hopefully) wiser, I developed a strategy whenever finding myself in new places: Keep my big mouth shut and drink a lot of water! (Translation: be quiet, look, listen, and learn.)

I had to learn to not impose my own behavioral rules and expectations on others. I had to learn *how to learn* about others instead of innocently—but inconsiderately—operating within a set of preconceptions based on my own Western value orientations. I was, after all, a guest in someone else's home!

Once I began to open my eyes and ears, to develop a sensitivity to the contrasting worlds of my new friends in South American jungles or on South Pacific islands, I, in turn, began to learn other important truths. From all the traveling, from these wondrous experiences, I was indeed learning about others but, more important, I was also learning about myself, about my own society's values, and about my place in the world of different realities.

The focus of the two original volumes dedicated to Ed Cook is not then on the significant "others" that are so important to the ethnographic enterprise. The focus is foremost on ourselves as anthropologists and the lessons we've learned in living with and trying to understand others.

The projects did not turn out entirely as Ed and I had envisioned. First of all, Ed died five months after we began the projects. In working to complete the memorial to a very special friend, I discovered that many of his colleagues did not wish to commit to writing those precious stories they had shared in a private forum. Second, in the seven years that it took to complete both collections, I'd discovered that, unlike Ed in his fieldwork and I in my maritime adventures, most anthropologists haven't really screwed up as much as we thought, or else they've chosen not to write about their misadventures.

However, as will become evident from the readings in this collection, we learn that much of what anthropologists learned about themselves and others was totally unanticipated. These lessons, none for which their academic training had prepared them, remain, perhaps, the most memorable and critical lessons of fieldwork. These are lessons about *us*, which we learned from *them*.

Originally, the longer I labored with the tasks of editing these articles, the more manifest became the sense of underlying structures. These were not stories about screwing up in the field. These were poignant tales of human experiences where, in most instances, the ethnographic stranger stumbled into a situation for which he or she had not been trained or was completely unprepared. Indeed, although we have been rigorously trained in structured ethnographic method, we so often do stumble upon cultural truths that arrive serendipitously, upon unexpected realities discovered accidentally, and upon a more lucid understanding of the values of the cultural "other." And in the experience, important lessons are learned: lessons about the contact culture, about the ethnographer, about the ethnographic process. Moreover, in nearly all cases, there are significant contrastive lessons learned about issues of cross-cultural humanity and humaneness, derived more often than not from accidental discovery than from the deliberate practice of social science. All of this is essentially part of the work of the cultural anthropologist.

It has been argued that American cultural anthropology, at least, lacks the rigorously defined methodological principles that are both traditionally and contemporarily part of archaeology, linguistics, and physical anthropology. We truly may be practitioners of a subdiscipline still in search of a methodology. These collections of fieldwork experiences represent new exercises in learning, in the epistemology of fieldwork. These exercises, to reflect on Gregory Bateson's (1942) concepts of deutero-learning, apply to the ethnographic processes. We may have to learn how to learn about how we learn as cultural anthropologists. Richard Feynman, in discussing his own discipline, physics, advises.

> In summary, the idea is to try to give *all* of the information to
> help others to judge the value of your contributions; not just

the information that leads to judgment in one particular direction or another. . . . But this long history of learning how not to fool ourselves—of having utter scientific integrity—is, I'm sorry to say, something that we haven't specifically included in any particular course that I know of. We just hope you've caught on by osmosis.

The first principle is that you must not fool yourself—and you are the easiest person to fool. So you have to be careful about that. You just have to be honest in a conventional way after that. (1985:312–313)

The late Nobel scientist could have been talking directly to the form and substance of these ethnographic reflections:

I would like to add something that's not essential to the science, but something I kind of believe, which is that you should not fool the laymen when you're talking as a scientist. . . . If you've made up your mind to test a theory, or you want to explain some idea, you should always decide to publish it, whichever way it comes out. If we only publish results of a certain kind, we can make the argument look good. We must publish *both* kinds of results. (1985:314)

There were many people responsible for the completion of the two earlier volumes dedicated to the memory of Edwin Aubrey Cook. The early, unwavering enthusiasm of Mac Marshall, Jim Watson, and Dorothy and David Counts was especially instrumental at a time when I was ready to scrap the projects in favor of a more traditional collection of ethnographic readings. Sue Pflanz Cook, a friend since graduate school, remained close to me at the annual meetings of the Association for Social Anthropology in Oceania, knowing full well, especially without Ed, that I was not comfortable at public gatherings. Jim Clifton's earliest commitment, support, and editorial efforts were cornerstones on which all of us were able to build. Jim Funaro, Alice Pomponio, and Miles Richardson must be thanked for their positive reviews of the original manuscripts. James Armstrong and Richard Robbins were continually and willingly supportive during the years in the development of the original volumes. For the latest reviews and insightful advice on this combined project, I again owe thanks to George Gmelch.

Perhaps more than anyone, Peg Adams must be thanked for her willingness to gamble on such nontraditional projects. Now, Tom Curtin, a respected friend for many years, is gambling. And, most important, I'd like to thank each of the anthropologists, including those not in this volume, for their patience and willingness to share their personal experiences in ethnographic fieldwork.

Philip R. DeVita
Naples, Florida

REFERENCES

APPELL, GEORGE N.

1989   British- vs American-Trained Ethnographers. Anthropology Newsletter. American Anthropological Association 30(9):48.

BATESON, GREGORY

1942   Social Planning and the Concept of "Deutero-learning." Conference on Science, Philosophy and Religion, Second Symposium. New York: Harper & Row.

BOHANNAN, LAURA

1966   Shakespeare in the Bush. Natural History 75(7):28–33.

CHAGNON, NAPOLEON A.

1983   Yanomamo: The Fierce People. New York: Holt, Rinehart, & Winston.

DEVITA, PHILIP R., ED.

1990   The Humbled Anthropologist: Tales from the Pacific. Belmont, CA: Wadsworth.

FEYNMAN, RICHARD P.

1985   "Surely You're Joking, Mr. Feynman!" Adventures of a Curious Character. New York: Norton.

HAYANO, DAVID M.

1990   Road Through the Rain Forest: Living Anthropology in Highland Papua New Guinea. Prospect Heights, IL: Waveland Press.

LEE, RICHARD BORSHAY

1969   Eating Christmas in the Kalahari. Natural History 78(10):14–27.

TURNBULL, COLIN

1962   The Forest People. New York: American Museum of Natural History.

WARD, MARTHA C.

1989   Nest in the Wind: Adventures in Anthropology on a Tropical Island. Prospect Heights, IL: Waveland Press.

🐚 An Anthropologist as Travel Writer

ROBERT TONKINSON

Some years ago, a friend who is a professional travel writer invited me to attempt something different from my accustomed ethnographic reporting by writing an article about the lighter side of doing fieldwork in Vanuatu. He thought that if I could put to paper some of my anecdotes about the ups and downs of immersion in a foreign culture, it would be of interest to a more general audience—*general* in this case referring to those airplane passengers who read in-flight magazines. I accepted the challenge and wrote the story I will present here. It remains substantially as written, but with some minor updating.

The story could be called ethnography in only the very broadest sense, being less a portrait of a society than a pen portrait of aspects of what it is like to conduct fieldwork in a small island in the South Pacific. The concentration is on the lighter side of doing ethnography, but there is also serious intent: acquainting the reader with what anthropology is and is not, and alluding to some of the ethical and political aspects of doing field research in a small-scale society. There is also an important parallel with the mission of anthropology in general—that is, the attempt to render our understandings about the human "other" accessible to Western society (cf. Burridge 1973).

The story was entitled "At Work in the Isles of Coral and Ash" (Tonkinson 1979). I will follow it with my thoughts on what was and was not being communicated in this attempt to address a nonanthropological audience.

"So you're an anthropologist. Oh yes, bones and stones. . . . Where do you dig?"

"Nowhere! I leave that to the archaeologists. I'm a cultural anthropologist," I reply, ready to explain further in case my questioner thinks this means I read Hegel, speak nine languages, and did a postdoctorate at the Sorbonne.

"Oh yes. You're the crazies who go and live with the natives in exotic spots at the end of the earth—escapees from the rat race. So where's your hideout?"

An immediate problem arises: whether or not to disabuse my questioner of the notion that anthropology equals the study of "the natives" in
far-off places, by pointing out the fact that most students today are doing
fieldwork in their own countries—and then risk a debate over the difference between anthropology and sociology—or press on regardless, eager
to talk about "my people." So I opt for the latter, hoping to get back to the
bigger issue of the scope of anthropology later in the conversation.

"I work in Vanuatu," I reply, and then quickly add, "Which is between
Fiji and Australia," since most people don't know where this ruggedly
scenic string of tropical islands hides in the vastness of the Western Pacific.
They may have read something about it during the turbulence surrounding the final move toward independence, which was achieved in 1980, but
more often than not Vanuatu is confused with New Caledonia, where
serious problems remain between the colonizers and the now-
outnumbered indigenous Melanesians, or "Kanaks."

The combination "anthropologist–South Pacific" is a surefire trigger
that evokes for many a romantic vision of a long and languorous idyll
beneath waving palms on remote golden sands, the epitome of getting
away from it all. There is truth in this vision, but it ignores certain realities.
No one who abandons the comforting familiarity of his or her own culture
for a year or two's immersion in a very different one does so without some
traumas of adjustment. So when the inevitable question comes—"What's it
like working there?"—my usual response mirrors the ups and downs that
virtually all anthropologists experience in the field: "Mostly I really love it,
but never every day, and there are times when I wonder what the hell I'm
doing there."

Given half a chance, I'll then regale my listener with the pros and cons
of fieldwork. I sometimes feel like the Ancient Mariner with the wedding
guest, except that my anecdotes generally favor the lighter side of research. For the most part I sidestep the weighty moral and ethical aspects
of fieldwork with which anthropologists, as very close-range voyeurs of the
lives of other peoples, must contend. In our dominant self-image we
champion respect for cultural difference and rigorously oppose any forms
of racism and the oppression of cultural minorities, particularly the more
powerless, among whom many of us have chosen to work. But anthropologists, the askers of a million questions, have been condemned in
some countries as being CIA agents. (Who else would be so nosy?) In
others, the close identification of anthropology with the colonial period
has rendered its practitioners suspect. And in some cases, the mistaken
belief that we study only "primitive" peoples leads to rejection, in favor of
those who designate their work "sociological."

I began research in Vanuatu in 1966, when colonialism was still in full
swing, and the country, then called New Hebrides, was in the thrall of a
unique (and seriously flawed) experiment in joint governance, the Anglo-
French Condominium. Typically, the necessary permission to actually

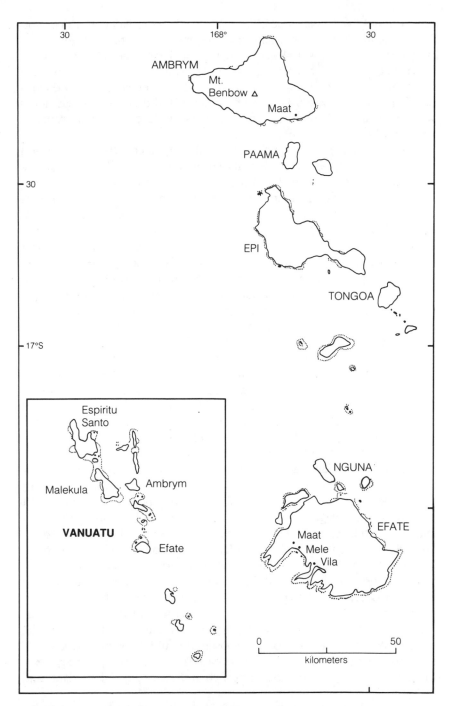

Ambrym, Epi, and Efate

carry out fieldwork had to be obtained from the colonial authorities, who had not consulted the villagers prior to my arrival—the villagers' concurrence was taken as a given, though it was left to me to carry out the actual negotiations. There were no problems, as it turned out, and since that time there have been no difficulties with my return and with continued fieldwork. My enthusiasm for the islands and their people has never weakened, and after more than twenty years the lure of Vanuatu remains undiminished.

The pace of change has quickened remarkably since independence, and greatly improved communications have opened up virtually all the islands to much greater contact with the outside world and with Western cultural influences generally. Tourism has become an important industry, but as yet not many visitors have managed to get to the southeast corner of Ambrym Island, where I do most of my fieldwork while in Vanuatu. Ambrym, in shape like a three-cornered hat, is centrally located about midway between the capital of Vila on Efate Island, and the second town, Santo, an Espirito Santo Island to the north. It measures about eighteen miles by twenty-seven and is dominated by two volcanic cones and a surrounding ash plain. The wide, flat two-thousand-foot-high plain gives Ambrym a cut-off look as one approaches it by sea. It is usually covered with a mantle of smoke and clouds that hides the pair of four-thousand-foot cones much of the time. The ash plain neatly divides the island into three habitation zones, each a distinct culture area with its own language. The volcanoes groan and rumble and glow pink some nights, but most of the time they behave. Major eruptions of lava are usually several decades apart, with periodic belches of ash emitted between times just to let the people know that the island's volcanic heart is slumbering, not dead.

About sixteen hundred people live in the southeastern part of the island, in fifteen villages and a number of small hamlets. Their lands are far from the two volcanoes, so they have little to fear from lava flows. The last one in the southeast was in 1888, spewing from a newly opened crater; it engulfed nine villages, but in leisurely fashion and apparently without fatalities. Ash-falls, however, have caused problems. The worst were in 1950–51 and resulted in the complete evacuation of the area. For ten months the southeast was blanketed with up to thirty-five feet of ash. It scorched the vegetation naked, fell as mud when mixed with rain, turned day into night, and lobbed grapefruit-sized chunks among the people from time to time. Life became quite uncomfortable and food was in short supply, but no one was killed and today people remember the funny side, such as confused chickens going to roost in the middle of the day. After the falls abated, the evacuees, unhappy at having been moved by the government to a nearby island, soon returned home to dig out, replant, and rebuild.

The people of one of the villages, Maat, did not go home. They remained on Efate Island in a new settlement they had built. Fifteen years later I went to live with them with the aim of attempting to gauge the effects of their resettlement, as part of a large Pacific Relocation Project being directed by Professor Homer Barnett out of the University of Oregon. So my initial field research was carried out in the new Maat Village, not far from the picturesque port and capital city of Vila. When I first visited Maat I had not yet mastered the country's lingua franca, Bislama, and though most villagers spoke some English, I had communication problems. I didn't realize this at the time, however, and only years later was I told the real reason some of the old women didn't want me to live in their village. The explanation I'd heard shortly after moving into Maat was the some of the older people feared that, having the "thin skin" of a European and living in a very malarial environment, I would be bitten badly by anopheles and probably die of malaria; the government would then blame the villagers and deport them to Ambrym as punishment. Such had been their limited and generally negative experience of colonial officialdom, they were bound to fear the worst.

The real reason, I later learned, stemmed from the fact that, before my first visit to Maat, I had copied a list of names (including those of deceased parents of villagers) from a census book in the Vila district agent's office. But once in the village and attempting to gain rapport by reference to the census list, I failed to make clear the source of my information. Who else but a returned spirit of the dead would know the names of the dead, reasoned the old ladies. And who would want such a *temat* (ghost) living cheek by jowl with them? Reassured by their menfolk, they later acquiesced to my request to live in the village. Fortunately, no one became ill after I moved in, so I was eventually accepted as a mere *metalo* (European) and not a potentially vengeful ancestral ghost.

The people of Maat proved to be most helpful, interested, and friendly hosts, which made the early months of settling in and language work relatively painless. Two of the community's most respected elders, Yonah Taso and Maxi Solomon, devoted much time to educating me, showing patience beyond the call of duty as I battled to assimilate a wealth of information. The villagers were very generous, and I received many gifts of food plus readily volunteered information. The kids, for every fieldworker the source of many blessings—and sometimes the odd curse—kept me, their first live-in European, under constant scrutiny. My self-appointed guides and informants reveled in the role of teacher and rarely let me out of their sight. I began to wonder who was studying whom. For a while at least, the villagers were at least as interested in me and my behavior as I was in them and theirs.

As the people of Maat on Efate had maintained close links with their homeland and most still continued to visit the old village from time to time, it was necessary for me to conduct part of my research in Ambrym. I needed to see how people's lives there compared with those of the resettled community in Efate. I went easily in 1967, accompanied by my two guardians, Yonah and Maxi. Ambrym had no airfields then but still looked like an easy place to reach. This is true of the sheltered western coast, but the southeast lies open to the full force of the prevailing trade winds, so getting ashore is a struggle most of the year.

The journey up from Vila is one of contrasts. Little interisland vessels (in times past, often of dubious seaworthiness and overloaded with cargo and passengers) peacefully cleave the calm waters in the lee of the islands en route, then fight what too often appears to be a losing battle with heavy seas in open waters. There is nowhere comfortable to sit, nothing much to hold on to, and the spray is drenching. I was always too preoccupied with thoughts of mortality to get seasick, but there is also an exhilaration as the boat rough-rides its way out of the hollow and crests the next big wave. The final half hour from Paama Island to Ambrym is across a wild stretch of water. Ahead is the low profile of southeast Ambrym, with its dense green forests and beaches of jet-black soil; to the east as you clear Paama towers the majestic, smoking cone of Lopevi, rising five thousand feet straight out of the ocean and capable of mounting spectacular eruptive displays for its Ambrymese audience a scant dozen miles to the north.

It was too rough that first time to allow our vessel to navigate the narrow, dangerous passage through the fringing reef, so we were put ashore in a dinghy—a wild, very scary wide as we almost surfed through the passage into the calmer waters near the beach. I scrambled ashore with shaking knees and great relief to be on terra firma with ourselves and my precious gear (swaddled in plastic bags, as is our custom) all safe. Cheery introductions followed, and there was embarrassment for me when some of the locals began talking rapidly to me in their language. They had taken my confident greeting in the vernacular to mean that I was a fluent speaker. I beat a hasty retreat into Bislama and we set off toward the old village of Maat, an hour's walk away and less than a mile inland from the coast. Many gardens were visible en route, as were the groves of coconut palms, which supply the raw material for copra, the area's only cash crop.

Excited to be home again, Yonah and Maxi gave me an impromptu botany lesson en route: "This is *nanggalat,* the stinging nettle; touch the top side of the leaves, go on! See, it's okay—only the underside stings, but better to keep right away. Over there, those nuts are called *tavu* . . . you can't stop eating them once you start; you'll see." We left the ocean and walked on the "main road"—a rough, black-sand track—through more groves interspersed with patches of thick jungle, from which much of the sun was blotted out. Suddenly, a fork in the road, a couple of huge mango trees, a clearing and an oval of blue sky, a cluster of decaying huts all overgrown, and another cluster of newer dwellings, surrounded by neatly cut grass. This was Maat, and one of its thatched-roofed, bamboo-walled huts would be my home for the next few months.

Yonah and Maxi took me on a guided tour of the entire southeast region and made my entry into the society an enjoyable and relaxed one. After more than six months in the country I was much less anxious about my situation and felt that I already knew a great deal about the home island of the Maat villagers with whom I'd been working near Vila. News of my presence in the Efate village had long since reached Ambrym, and the people knew I was coming. My mentors undertook to explain my work and my research objectives, thus relieving me of a very difficult task. Few anthropologists are so lucky, and many have a hard time establishing themselves in the field. They are fortunate that in so many cases the local people give up trying to work out why the fieldworker is *really* there. Instead, they take them as they find them and make judgments on the basis of their behavior as individuals.

Ambrymese still ask me if I'm there on vacation, since nothing I do fits their notion of work. (As academics, we have these same credibility problems with sections of our own society!) What are the locals to make of someone who wanders from village to village, always questioning, scribbling notes, counting things, clicking a camera, recording stories, measuring garden plots, gossiping, and watching the world of the village go by? This outsider of insatiable curiosity stays for months at a time, not like the few government officials who drop in very infrequently and usually for only a day or two. The anthropologist appears to be harmless, though small children flee in terror on first encounter; he or she must be the white man their parents are always warning will "get" them if they're naughty.

Unless they are given good reason not to, the villagers treat the few outsiders who visit with unfailing courtesy and hospitality. I was accorded the same treatment but was regarded as different because I had learned some of their language. Also, I maintained contact with several people through letters while away from Vanuatu and kept on returning regularly. These things were taken as indications of a serious interest in Ambrym and in continuing my relationships with its people.

For anthropologists it is essential to join in the lives of the people studied and to observe as faithfully as possible the local customs and rules of etiquette. But this does not mean "going native" and attempting to do everything the locals do. I have brown thumbs, not green, for a start, so gardening would have been a lost cause. My early attempts to wield a machete—say, when opening a green coconut for a drink of its delicious water—usually resulted in a small child relieving me of the knife and deftly showing how it should be done. I think many anthropologists provide the people among whom they live with a measure of reassurance by demonstrating what hopeless incompetents Westerners can be. Have you ever tried to paddle an outrigger canoe in a straight line? Or hit a fleeing chicken at forty paces with an arrow? Or spear a fish when your far point of clear vision without glasses is about a foot? Some day soon "my" Ambrymese are going to have a comic best-seller on their hands by telling about "their" anthropologist's search for knowledge in the tricky shoals of another culture.

Southeast Ambrymese, like many other peoples, tend to judge foreign visitors to a large extent on how well they take to the local diet. Ash-falls and the occasional hurricane aside, Ambrym is very well served by Mother Nature. A combination of high rainfall and very fertile soil ensures an abundance of tropical fruits, nuts, and wild bush foods to supplement the highly productive gardens. The fresh meat staple is chicken, and every family feeds a large flock on coconuts and food scraps. There are also a lot of cattle and pigs, usually reserved for special occasions, such as wedding feasts. Men sometimes hunt, with rifles and bows and arrows, for wild pigs, birds, flying fox, and for wild cattle up on the ash-plain. The ocean and fringing reefs are a convenient source of protein, and fishing is a popular leisure-time activity that also provides food.

Getting used to the likes of mangoes, papayas, an array of delicious nuts, fresh fish, lobster, and chicken was really no effort. Some of the staple root crops took me longer to develop a liking for, especially when boiled or roasted in large chunks. Fortunately tubers such as yam, taro, manioc, and sweet potato are often cooked as *lap-lap* puddings, some varieties of which are very tasty. The vegetables are peeled, grated, mixed with coconut milk, perhaps garnished with "bush cabbage" and fresh meat or shellfish, wrapped in leaves, and steamed slowly in an earth oven over hot stones. Manioc *lap-lap* topped with coconut cream is excellent, especially when baked with octopus fresh from the reef. Another mouth-watering seasonal staple is *huhu,* a bright yellow paste of pounded breadfruit. The preparation of *huhu* involves much effort and many workers, so it is often prepared in a communal kitchen and the whole affair can take on the aura of a happening. An addict, I listen for the rhythmic pounding of the freshly roasted fruit on huge oval platters. The rolling pin is a green coconut, and when the pastrylike ball is flattened to cover the board in a half-inch-thick layer, thickened coconut cream is splashed over it. A sliver of bamboo is used to cut the pastry on the diagonal, producing diamond-shaped pieces. Everyone then sits around the board and within minutes reduces it to an empty, cream-spattered expanse.

Some local foods such as flying fox, edible grubs, green bananas, *lap-lap,* and porkfat will not appeal to most foreigners. I heard protests from the French about flying fox, since *rousettes au vin rouge* is a delicacy they aver. Personally, I can live without the simple pan-fried version.

As in many parts of the Pacific, some of the foods favored by the Ambrymese are not at all exotic: white rice and canned meat and fish! Even where local foods abound, these imports are often preferred, largely because they are convenient and easily prepared. Many people have gardens quite a walk from the village, so after a hard day cutting copra the cooks prefer something quick and easy. As to why children, especially, adore plain boiled white rice, I have no idea; but I do know that it was a source of amazement to the villagers that a five-year-old child could eat much more of it than I ever could.

There are no fast-food joints on Ambrym. And one look at the stock in the local village stores would send a suburban shopper into a tizzy. The wise Ambrymese have never been bitten by the consumerism bug, and their shops reflect this disinterest. Tea, sugar, tobacco, kerosene, batteries, matches, cloth, and clothing are among the important basics. On the island there is very little else to spend their money on, so people who want luxury items such as radios must go to the towns or else wait for trading vessels with on-board stores.

When people need cash they make copra, especially when its price on the world market is high. The villagers like to organize work parties. Tackling the coconuts communally allows people to socialize as they work and lessens the boredom of repetitive activity out in the groves. The Ambrymese are their own bosses, free to work when they choose and at their own pace. Some of their gardening chores are arduous and their slash-and-burn technique requires that new areas be cleared and planted each year, but there are times when the gardens need very little attention. Every village has communal workdays devoted to keeping the site clean and tidy, or to some project such as repairing the church or digging a well, but there is still plenty of time for people to pursue a variety of different activities, ranging from visits to kin and friends in distant villages, to building a new kitchen, to preparing and drinking kava (a man-only pastime that has swept the nation since independence).

By anyone's standards it's a good life, and the people of southeast Ambrym appreciate its leisurely pace. Listening on their radios to the woes of the rest of the planet, they often remark to me about how lucky they are. Their society is remarkably peaceful and tranquil. There has not been a homicide in decades, and an easygoing politeness, devoid of aggression, dominates people's interaction. Until the 1970s, however, the good life was marred by a lot of anxiety. This was generated by the alleged presence of sorcery, an antisocial activity that a number of the local men were believed to practice in secret. Severe illness and sudden deaths were taken as proofs of the presence of sorcerers in the society. In Melanesian thought, volcanoes are associated with heat, and heat with magical potency. Ambrymese have always been feared as sorcerers by other non-Vanuatu, and for this reason were allegedly never employable as cooks on European-owned copra plantations because of the workers' fears of being poisoned. People of neighboring islands also avoided Ambrym because its volcanoes were said to be the homes of malevolent spirits of the dead. An outsider may begin by being quite skeptical, but a walk alone through the forest, with its black soil, eerie silences, and atmosphere of foreboding can arouse disquiet, especially at night. Twice, in exactly the same spot on a moonless evening, coconuts crashed to the ground right beside me as I was walking home from a nearby village. Coincidence, of course, but I was unnerved and came close to conversion both times. When I told my mentors, they were certain I had been attacked and forbade me to travel alone again at night.

I was fortunate to be back on Ambrym in 1973 in time to witness what happened when local church leaders declared war on sorcery. They organized an evangelical campaign, which was a spectacular success. Great euphoria followed, and people talked confidently of the victory of the Holy Spirit over the forces of evil. A lot of the old fears subsided and the change in the society was palpable: People moved about with a new confidence and talked openly about a once-secretive topic. It was too much for a cynical social scientist to expect that the change would be long-lived. Yet as recently as 1986 there still had not been any resurgence of sorcery in southeast Ambrym. Development, in the form of new schools and clinics, a water supply, a local government council, and better communications, has finally begun in this isolated and long-neglected area.

The Ambrym of today is a far cry from "uncivilized" times, and the tourist in search of the proverbial unspoiled "savage" would be disappointed. Before the Europeans came, people lived in small fortified hamlets scattered throughout the bush. Feuds and ambushes were apparently common elements in the social scene, and alliances were flimsy, uncertain things. With traders and labor recruiters came rifles to change the technology of the feud. The death rate escalated as the haves massacred the have-nots. Not everyone was a crack shot, however. A chief of the old Maat Village is said to have shot at James Taltasso and missed him at point-blank range. A fateful miss, this, because James was a west Ambrym man who arrived about the turn of the century to convert the heathen southeasterners. James was quick to attribute his miraculous escape to the power of the Christian god. At about the same time the locals refused to hand over an escaped plantation worker to his European master. The irate planter threatened the southeast Ambrymese with punishment: bombardment of their villages by a French or British warship. As the local people now relate the story, James ordered prayers, the planter died suddenly shortly after, the warship failed to arrive, and Christianity became the hit of the day.

In the twenty years that followed, the traditional society was rapidly transformed. Many of the old customs were abandoned; for instance, women no longer walked on their knees in the presence of certain male relatives. Many of the old crafts fell into disuse. The magnificent carved slit-gongs that surrounded their dancing grounds were burned and the grounds razed. People built new villages around churches and sought to please the new god by putting aside all reminders of the Time of Darkness. Today, in a still-young republic, where the need to forge a strong sense of national unity remains, leaders are searching for what is left of their traditional past. In southeast Ambrym, as elsewhere, old people are being urged to tell all they know of the old days and the old life. The Ambrymese want to revive elements of their traditional culture that are compatible with Christian values and with modern life. The new, postcolonial society is an lively amalgamation of Christian and *kastom* (tradition) elements.

There is an excitement and dynamism in the Vanuatu of today. This is part of what draws me back, as does the same anthropological curiosity that lured me there in the first place. Anthropologists everywhere study two sides of the same societal coin: continuities and change. The continuities are the essential and precious threads that give direction, purpose, and a sense of security to our lives. Changes force us to adapt continually as we must make new choices and learn to live with the consequences. So far the people of southeast Ambrym, somewhat cushioned by their isolation, have been able to balance the new and old very well.

There are by now twenty-one years since my first visit, and I have many reasons to go back to Ambrym: a great desire to be reunited with old friends, obligations to be lived up to, and a readiness to be of some assistance if I can. There are changes to be noted and make sense of, true, but it is always reassuring to see just how much the place and its people remain the same. The experience of immersing yourself in another culture is never without some pain, but the enormity of the satisfactions to be gained overwhelms the minuses of the adventure. I once asked a friend, newly returned from two years' fieldwork on a tiny Micronesian atoll, how it went. "Great!" he replied. Then he added after a thoughtful pause, "I'm still not sure how much I learned about the islanders, but I sure as hell learned a lot about myself." For many of us who are anthropologists, that is perhaps what the long journey into otherness is really all about.

No matter what the intended audience for our product, selective reporting of some kind is essential to the distillation of a mass of disparate data from the wealth of observed and reported events, both real and imagined, that constitute human social process (cf. Marcus and Fischer 1986). Given the target audience for my story, it was inevitable that I could not dwell on the heavier side of the anthropologist's role, though I was determined to allude to some of the ethnographic problems. The story was written immediately before Vanuatu's independence, and what has happened since regarding the status of foreign researchers in the country highlights the enormous difference between our privileged access in colonial times (provided we agreed not to openly foment revolution) and the bureaucratic hurdles placed before us now by indigenous governments decidedly ambivalent about the relevance of our research to their aspirations. A more serious and scholarly article would have necessarily dwelt on the debate over whether or not anthropologists have been tools of colonialism or defenders of oppressed minorities. At the least, it would be mindful that the romance and adventure of the search for the "other" never took place in an apolitical vacuum, and that at base "our people" were for us as much of a commodity as they were for the labor recruiters or missionaries we frequently criticize.

In this story I wanted to amuse, but not to amuse at the expense of the Melanesians. No, the target must be the writer, whose ignorance of the alien culture (and consequent missteps as, babylike, he attempts to master a particular task but so often discovers himself awkward and stumbling) is used to reverse the stereotype of the "ignorant native" bedeviled by Western technology. Nigel Barley (1983), in his wickedly funny book about doing fieldwork in West Africa, adopts a more evenhanded approach: Everyone gets it in the neck at some stage, including "his" people. But then, fieldwork in Vanuatu was a breeze compared to what Barley claims to have endured in the Cameroons, and for all my frustration at aspects of colonial rule, I most truly had an easy time of it. Also, unless I've totally suppressed it, I suffered no traumas at the hands of vindictive locals, either, so there was no desire whatsoever to satirize them. I was never physically threatened, or robbed, or thrown out of a village, (or a dinghy, for that matter), or openly denied access to information, and my comments about missing the island and the people while away were absolutely true.

The concentration on food was based on my experience of being asked frequently by people in my own society about this aspect of doing fieldwork. It also allowed me to give readers some idea of the range of local food resources. The brief discussions of subsistence and of cash-cropping likewise address the common question, "What do the people there do for a living?" and my exposition of the uneven rhythm of work and leisure is in implicit contrast to the vastly more regimented lives of most outsiders. Had I remembered, I would have related my chiding of islanders who wore, or wanted, wristwatches, warning them that this object is our own "god" and master, and urging them to avoid that kind of partitioning of their existence.

The discussion concerning problems with establishing my identity and motives was included for the interest value of the particulars, but also because it highlights an important aspect of entering the field in cultures unlike our own. We cannot ever know fully what "our people" are making of us when we go to live with them, and the disjunction between our motives and explanations, and their interpretations of them, are at the root of many of our difficulties in the field, at least in the early stages. The obvious (to us, as anthropologists) ethical and moral issues that surround and lie beneath our self-presentations, and vexed issues of unmeetable expectations and the constitution of "adequate" or "just" reciprocity, lie in the realm of the deep issues which cannot be part of a discourse aimed at the kind of general audience addressed in the foregoing article.

We are often accused of not writing for, and reaching, an audience beyond the social sciences and humanities. Perhaps some of the issues I've mentioned are better not given a wider airing, lest we end up with "anthropology on trial," without the opportunity to answer our critics immediately and forcefully. That said, I would still respond positively to any request to write the same kind of story for a general audience again—and not simply because there is monetary reward, but because the act of doing it heightens one's awareness of what is entailed in rendering "things anthropological" accessible to the nonspecialist reader. It turned out to be more difficult than I had envisaged, but it was also quite refreshing to write in a looser and more creative mode. The need for us to reach a much wider audience, to put our skills as cultural translators to better use in making what is alien and exotic meaningful and logical in Western cultural terms, remains as strong as ever.

SUGGESTED READINGS

BARLEY, NIGEL

1983   The Innocent Anthropologist. Baltimore: Penguin.

BURRIDGE, K. O. L.

1973   Encountering Aborigines: Anthropology and the Australian Aboriginal. New York: Pergamon.

CLIFFORD, J., AND G. E. MARCUS, EDS.

1986   Writing Culture: The Poetics and Politics of Ethnography. Berkeley: University of California Press.

JOLLY, M.

1982   Birds and Banyans of South Pentecost: *Kastom* in Anti-colonial Struggle. Mankind 13(4):338–356.

MARCUS, G. E., AND M. J. FISCHER

1986   Anthropology as Cultural Critique: An Experimental Moment in the Human Sciences. Chicago: University of Chicago Press.

TONKINSON, R.

1979   At Work in the Isles of Coral and Ash. Pacific 8(4):50–59.
1982a *Kastom* in Melanesia: Introduction. Mankind 13(4):302–305.
1982b National Identity and the Problem of *Kastom* in Vanuatu. Mankind 13(4):306–315.

PART ONE

Unexpected Welcomes to Other Worlds

🦋 Getting Below the Surface

DOUGLAS RAYBECK

INTRODUCTION[1]

Beginning fieldwork in a foreign culture is a bit like diving into an un-familiar pond in which you suspect there may be underwater hazards. You may examine the surface of the pond at length (and breadth and width for that matter); you may even review the observations of others who have swum in the pond, yet when you leap in yourself, you still have an excellent chance of landing headfirst on a submerged boulder. This essay describes a few such accidents as well as the understanding, humility, and of course, bruises that such experiences leave behind. Ultimately, it also relates a process of becoming familiar with the uneven cultural terrain that lies below the seeming placidity of the surface. As fieldwork is a very personal experience, so will this be a personal tale of misperception and insight, of innocence and guile, culminating in a bit of personal growth and some painfully acquired self-knowledge.

Interested in Southeast Asia, I did my graduate work in anthropology in the mid-60s at Cornell University, a school noted for its excellent Southeast Asia Program. While there, various members of the anthro-pology faculty impressed me, and other graduate students, with the mystique of fieldwork. We were informed that it was a singularly im-portant and necessary part of becoming an anthropologist (library theses were discouraged). We were given the impression that this rite de passage transformed one from a pedestrian scholar to a sensitive and percep-tive observer of the human condition, possessed of increased wisdom and maturity.[2]

Despite the centrality of fieldwork to our chosen profession, I and other graduate students received no instruction in what it was or how to do it. Indeed, when I, attempting to improve my grasp of this impalp-able method, enrolled in a seminar titled "Methods in Anthropology," I found that it involved reading most of the writings of Malinowski. While such works as *The Sexual Life of Savages* were interesting and even edifying, they did little to reduce the mysteries surrounding fieldwork. Even reading the then recently published (and expurgated) field diary of Malinowski provided few pointers beyond the obvious:

Fieldwork was a difficult, lonely experience that could exacerbate personal problems.

I had decided to carry out my fieldwork in the state of Kelantan on the east coast of the Malay Peninsula. It met all of the requirements that I understood were necessary for a successful fieldwork experience. It was exotic, little studied, and reasonably accessible. Also, the Malay language is one of the easiest to master in Southeast Asia, although Kelantanese were reputed to speak a somewhat difficult dialect of Malay. Furthermore, compared to the states on the west coast, Kelantan was comparatively undeveloped and possessed of a traditional Malay culture that elsewhere had been adulterated by modernization and exposure to other cultural influences.[3]

In preparation for my field experience, I spent two years studying Malay (actually Indonesian, which is essentially the same language). I also read virtually all of the anthropology and much other literature written about Kelantan (a relatively modest task in the mid-60s), and I obtained a field research grant from the National Institute of Mental Health. I even managed to arrange a semester in London prior to entering the field. There I had the good fortune to study some of the Kelantanese dialect at the School of Oriental and African Studies with Amin Sweeney, at that time a graduate student about to undertake his dissertation research. Amin was and is a singular person who figured prominently in my fieldwork experiences. Finally, I contacted Raymond Firth who, together with his wife Rosemary, had worked in Kelantan. I have a very high regard for Firth's unassuming brilliance and for his kind and gentle manner toward the most fumbling of graduate students. He generously provided me with assistance and my first real advice about the fieldwork process.

Suitably armored against ignorance and error, I arrived with my wife at Kota Bharu, the capital of Kelantan, on January 9, 1968. We took up temporary residence in the Hotel Rex, a cubical-stucco compromise between comfort and going native, while I set about trying to familiarize myself with the city, buy a secondhand motorcycle, locate a suitable field site and, coincidentally, understand what was being said to me. It seems that people could understand my halting standard Malay, but insisted on answering in machine-gun bursts of plosives, fricatives, and sibilants that bore little relation to the language I had learned at Cornell, and that was both much more rapid and much less intelligible than the kindly paced and carefully articulated phrases Amin had exposed me to only months earlier.

Amidst considerable frustration, persistent dysentery, occasional heat prostration (we were approximately six degrees north of the equator), and continuing bewilderment, there was one precious asset, an experienced pilot to assist in navigating these unfamiliar waters—Amin Sweeney—who had arrived in Kelantan a month before us and who

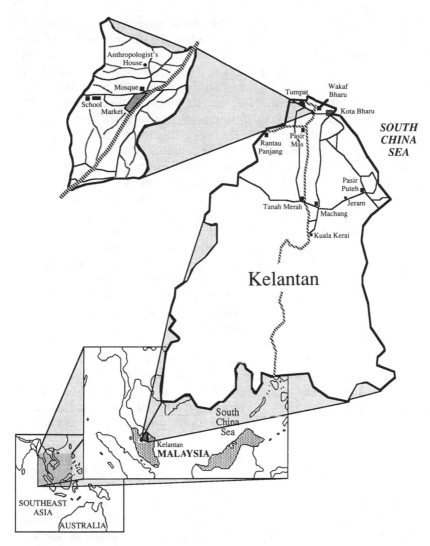

Wakaf Bharu, Kelantan, Malaysia.

charitably provided his time, assistance, and friendship throughout the fieldwork period. Born in England, Amin had lived for years in Kelantan, married a local woman, learned both the native language and the customs, and was exceptionally well suited to assist wandering would-be anthropologists in search of truth and beauty.

The problem with fieldwork is not that *things* are different; one expects *things* to be different. The difficulty is that nearly all *things* are or can be different, and the neophyte has no means of anticipating which *things* require special attention. It is not the big questions that exhaust you; those have been planned for and are, at least in part, anticipated. It is the little, commonplace experiences that would ordinarily be taken for granted that are the source of unending concern. People smile. Why did they smile? Are they simply being friendly, or did I do something foolish? Should I smile back? How long? How broadly? Am I too concerned about this? I cannot detail here the myriad ways in which Amin and his wife, Zainab, eased the initial shock of fieldwork and provided a psychological haven from the storms of insecurity that attend such endeavors, but the debt is both significant and enduring.

The choice of a field site is among the most important decisions made in the initial stages of fieldwork. It takes months even to start becoming familiar with a community, to build rapport, and to develop a sense of mutual trust between participant-observer and observed. Choose an inappropriate setting and those months are largely wasted.

Since my research was to focus principally upon traditional values and deviance, I knew that I would have to invest a good deal of time gaining the acceptance and trust of those with whom I would be living for a year and a half. I also knew the qualities of the community I was seeking: It should be a reasonably typical, traditional peasant village subsisting on wet rice agriculture; it should possess a standard market and thus serve as a locus of activity for surrounding communities; and it should have a fair-sized Chinese population as interethnic relations was one of the topics in which I was interested. All of these were good, objective, professional considerations, but in addition, my wife and I were hoping to be near the state capital where we could buy such necessary provisions as film, canned food, pocket books, and ice cream, and where we could see the occasional movie.

On my well-used and underpowered Yamaha, I began to explore roads, paths, and trails in search of an appropriate village (*kampong*). The strategy was both simple and ineffective. When I came across a promising village, I would stop at a local coffee shop, which both my reading and Amin assured me was a center for local gossip and information. I would make inquiries concerning the nature of the village and whether or not there was a house to rent. This slapdash approach led to numerous conversations with assorted villagers of a semi-intelligible nature. They could generally understand me; I seldom understood them. Finally, in a fit of humility, I asked Amin for suggestions and he recommended Wakaf Bharu, a village that met the criteria above and was situated on Kelantan's lone railway just across the Kelantan River only eight miles from Kota Bharu, the state capital.

One of the few fieldwork recommendations with which I was familiar was to contact a local person of high status prior to entering a fieldwork setting. Thus, with the assistance of Amin I met with the local *Imam,* the Islamic priest, and learned that, in addition to the characteristics enumerated above, Wakaf Bharu also possessed a mosque, a grade school, and a small police post that kept local demographic records (more or less, as I was to discover later). The population was just over 2,000, a bit large but not unmanageable, since my research did not require detailed household registries and the like, and there was a nice, new house that could be rented for a reasonable sum. In short, the village appeared very appropriate for my research needs.

JUMPING IN

With practically no acquaintance with the village, my wife and I moved in on a Thursday afternoon on February first, three weeks after arriving in the country. Our initial discovery was easily made: The villagers of Wakaf Bharu were as interested in us as we were in them. We are both Caucasian and my wife at five-feet-five was taller than most Malay males, while I at six-feet-four was an extreme oddity. People surrounded the house to watch us unpack. Little children ran through the house checking our belongings and reporting back to their better-mannered parents. We had not quite finished unpacking when I had to attend to my first social obligation in the village. Prior to our arrival, I had made an arrangement with the man whose house we had rented that proved to be very valuable.

For complex current and historical reasons, Kelantanese villagers distrust outsiders, especially representatives of authority, and prefer to address their own problems independently. During a nine-month period preceding our arrival, Wakaf Bharu villagers had suffered a number of break-ins and thefts, but unlike a U.S. community, which would have summoned the police, they determined to deal with the problem themselves. The village mounted a guard (*jaga*) consisting of male volunteers, mostly younger married men, who would give one or two evenings a week to safeguard the village. Thus, each night several Malay males armed with clubs would patrol village pathways from ten in the evening to four in the morning seeking evildoers. Since the man from whom I was renting the house was scheduled to do guard duty on Tuesday and Thursday evenings, I had (rather cleverly) arranged to take on his obligation, thereby making a statement to the village that I was not simply an interloper but was willing to assume some responsibilities for the privilege of residence there.

Thus, at approximately ten o'clock on my first evening in the village four Malay males arrived at my front door and announced in a quiet fashion that it was time to patrol the village. Two of the four were to become close friends and valuable, if not always subtle, sources of information. Yusof, a stolid, strongly built man in his early twenties with an open and (for a Kelantanese) somewhat assertive style, had been known for youthful misbehavior but, recently married, seemed to have settled down to a degree. Mat, a clever, wiry young man possessing a quick sense of humor and an occasionally mischievous manner, was a frequent companion of Yusof, and the two, as I was to discover, were still capable of the sporadic solecism.

The four young men introduced themselves, waited while I located a suitable pick-axe handle, and then set off to escort me through the twisting maze of arteries and capillaries linking the houses and neighborhoods of the village organism. Thoroughly lost and bemused by the barrage of questions I was continually encountering, I was delighted to discover that the formidable *jaga* was, at least for the first two hours of its operation, largely a social affair. As we passed by houses, we were frequently invited to stop in for coffee and conversation. I don't doubt my presence increased the frequency of the invitations, but I found that this was customary even in my absence. Thus, I was presented to villagers, not simply as a nosey busybody (it became clear later that such was my true calling) but a visitor willing to share in the social life and responsibilities of the village. Further, the continuing association with the young men of the *jaga* was to lead to my first real success in delving below the surface calm of Kelantanese village culture.

Arising early the next morning, I found my first hazard waiting outside our front door wearing a broad grin and a dirty sarong. His manner was expansive and his language incomprehensible. Gradually he made it apparent that he wished to offer me a tour of the village and that his name was Ché Din. Quite reasonably, I attributed our communication difficulties to my unfamiliarity with the Kelantanese dialect and with local customs. Pleased at the friendly offer and the prospect of beginning to become familiar with the tortuous network that comprised the village pathways, I told my wife that I would skip breakfast and headed off after Ché Din.

Thoroughly lost and bemused by the barrage of comments (does this sound familiar?) that Ché Din kept up concerning people and houses we were passing, I nodded and smiled at everyone we passed or chanced across. Villagers returned my smile with broad grins and quizzical looks probably, I thought, occasioned by my odd appearance. As we wound our way among the maze of trails, we came to a remarkably dilapidated house that had buckling sides and only part of its thatch roof. Ché Din indicated with some pride that this was his home and I nodded, confirming my initial and professionally sensitive judgment that he was not a wealthy man.

After more than an hour, with the sun suggesting that we were traveling back toward our point of departure, we came across three children playing in their yard near the path. The oldest boy looked up, pointed directly at my companion, laughed, and shouted, quite clearly *"orang nakal!"* Now, my reading had informed me that Malay parents took great pains to train their children to be very polite toward adults. Nonetheless,

a Kelantanese youth had just called my guide a "naughty person," raising the not inappropriate question: Just who the hell was I walking
around with, anyhow?

Despite my increasing unease, nothing untoward transpired and we
arrived back at my house shortly after having encountered the children.
With my thanks and to my relief, Ché Din soon took his leave, whereupon Hussein, my next-door neighbor, walked over with a smile and
the inquiry "Why were you going about the village with *tiga-suku*?"
Tiga-suku translates as three-quarters and is a colloquial Kelantanese term
for someone who is intellectually impaired. I had just been squired about
the community by the village half-wit.

What makes this occurrence particularly poignant, and perhaps even
educational, is that I genuinely thought Ché Din was simply a poor
Kelantanese. I had studied the language for two years, read all of the
anthropology written on the area, worked in a profession that sensitizes
one to interpersonal behaviors, and I still couldn't perceive the difference
between a typical Kelantanese and one who was mentally disabled. Lacking a sound basis for comparison, I assumed that Ché Din was simply
poor and perhaps a bit odd, but maybe many Kelantanese appeared a
bit odd to outsiders.

LEARNING TO SWIM

My difficulties in making such simple discriminations as the difference
between normal and abnormal villagers should provide some sense of
the bewilderment that often accompanies fieldwork. In many respects,
it involves a return to childhood when little is known and less is
understood. Happily, the villagers of Wakaf Bharu proved to be tolerant
and helpful parents who undertook my education with enthusiasm and
good humor.

Their good humor was usually occasioned by one of my gaffes, which
tended to be of two sorts: those which could be attributed to absolute
ignorance often coupled with a tendency to transpose assumptions from
U.S. to Kelantanese culture, and those which arose from well-meaning,
but imperfectly executed, efforts to adapt to village society. Two examples will illustrate the differing ways in which I learned humility,
though I would entreat the reader not to view these as typical of my
fieldwork.

Very early in my fieldwork I was invited to attend a traditional Kelantanese wedding. Following the wedding, I was seated cross-legged on
a woven pandanus mat in a circle of five males preparing to enjoy the
postwedding feast. There was shallow bowl before me and a glass of
clear, cool water by my right hand. I was the only one in the circle so
equipped, but I assumed that my companions were simply making life

easy for me as they had done several times already. As it was a hot after-noon (it seemed they all were), I picked up the glass and took a long drink, noticing gradually the somewhat curious looks my associates were giving me. Finally, one of my companions leaned toward me and whispered some useful information. It seems Malyas eat with their right hands and prior to meals (why wasn't this in any of the ethnographies I had read?) they wash the right hand by pouring water over it into a shallow bowl. I had just drunk the wash water, an act akin to sipping from a finger bowl.

The second class of gaffe is illustrated by a series of events that occurred after two months in Wakaf Bharu, when some of my village friends suggested I might be more comfortable wearing a local sarong (*kain pelékat*) rather than the hotter and more confining trousers I had worn to that point. Attracted by an invitation that seemed to suggest increasing acceptance of me (it did), I went with a friend to purchase several *kain* at the local market.

Most *kain* are imported, preferably from India but increasingly from Japan, and are a standard length of approximately four feet. They are sewn longitudinally forming a tube which is donned over the head, snugged with two center tucks, and then folded down until a roll of fabric forms a natural belt. Kelantanese males pull their *kain* up just under their armpits and then roll the fabric down to their waists where it supplies stability and insurance against embarrassment. This leaves them with the bottom of the *kain* just brushing the top of the feet; only a crude and uneducated hick (*orang darat*) would wear his *kain* halfway up his ankles.

Now the average Kelantanese male is about five-feet-four and I am a foot taller. This simple fact created a simple dilemma. Being tall, I could not begin to roll my *kain* under my armpits and still have the bottom anywhere in the vicinity of my feet. I could either wear my *kain* according to the dictates of fashion or wear it securely, but not both. I opted for social acceptance and wore my *kain* as low as possible, allowing myself only two fragile rolls of the material to secure my modesty. In the process of accustoming myself to wearing a *kain*, I made some important and expensive discoveries: Sarongs are remarkably poorly suited for motorcycle riding and, as most women already know, when climbing stairs, the hem of a long garment should be lifted. My "discoveries" were invariably accompanied by a good deal of amusement on the part of villagers, but they seemed to appreciate that I was making a genuine, if frequently inept, attempt to adapt to their mores. Adding fuel to a well-tended fire, I further agreed to wear a *baju Melayu*, a Malay-style overshirt of light cotton that is cut full with a belled waist and belled sleeves. Kelantanese, being of modest stature, look quite attractive in such garb. However, I am long and lanky and when attired in sarong and *baju Melayu* my mirror informed me that, despite the compliments

I received from villagers, I most closely resembled a becalmed sailing ship.

Fortunately for me and my few tatters of remaining dignity, some villagers actively, albeit indirectly, instructed me in the niceties of social behavior.

Malays in general and Kelantanese in particular are very sensitive to interpersonal relations, and they are quite concerned with maintaining interpersonal harmony within the village context. To facilitate harmonious relations, all villagers are schooled in a well-developed courtesy code (*budi bahasa*). This involves not only a set of rules for proper behavior but also the cultivation of a proper demeanor characterized by humility and indirection.

Hussein was my next-door neighbor, a particularly small and swarthy man possessing a quick intelligence and an excellent familiarity with *budi bahasa*. He was also one of few villagers willing to give me advice concerning social matters, a mission that he carried out with great sensitivity and tact. Rather than provide direct advice, a behavior that risks embarrassing both the giver and the receiver, Hussein would use personal references of transparent relevance. On one occasion when he wished to suggest that my behavior was not as tactful as it might have been he made the following observation:

> I was not born here and I do not have my relatives here. I have to
> be careful of my behavior. When you go to live in a place where you
> weren't born, you behave like a hen, not like a rooster. This is proper.
> In my own kampong I can behave more importantly, but here I must
> be careful not to give offense.

I got the idea.

Such solicitous assistance saved me numerous blunders during the first months of fieldwork. Villagers had responded positively to my explanation that I was a student of their culture who would return to the United States to teach others about the customs of the Kelantanese. Kelantanese are aware and proud that they maintain a rich, traditional Malay culture that elsewhere on the peninsula has largely succumbed to other cultural influences and to modernization.[4] Things seemed to be going well. My note cards multiplied at an appropriate rate, and people were quite helpful concerning many of my questions. I quickly discovered, however, that there were distinct limits on the kinds of questions with which I could expect assistance.

Those questions which concerned factual minutiae pertaining to such mundane activities as planting, family life, common rituals, and the like, were answered readily and fully. However, since my major interests dealt with values and deviant behavior, I also somewhat naively asked about the existence of misbehaviors such as gambling, drinking, premarital sex, and so forth. My friends and acquaintances gave me to believe that

Kelantanese were among the most law-abiding and proper individuals on the planet. No one drank, gambled, fooled around or, it seemed, even spoke ill of others.

My suspicions that people were being less than candid with me were exacerbated one day when I attempted to ascertain the reasons behind a heated and loud quarrel between a man and a woman that I had heard the preceding evening. I inquired of a variety of villagers, whom I knew to be closer to the disturbance than I had been, what the argument concerned and who the principals were. I received a notably uniform reply: "What argument? Sorry, but I didn't hear any argument." I realized that I was still not sufficiently trusted to be made privy to the sensitive and sometimes less than ideal social life of the village. Access to such information would give me a means to harm village interests, and as I was still seen largely as an outsider, villagers could not be certain I wouldn't use such means against their interests.

Presented with an image of a deceptive exterior calm, I needed a means to delve below the surface boundaries of village life where I might encounter the muddiness and unevenness that constitutes a portion of all human relationships. As in most aspects of fieldwork, the solution to my problem came in an unforeseen manner, from an unexpected source, and owed little to the anthropologist's intelligence.

GETTING BELOW THE SURFACE

Gaining the trust of those with whom you work is a slow process generally characterized by numerous small exchanges that gradually add to mutual understanding and acceptance. Seldom are there breakthroughs in trust of the sort to which one can point. Nonetheless, I can date exactly when I was enabled to dive below the surface calm of village society: March 18, 1968, a Monday.

Throughout the early months of fieldwork, I continued to participate in the evening guard (*jaga*) twice a week. This regularly placed me in the company of married males a few years younger than myself with whom I shared several interests. As time progressed and they, especially Mat and Yusof, grew more comfortable with me, they asked questions about that preeminent concern of young males—sex. They wished to know about the sexual mores of contemporary U.S. society, which in the 60s had rather a lurid reputation. I answered their questions candidly and responded with queries of my own. They began giving me my first evidence that Kelantanese were as fraillly human as the rest of us.

Eventually we even exchanged swearwords, an extremely important aspect of language, curiously absent from language classes. They traded Kelantanese curses for English profanities and seemed pleased with the secret power the words conferred. Mat, the more playful of the two, delighted in approaching young women, smiling and saying "Fook!" (his pronunciation lacked total accuracy) before cackling and running away.

After months of this sort of banter, we had become quite comfortable with each other and were developing close friendships. One Thursday evening as we were ending our *jaga*, Yusof asked me if it would be possible for three people to travel on my motorcycle. I remarked that it probably was feasible and asked why he wished to know. His response was both opaque and promising: He asked me to meet Mat and him Monday evening on the main road at the edge of the village and commented that there was something he wanted to show me.

That Monday night I met Mat and Yusof at the designated location and the three of us set off on my motorcycle under Yusof's direction. Questions concerning our destination were greeted with smiles, and directions were confined to immediate turns. I was guided into the capital, Kota Bharu, down a side street, through a maze of paths, and into a dark, dead-end alley where we dismounted. Yusof beckoned me to follow him, which I did with only a slight frisson of apprehension.

We approached the side a of darkened building where Yusof opened a door and ushered me into a noisy, dingy, low-ceilinged room occupied by both men and women. Within three minutes, Yusof had purchased beers for all of us and had a "waitress" sitting on my lap. With both he and Mat watching me closely, I realized the significance of the risk they were taking and the importance of my response. I drank the beer, joked with the waitress and thanked them for both opportunities. After I declined their kind invitation to retire with my waitress to a loft over the room, we settled in for some pleasant drinking and conversation.

It seems that there were numerous "bars" of the same sort throughout Kota Bharu. People from a given village tended to patronize a single location, thus ensuring a degree of confidentiality. Villagers engaged in similar deviance at a shared locale were unlikely to inform on one another, partly due to bonds of solidarity and partly because doing so would raise questions regarding how one knew of the behavior. Indeed, I learned later that Yusof and Mat were very interested in compromising me as soon as possible and were somewhat disappointed that I hadn't taken the waitress upstairs. Had I done so, they would have had even greater insurance that I would not mention our recent activities upon returning to the village.

That evening perceptibly changed my relationship with Yusof and Mat. I now had two friends who had taken me below the surface and who counted on me to be circumspect about the experience. They had invested their trust in me and we had shared solecisms. Each possessed information that could be detrimental to the others, were it to enter the ever-active village gossip network. That evening also represented a major breakthrough in my fieldwork. Soon I could approach Yusof and Mat with questions concerning subsurface elements of village behavior, and they would delight in telling me whatever relevant gossip they knew. As gossiping is a favored pastime, they usually had useful information concerning any event about which I might ask.

Information garnered from Yusof and Mat allowed me to ask very different and far more successful questions of other villagers. Instead of asking open-ended questions betraying my near total ignorance of a situation, I could now inquire about events in a manner suggesting I was already privy to the main issues and only wished clarification of details. Instead of asking "What was that argument last night and who took part in it?" I could now inquire, "Were Minah and Dir arguing about her sister's inheritance again?"

This approach immediately placed me below the surface, for I could not be familiar with such information unless other villagers already trusted me. In this fashion, I rapidly increased my access to information that hitherto had been denied me, and as it became increasingly apparent that I neither disclosed nor abused this knowledge, other villagers began to accord me a trust similar, but not identical, to that which Yusof and Mat had displayed.

From this point forward, my work progressed nicely. The more time spent delving below the boundary between surface ideals and subsurface reality, the more familiar the terrain became and the easier it was to navigate among half-hidden forms.

CONCLUSION

I suggested at the beginning of this essay that fieldwork changes the anthropologist in ways that can be only imperfectly understood. For a period of time, the investigator knows what it is to be a member of a minority denied full access to the surrounding society. One is forced to acknowledge weaknesses and encouraged to discover strengths in ways that are more often mundane than exotic. Similarly, the anthropologist comes face-to-face with the limitations of both science and one's ability to determine the outcome of events.

Certainly, an increasing sensitivity to others is one of the benefits of the fieldwork experience. Equally likely gains are improved self-knowledge and a finer sense of humility (though I confess the writings of some anthropologists belie this assertion). A major result of my fieldwork, as my teachers had suggested, was to transform me into a more sensitive and perceptive observer of the human condition, possessed of increased wisdom and maturity. (Note I didn't say how greatly increased.) At the very least, I learned that the evolution of trust involves mutual vulnerability. I can never forget that I owe much of my fieldwork success less to my own professional acumen than to a night out on the town in the company of good friends.

NOTES

1. The information on which this essay is based was gathered during eighteen months of fieldwork beginning January, 1968, in Kelantan, Malaysia. I am grateful for the National Institute of Mental Health Grant (NH 11486) that supported this research. I also want to thank the Southeast Asia Program, and especially Tom Kirsch and the Department of Anthropology of Cornell University for providing me with a quiet and comfortable place to complete this and other writings. Finally, I want to express my deep appreciation for the efforts of my wife, Karen, who not only steadfastly endured an experience she found less than enthralling but who also had the good sense to maintain a daily journal in which she noted many details that escaped my field notes.

2. So that you will be apprised of my biases, I should inform you that I have come to share this assessment in large degree, though I would not argue, as would some, that it is necessary to carry out fieldwork in a foreign and preferably exotic land in order to enjoy such benefits.

3. This essay is clearly not an ethnographic study of the Kelantanese, and the interested reader might wish to examine works by Raymond Firth (1966), Rosemary Firth (1966), Clive Kessler (1978), and William Roff (1974) among others.

4. An excellent example of traditional culture preserved in Kelantan and not elsewhere is a curing ceremony, *main puteri*, which combines both traditional healing and spirit beliefs (see Firth 1967, 1974, Kessler 1977, Raybeck 1974).

REFERENCES

FIRTH, RAYMOND W.
1966   Malay Fishermen: Their Peasant Economy. London: Routledge & Kegan Paul Ltd. (first publ. 1946).
1967   Ritual and Drama in Malay Spirit Mediumship. Comparative Studies in Society and History 9:190–207.
1974   Faith and Scepticism in Kelantan Village Magic. *In* Kelantan: Religion, Society and Politics in a Malay State. W. R. Roff, ed. Kuala Lumpur: Oxford University Press.

FIRTH, ROSEMARY
1966   Housekeeping Among Malay Peasants. 2d ed. London: Athalone Press (first publ. 1943).

KESSLER, CLIVE
1977   Conflict and Sovereignty in Kelantanese Malay Spirit Seances. *In* Case Studies in Spirit Possession. V. Crapanzano and V. Garrison, eds. New York: John Wiley & Sons.
1978   Islam and Politics in a Malay State: Kelantan 1838–1969. Ithaca, NY: Cornell University Press.

RAYBECK, DOUGLAS
1974   Social Stress and Social Structure in Kelantan Village Life. *In* Kelantan: Religion, Society and Politics in a Malay State. W. R. Roff, ed. Kuala Lumpur: Oxford University Press.

ROFF, WILLIAM
1974   Kelantan: Religion, Society and Politics in a Malay State. Kuala Lumpur: Oxford University Press.

SUGGESTED READINGS

CHAN SU MING
1965   Kelantan and Trengganu, 1909–1939. Journal of the Malaysian Branch of the Royal Asiatic Society 38:159–198.

DOWNS, RICHARD
1967   A Kelantanese Village of Malaysia. *In* Contemporary Change in Traditional Societies. Asian Rural Societies, Vol. 2. Julian Steward, ed. Urbana: University of Illinois Press.

RAYBECK, DOUGLAS
1975   The Semantic Differential and Kelantanese Malay Values: A Methodological Innovation in the Study of Social and Cultural Values. Doctoral dissertation, Cornell University, Ithaca, NY.
1980   Ethnicity and Accommodation: Malay-Chinese Relations in Kelantan, Malaysia. Ethnic Groups 2:241–268.
1980–   The Ideal and the Real: The Status of Women in Kelantan Malay Society.
  1981 Women and Politics 1:7–21.
1986   The Elastic Rule: Conformity and Deviance in Kelantan Village Life. *In* Cultural Identity in Northern Peninsular Malaysia. S. Carstens, ed. Athens, OH: Ohio University Press.
1996   Mad Dogs, Englishmen, and the Errant Anthropologist: Fieldwork in Malaysia. Prospect Heights, IL: Waveland Press.

WILSON, PETER
1967   A Malay Village and Malaysia. New Haven: HRAF Press.

THREE

Of Softball Bats and Fishnets: A Summer in the Alaskan Bush

GEORGE GMELCH

I was in Yakutat, the only settlement along a three-hundred-mile stretch of remote coastline in southeastern Alaska. I planned to spend a week there to get acquainted with some of the Tlingit Indians before traveling fifty miles down the coast to begin a study of Indian and white salmon fishermen. And, I was to meet with village leaders to explain my research and to obtain their approval.

But even before I met with the leaders, I noticed that people were decidedly cool toward me. My greetings to passersby, for example, were often not returned. One morning, while I was walking along the dirt road from the village to the pier, a man came into view walking toward me. We were the only people on the road, yet when he came to within thirty yards of me he swung over to the other side of the road and as we passed he turned his head and looked off into the distance. Each time I entered Flo's, the small village café, the patrons lowered their voices. And when new customers came in, they routinely took the tables furthest from mine—or so it seemed.

Damn, I thought, what have I done to bring this on? Mentally I reviewed my first few days in the village, searching for anything that might explain the cool reception I was getting. I remembered having jotted down some notes to myself in the café a couple of days before, mainly a list of things I needed to do. Perhaps that had aroused suspicion? I thought about how writing notes might have been perceived—an unknown man walking around the village at all times of day, then taking notes in the café.

I was no stranger to this situation; I had been the object of suspicion before. As a graduate student I had lived for a summer in a village in the Mexican highlands taking part in an anthropology field training program. My wife, Sharon, and I had arrived in the village of San Antonio Acuamanala in the middle of a fiesta, and I remember how the crowd watched curiously as we unloaded our gear. Over the next few days, we were asked many questions about our religion. It seemed to take a long time before the people of San Antonio began to warm up and

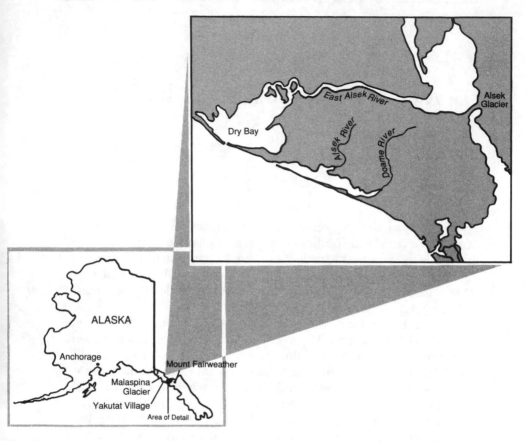

Dry Bay area, southeastern Alaska

talk to us willingly. Later, Celia Sanchez, the village paramedic who became our friend, revealed to us that the week before our arrival a light plane had flown over the village dropping leaflets promoting Seventh-Day Adventism. In this Catholic village, we had been mistaken for Protestant missionaries.

Were the people of Yakutat mistaking me for someone else? The next morning I went to the U.S. Forest Service office to ask about some aerial photographs of Dry Bay. As soon as I explained who I was and what I wanted, the woman at the desk burst into laughter. "Everyone in town," she said, "thinks you're with the IRS. They think you're here looking for unreported income."

When the village council meeting took place, John Chapman, head of Glacier Bay National Park, was with me. Park Service officials had already had one meeting with the council, but he explained again that the Park Service was being required by the U.S. Congress to do this study. In 1980 the Dry Bay area had been designated a "preserve" and added to Glacier Bay National Park. Park planners anticipated problems in trying to oversee the activities of commercial fishermen, trappers, and big-game hunters, particularly given the tensions that existed between the Tlingits and the non-natives who competed for the same resources. They had even tried to trade the Dry Bay area to the State of Alaska for another parcel of land, but the deal had fallen through.

I explained to the council how I would go about doing the research: that like most anthropologists I would live in Dry Bay among the people and observe and participate in the activities which took place there and that I would write up my observations and the things people told me in field notes which would later be used to write my "report." A Tlingit elder spoke, implying that native fishermen might be less than eager to participate in the study. I knew of the interethnic tension, and I could imagine his skepticism about an outsider really understanding the Tlingit point of view. Nevertheless, I remained enthusiastic. I was excited about the prospect of working in the Alaskan wilderness and of comparing how different peoples—Tlingits and whites—fished and used resources.

I chartered a small plane to take me to Dry Bay. Sitting in the copilot's seat I got a good look at the terrain, which directly below us was a flat coastal foreland latticed with rivers and small streams flowing to the ocean through muskeg and spruce forest. From their milky appearance, I could tell which rivers were fed by runoff from the glaciers. I counted three brown bears and four moose. In no hurry to return to Yakutat, and proud of the dazzling scenery, the young pilot turned inland toward the mountains. Within a few minutes we were over the snow-covered peaks of the Brabazon Range. Glaciers descended from U-shaped valleys, the ice and snow streaked black, dirtied with stone and rock debris.

We landed in a clearing near the small cabin where Clarence, the ranger in Yakutat, had recommended I stay. Within minutes I had unloaded my gear and stood watching as the plane disappeared over the horizon. The only sound was the distant hum of its engine. It was a lonely feeling. As I lugged my gear toward the cabin, I noticed bear tracks in the sandy soil, then claw marks on the cabin door and window frame. I got out my shotgun. I had been warned to carry it whenever I left camp and to put it near my sleeping bag at night. "Put the buckshot in first and then the slugs," explained one Park Service official, "because if you have a bear inside your tent at night, you won't be able to see him well and you'll want a wider pattern of shot to make sure you hit something." I was also counseled to "wear bells, carry a whistle, and make lots of noise" when hiking, and *never run* should I encounter a bear, for that could trigger their chase instinct. I thought of Clarence, who had told me how important it is in Alaska to be cautious and prepared. "Small mistakes," he had said, "that are inconsequential in the Lower 48 can be fatal in the north." I had dutifully recorded all of their advice in my notebook, but privately I thought they were overdoing it. Now I wasn't so sure.

The next morning I set out downriver, shotgun over my shoulder, to meet some of the local fishermen. I walked several miles before reaching the first camp, the next camp was another mile away. It was immediately apparent that the Yakutat ranger who had recommended that I live at the cabin didn't understand my research, that anthropologists like to live *among* the people they study rather than commute. Or perhaps it had been a perverse joke, as I now faced the prospect of having to move all of my gear by foot six miles to the only suitable location for my research—a small fish-processing station where the fishermen gathered to sell their fish. It was here that the salmon were gutted and iced before being flown out to Yakutat in an old DC-3, and fishermen spent some time relaxing and socializing.

In Dry Bay, unlike Yakutat, there was no confusion about who I was or what I was going to do. Again, however, I was to meet with hostility of a different sort. The Park Service had sent all of the fishermen a letter explaining the nature of my research and who I was—an anthropology professor from New York. In this case, I might have gotten a better reception if I had been an IRS inspector. The fishermen had been almost unanimously opposed to the Dry Bay area becoming part of the national park system. The land had previously been under the jurisdiction of the U.S. Forest Service, which in large measure had left the fishermen alone. Now they feared there would be new regulations restricting their activities. And they did not want anyone, least of all the federal government, telling them what they could or could not do. As one fisherman put it, "I came here to get *away* from Big Brother."

My job was to document the very activities—hunting and fishing—they feared might be restricted. Worse still, from their perspective, I was a college professor "from back East," New York no less. "A pointy-headed intellectual," I overheard one man say. Maybe if I had been from the University of Wyoming or Idaho I would have been more acceptable. One day during my first week, a young, grizzled fisherman, high on pot, alcohol, or both, came into my camp on his three-wheeler, pistol visibly at his side. "Keep your nose out of my business or there'll be trouble," he threatened. I tried to explain calmly what anthropologists do and why the Park Service had to do this study, but he sped off before I could finish.

The other white fishermen were not overtly threatening, but they, too, made it clear that they were opposed to the research. It was "unnecessary," they said, and "a waste of taxpayers' money." They also said I could not possibly learn enough in one summer to make it worthwhile.

At first I had little contact with the Tlingit fishermen because few came to fish in the area until July, when the sockeye arrived. Unlike the non-natives, who fish in the Dry Bay area all summer long, the Tlingit move between a number of rivers and fish according to when the different species of salmon (king, sockeye, silver, pink, and chum) begin their spawning migrations.

Competition between the Tlingits and whites over fishing sites in the Dry Bay area had strained relations between the two peoples with some nasty results. Over the previous four years, Tlingit fishermen were fired at several times in an attempt to drive them away. One Tlingit fish camp had been set on fire, and the helicopter used to haul the Indians' catch to the fish processor had been shot and disabled.

Although each group was distrustful of the other, my study required that I develop rapport and gather information from both. I tried to divide my time between them, but some individuals always viewed me with suspicion whenever they saw me interacting with members of the other group.

During the first week or two, I noticed that when I approached a group of white fishermen, one by one they walked off, only to regroup somewhere else. After the summer was over I learned more about what the fishermen had thought of me from the backcountry ranger based at Dry Bay who heard much of the gossip. They joked about my appearance—I wore tennis shoes instead of rubber boots—and they said that my speech, like my clothes, was too clean. The rumor was that I lived near the safety of the fish processor because I was afraid of bears. The ranger also told me what he had observed in my interactions with the fishermen: "Your body language just didn't fit with theirs. . . . You stood too erect while they tend to slouch with their thumbs cocked in their pockets. And you made too much eye contact while they prefer to look away and fidget."

Though the Tlingits never walked away from me when I approached them, they didn't make me feel welcome either. My early attempts at conversation were often met with the most minimal responses, and sometimes with silence. The Tlingits are a reserved and private people, unaccustomed to asking or being asked questions. And in the beginning I didn't have enough knowledge of Alaska, the region, or the issues that concerned the Tlingits to have an informal conversation without asking questions. When I arrived at one of their tents I always had the sinking feeling that I was intruding, that they were busy and didn't have the time to chat.

Nevertheless, my rapport with members of both groups gradually improved. At the fish processor, after each fisherman unloaded his catch, he usually hung around to talk and learn how the other fishermen were doing before returning to the solitary life of the fish camp. In addition to the little things that any stranger in a new setting does to develop good relations with local people, I drew the younger men into playing frisbee, pitching horseshoes, or shooting baskets on a makeshift backboard. The games often ended up in a relaxed conversation, sometimes over beer.

I tried to demonstrate to both Tlingit and white fishermen alike that I respected their knowledge and capabilities: the way in which they dealt with the hazards of bears and of fishing in small boats in the swift, frigid waters of the Alsek where floating logs and chunks of ice from calving glaciers upriver could destroy a person's nets and where falling overboard could easily mean death. I listened attentively to what they said, like a conscientious schoolboy. They were, indeed, my teachers. I told each fisherman that everything I learned from them was confidential and that even in my own field notes I was not using their real names. I promised to let each of them read and comment on the first draft of my report and that if they disagreed with some point I had made but could not convince me that I was wrong, that I would include their objections in the report.

The fishermen, Tlingits and non-natives, gradually came to accept that I had an open mind about them and their activities, that I had not come with fixed ideas about the appropriateness of fishing and hunting or of building cabins and airstrips in a protected wilderness area. Ultimately, a few fishermen invited me to their fish camps for a meal.

My wife Sharon's arrival in Dry Bay several weeks into the fieldwork also seemed to help. While the wives of most fishermen did not come to Dry Bay, mine had and she was seven months pregnant. She hiked with me to visit distant fish camps and took an unexpectedly severe pounding in a boat while ascending swift water miles up the Alsek River. Some thought she was foolish to come to Dry Bay in her "condition," where storms can ground airplanes for days putting medical attention out of reach. But whatever the wisdom of her being there, her presence seemed to make it easier for people to accept me. Perhaps because with a wife and a child on the way I was seen as a family man, something to which the fishermen could relate.

But the turning point in my rapport with local fishermen happened on the Fourth of July. All of the non-native fishermen gathered at the fish processor to celebrate; the height of the festivities was a softball game played on a bluff above the river. I had once played baseball for a living and still enjoyed the game. In my first two at bats I hit the ball hard and far, making two home runs. In the sixth inning, when our only bat broke nearly in half, I helped one of the fishermen repair it with screws and plenty of tape, and with choked grips we resumed play. In the field, with the enthusiasm of play and forgetting for the moment my low status among the fishermen, I gave the other fielders directions on which cut-off man to throw to. When a debate broke out over a quirky play, I knew the rule that resolved the disagreement. Being able to play ball was the accidental key to acceptance. Following the game there was some good-natured joking about my play, and the fishermen seemed decidedly friendlier. During the game, the ranger, without my knowing, had told some of the fishermen that I had once played professionally.

In earlier research I had often played sports with the people I was living among as a way of getting to know them better, but also for fun and exercise. It always seemed to me to make a difference in their attitudes toward me, but I had never really known for certain. This time, at the end of the summer when I was at the Park Service headquarters in Glacier Bay reviewing the summer's fieldwork, I had a long chat about my fieldwork with Richard Steele, the back-country ranger. "The ice breaker," he said, "was the softball game. When they saw how hard you hit the ball and that you really knew how to play the game, you became a regular guy. . . . You were no longer just a weirdo professor from back East who wore tennis shoes and clean clothes and had good posture."

What the ranger's observations also revealed to me was that I had failed to realize how differences in *class* can be as big an obstacle to developing rapport as differences in *culture*. When arriving in Dry Bay I had unconsciously assumed that I would have little difficulty making friends among the white fishermen, who ostensibly were from the same mainstream American culture as I. It would take more understanding and effort, I thought, to get to know the Tlingits. But the differences in class between me—white-collar academic—and the largely blue-collar fishermen were no less tractable.

While I received confirmation from the ranger that I had been accepted by the whites, I wasn't totally sure what the Tlingits thought of me and my research until several years later when I got a phone call from an Alaskan attorney who was representing twelve Yakutat fishermen in a suit against the State of Alaska over fishing rights. The Tlingit fishermen wanted to know if I would come to Alaska and help them. They wanted to know if I would testify in court as an "expert witness" on the history of their fishing in the Dry Bay area. The Alaska Department of Fish and Game had banned "surf fishing," that is, fishing the ocean waters outside the mouths of the Alsek and East rivers. Since only the natives fished in the surf, they believed the banning of the fishing there was discriminatory. The department justified its actions, in part, by claiming that surf fishing was not "traditional" among the Tlingits. The Indians knew it was and hoped that I knew enough about the history of their fishery to back them up.

In November 1987 I testified for the Tlingits in the Alaska Superior Court. It was the final irony—a complete reversal of roles. There I sat in the witness stand giving "expert" testimony on various aspects of Tlingit fishing and culture while in the gallery sat the real experts, the Tlingit fishermen who had taught me virtually everything I knew about them and their fishery. Later, outside the courtroom, after two hours of testimony and cross-examination by the State's attorney, they informed me that I had gotten it *right*.

ACKNOWLEDGMENTS

I wish to thank Anna Allen, Phil DeVita, Sharon Gmelch, Chase Henzel, Miriam Lee Kaprow, Phyllis Morrow, Trecie Melnick, Richard Nelson, and Richard Steele for their excellent comments on earlier drafts of this paper.

FOUR

🌺 The First Rotumans

ALAN HOWARD

Even after twenty-five years it is not difficult to recreate the mixture of feelings that overcame me when the plane I had taken from Hawaii, itself rather exotic in my eyes, landed at Nandi in Fiji. The Qantas flight arrived at five in the morning, and while we were disembarking the glow of dawn made its appearance. The air was soft and tropical, but still cool, and the Fijian policemen, whose presence (in the theatrical sense) was most impressive, added drama to the scene. A mixture of strange smells, some sweet, others pungent, filled my nostrils. I was overcome with a sense of being in an exotic place and, my anthropological training notwithstanding, was overcome with a mixture of excited anticipation and anxiety. I was twenty-five years old, naive and full of wonder for the mysteries of cultural differences. The airport experience did nothing to dispel the images I had in my mind of the culture I was planning to study, or what "my subjects" would be like. If anything, the island of Rotuma, which was governed from Fiji by the colonial administration, would be more exotic, and more primitive, than Fiji. I had read the meager literature describing Rotuman culture, and something about its history, and it left no doubt that I would find a people steeped in traditions and beliefs I would find initially bizarre and irrational. But I would work hard and eventually unravel their twisted logic so that it would appear sensible. I would be translator for these people, would transform their exotic remoteness to comfortable familiarity. It was a mission of sorts, born of a need to make sense out of a world I was (and still am) struggling to understand. I could not help but run over the rules I had set for myself:

Be observant and careful not to offend.

Do not show disapproval, no matter how strange the behavior or how silly the beliefs (which recalls a dictum I read in an early version of *Notes and Queries in Anthropology,* the fieldwork manual published by the Royal Anthropological Institute of Great Britain and Ireland, that an anthropologist should not show his revulsion, no matter how disgusting the customs of the natives really are).

Concentrate on communicating, by learning the Rotuman language and being careful to talk simply and clearly when using English.

There were other rules—there must have been, for I remember re-hearsals as taking quite some time—but I have forgotten what they were. In retrospect it seems they helped me deal with anxiety, but they were soon displaced by the realities of interaction, which made any pre-conceived code of conduct untenable.

It was in this frame of mind that I met, quite fortuitously, my first Rotuman. I had left Nandi and taken a taxi to Korolevu, a resort on the way to Suva where I would later have to confront colonial officials, for whom I had prepared another set of preconceived behaviors. In Suva I would have to be on my best behavior and would have to recall all the rules of etiquette and table manners my mother tried to teach me as a child. With them I would use the elegant parts of my vocabulary (learned mostly in studying for my entrance exam to Stanford) so as not to sound like a dolt. My advisor had suggested that I buy a tuxedo and dinner jacket, which I couldn't afford, just in case I got invited to formal affairs in Suva. Lacking the right attire, I was even more determined to talk properly. With Rotu-mans I would talk simply and clearly, with colonial officials I would turn into a pedant.

But before facing these ordeals I would spend a day at Korolevu, which lived up to its advertisements as a resort that captured the full flavor of Fiji. The hotel was located on a splendid beach, with palm trees and all the other romantic symbols of the South Seas. The hotel rooms were *bures* (thatched huts) and the service personnel were frizzy-headed Fijians who by physique and bearing gave new meaning to my visions of "the noble savage." I was enthralled, to say the least. After dinner—itself an exotic experience for me, although the fare was curry rather than dalo and roast pig—I got into a conversation with one of the hotel clerks. He asked what I was doing in Fiji and I when I told him about my plans for doing research on Rotuma he said, "Oh, we have a Rotuman working here as maintenance manager. Would you like to meet him?" My heart skipped a beat. "Sure," I replied, and quickly rehearsed the rules. So I was taken to meet my first Rotuman.

Alex Rae was an impressive-looking man by any cultural standard. He stood about six-feet-four and had a mane of white wavy hair and a beautifully bronzed complexion. Despite his casual European clothes he appeared the epitome of the Polynesian chief. He was in his mid-sixties at the time—a very handsome man indeed. As soon as he spoke I realized my rules were a waste of time, for his speech was as elegant as his appearance. To my untutored ear it sounded like Cambridge or Oxford, but it turned out to be simply good Fijian English. Mr. Rae was a charming and gentle man, who made me feel at ease right away. I guess I learned my initial important lesson from him in the first few minutes of our encounter—that Rotumans were gracious, perceptive hosts, and that any attempt on my part to act the role of anthropologist would be ludicrous.

He held full command of our conversation, asking first one question, then another. He listened patiently to my answers and showed a full appreciation for my purposes. We started out slowly, talking about practical matters related to life on Rotuma, and then he gradually shifted toward more theoretical concerns. I don't remember the specifics, for in retrospect it was his sophistication and style of conversing that sticks in my mind. However, I do remember my first blunder. We were talking about the issue of Polynesian migrations and he mentioned some of Peter Buck's theories. I seized that moment to make one of those Batesonian statements—a statement framed in such a way as to carry an implicit message about our developing relationship—that one is often tempted to make to people one is patronizing. I said, simply and as a matter of fact, that Peter Buck was a Maori, that his true name was Te Rangi Hiroa. What I was trying to do, of course, was to use Peter Buck as a common denominator between us. I am an anthropologist; Peter Buck was an anthropologist; Peter Buck was Te Rangi Hiroa, a Polynesian; you, Alex Rae, are a Polynesian; therefore there is a social equivalence between us. I am not really your social superior by virtue of being white.

Perhaps I am making myself sound more arrogant than I in fact was, for my manner was gentle and appreciative of his obvious intelligence. I was simply trying to consolidate our developing relationship. His response caught me off guard, for he corrected my error. I don't remember his exact words, but the message was that I was not quite right, that Te Rangi Hiroa was only half Polynesian. His mother was a New Zealand Maori but his father was Irish. In truth I did not know this, or if I once did had forgotten it, and felt properly chastised. I don't think Mr. Rae was trying to chastise me or was making a statement about our relationship by correcting my error. I think he was much more at ease and less self-conscious than I was during the entire encounter. But his remark made me aware of how inappropriate my initial framework had been for our interaction. Lesson two: Don't assume I know more than another person, Rotumans included, unless I'm prepared to be embarrassed.

Our conversation extended for hours and I enjoyed it immensely. It was in no sense an anthropological interview. If I had entertained that thought to begin with it soon dissolved in the sheer pleasure of conversing with a delightful and knowledgeable companion. This simply wasn't the context I had associated with anthropological interviewing. I could not see Alex Rae as a "subject," only as a remarkable human being. He did talk about his life, especially about the period in his youth when he became a professional boxer. This led him to discuss various professional boxers, past and present, and to my astonishment he knew the succession of world champions in every major weight division from the beginning of records to the present. Since I took pride in my own knowledge of sports trivia—I could recite the New York Yankees lineups back to the 1920s—Rae's knowledge of boxing was the final persuader. Here was a formidable intellect—a man from whom I could, and did, learn much.

I left Korolevu in a rather different frame of mind from the one I had brought to Fiji. The landscape was still exotic enough, but I was no longer burdened by notions of "primitive" natives. In Suva I met Alex Rae's sister, Faga, her son, Oscar, and her daughter, Liebling. All were sophisticated urbanites who further demolished my preconceptions. Liebling had been the first Miss Hibiscus and had traveled extensively abroad; Oscar was a draftsman for a government agency. Perhaps it was one of the jokes Oscar told me that put the final nail in the coffin of my ill-conceived notions. It went like this:

There were two men who were fond of poetry. One man was an ardent fan of Tennyson, the other was equally committed to the poetry of Shakespeare. They would frequently go on walks together and when they came upon interesting scenes would make up poems in the style of their favorite bards. One day when they were on such an excursion they saw before them a man approaching with a severe hernia. The Shakespearean turned to his companion and asked, "How would Tennyson describe this scene?"

With only a moment's hesitation the second man offered his verse:

"Down yonder hill there comes a wag,
legs spread apart,
balls in a bag."

"Not bad," remarked the first man. His friend then challenged him to compose a poem in the Shakespearean manner, and without hesitation he came forth with his composition:

"Lo! What manner of man is this,
that comes with his balls in parenthesis?"

As it turned out, Alex Rae and his sister, Faga, were by genealogical reckoning among the highest ranking Rotumans alive at the time. They were grandchildren of the great chief Marafu, who was in power when the island was ceded to Great Britain in 1881. It was, I think, fortunate that I met them first, since it might have been easier to maintain my illusions had I gone directly to Rotuma. Not all Rotumans were as sophisticated as Alex or Oscar, but then again, I have met few people since who can match them.

SUGGESTED READINGS

HOWARD, ALAN

1970 Learning to Be Rotuman. New York: Columbia Teachers College Press.

PLANT, CHRIS, ED.

1977 Rotuma: Split Island. Suva, Fiji: Institute of Pacific Studies, University of the South Pacific.

FIVE

Navigating Nigerian Bureaucracies; or, "Why Can't You Beg?" She Demanded[1]

ELIZABETH A. EAMES
Bates College

Americans have a saying: "It's not what you know, it's who you know." This aphorism captures the—usually subtle—use of old-boy networks for personal advancement in this country. But what happens when this principle becomes the primary dynamic of an entire social system? The period of three years I spent pursuing anthropological field research in a small Nigerian city was one of continual adjustment and reordering of expectations. This essay discusses a single case—how I discovered the importance personal ties have for Nigerian bureaucrats—but also illustrates the general process by which any open-minded visitor to a foreign land might decipher the rules of proper behavior. I was already familiar with Max Weber's work on bureaucracy and patrimony, yet its tremendous significance and explanatory power became clear to me only following the incidents discussed below.

I heard the same comment from every expatriate I met during my three years in Nigeria—U.S. foreign service officers, U.N. "experts," and visiting business consultants alike: "If you survive a stint in Nigeria, you can survive anywhere." The negative implications of this statement stem from outsiders' futile attempts to apply, in a new social setting, home-grown notions of how bureaucratic organizations function. This is indeed a natural inclination and all the more tempting where organizational structure appears bureaucratic. Yet in Nigeria, the officeholders behaved according to different rules; their attitudes and sentiments reflected a different moral code. A bureaucratic organizational structure coexisted with an incompatible set of moral imperatives. The resulting unwieldy, inflexible structure may be singled out as one of British colonialism's most devastating legacies.

Please bear in mind the problem of understanding that another culture works both ways. Any Nigerian student reading for the first time the following passage by a prominent American sociologist would probably howl with laughter:

The chief merit of a bureaucracy is its technical efficiency, with a premium placed on precision, speed, expert control, continuity, discretion and optimal returns on input. The structure is one which approaches the complete elimination of personalized relationships and nonrational considerations (hostility, anxiety, affectual involvements, etc.). (Merton 1968:250)

Even those well-educated administrative Nigerian officers who had once been required to incorporate such notions into their papers and exams do not live by them.

To many foreigners who have spent time in Nigeria, "the system" remains a mystery. What motivating principles explain the behavior of Nigerian administrative officers? How do local people understand the behavior of their fellow workers? Why do some people successfully maneuver their way through the system while others founder?

Recently I attended a party. As often happens at a gathering of anthropologists, we started swapping fieldwork stories and meandered onto the topic of our most unpleasant sensation or unsettling experience. That night, I heard tales of surviving strange diseases, eating repulsive foods, losing one's way in the rain forest, being caught between hostile rebel factions or kidnapped by guerrilla fighters. As for me? All that came to mind were exasperating encounters with intransigent clerks and secretaries. I began to ponder why these interactions had proved so unsettling.

My discipline—social anthropology—hinges on the practice of "participant-observation." To a fledgling anthropologist, the "fieldwork" research experience takes on all of the connotations of initiation into full membership. For some, a vision-quest; for others, perhaps, a trial-by-ordeal: The goal is to experience another way of life from the inside and to internalize, as does a growing child, the accumulating lessons of daily life. But the anthropologist is not a child; therefore, she or he experiences not conversion but self-revelation.

I came to understand my American-ness during the period spent coming to terms with Nigerian-ness. I found that I believed in my right to fair treatment and justice simply because I was a human being. I believed in equal protection under the law. But my Nigerian friends did not. What I found was a social system where status, relationships, and rights were fundamentally negotiable and justice was never impartial. In the United States, impersonalized bureaucracies are the norm: We do not question them, our behavior automatically adjusts to them. But imagine spending a year working in a corporation where none of these rules applied.

You see, a Nigerian immigration officer will sign your form only if doing so will perpetuate some mutually beneficial relationship or if she or he wishes to initiate a relationship by putting you in her or his debt.

For those unlucky enough to be without connections (this must necessarily include most foreigners), the only other option is bribery—where the supplicant initiates a personal relationship of sorts and the ensuing favor evens matters up.

Hence, Nigeria becomes labeled "inefficient," "tribalistic," and "corrupt." And so it is. Yet this system exists and persists for a profound reason: Whereas in Europe and Asia power and authority always derived from ownership of landed property, in West Africa the key ingredient was a large number of loyal dependents. Because land was plentiful and agriculture was of the extensive slash-and-burn variety, discontented subordinates could simply move on. The trick was to maintain power over subordinates through ostentatious displays of generosity. This meant more than simply putting on a lavish feast: You must demonstrate a willingness to use your influence to support others in times of need. Even now, all Nigerians participate in such patron-client relationships. In fact, all legitimate authority derives from being in a position to grant favors and not the other way around.

Actually, only a miniscule portion of my time in the field was spent dealing with Nigeria's "formal sector." My research entailed living within an extended family household (approximately a dozen adults and two dozen children), chatting with friends, visiting women in their market stalls, even at times conducting formal or informal interviews. And during the years spent researching women's economic resources and domestic responsibilities, I came to understand—indeed, to deeply admire—their sense of moral responsibility to a wide-ranging network of kin, colleagues, neighbors, friends, and acquaintances. Even now, I often take the time to recall someone's overwhelming hospitality, a friendly greeting, the sharing and eating together. Such warm interpersonal relations more than made up for the lack of amenities.

The longer I stayed, however, the clearer it became that what I loved most and what I found most distressing about life in Nigeria were two sides of the same coin, inextricably related.

The first few months in a new place can be instructive for those with an open mind:

LESSON ONE: THE STRENGTH OF WEAK TIES

My first exposure to Nigerian civil servants occurred when, after waiting several months prior to departure from the United States, I realized my visa application was stalled somewhere in the New York Consulate. Letter writing and telephoning proved futile, and as my departure date approached, panic made me plan a personal visit.

The waiting room was populated by sullen, miserable people—a roomful of hostile eyes fixed on the uniformed man guarding the office door. They had been waiting for hours on end. Any passing official was simultaneously accosted by half a dozen supplicants, much as a political celebrity is accosted by the news media. Everyone's immediate goal was to enter through that door to the inner sanctum; so far, they had failed. But I was lucky: I had the name of an acquaintance's wife's schoolmate currently employed at the consulate. After some discussion, the guard allowed me to telephone her.

Mrs. Ojo greeted me cordially, then—quickly, quietly—she coaxed my application forms through the maze of cubicles. It was a miracle!

"What a wonderful woman," I thought to myself. "She understands." I thought she had taken pity on me and acted out of disgust for her colleagues' mishandling of my application. I now realize that by helping me she was reinforcing a relationship with her schoolmate. Needless to say, my gratitude extended to her schoolmate's husband, my acquaintance. As I later came to understand it, this natural emotional reaction—gratitude for favors granted—is the currency fueling the system. Even we Americans have an appropriate saying: "What goes around comes around." But at this point, I had merely learned that, here as elsewhere, connections open doors.

LESSON TWO: NO IMPERSONAL TRANSACTIONS ALLOWED

Once on Nigerian soil I confronted the mayhem of Muritala Muhammad airport. Joining the crowd surrounding one officer's station, jostled slowly forward, I finally confronted her face-to-face. Apparently I was missing the requisite currency form. No, sorry, there were none available that day. "Stand back," she declared. "You can't pass here today." I waited squeamishly. If I could only catch her eye once more! But then what? After some time, a fellow passenger asked me what the problem was. At this point, the officer, stealing a glance at me while processing someone else, inquired: "Why can't you beg?" The person being processed proclaimed: "She doesn't know how to beg! Please, O! Let her go." And I was waved on.

A young post office clerk soon reinforced my conclusion that being employed in a given capacity did not in and of itself mean one performed it. Additional incentive was required. Again, I was confronted with a mass of people crowded round a window. Everyone was trying to catch the clerk's attention, but the young man was adept at avoiding eye contact. Clients were calling him by name, invoking the name of mutual friends, and so on. After some time, he noticed me, and I grabbed the opportunity to ask for stamps. In a voice full of recrimination, yet tinged with regret, he announced more to the crowd than to me: "Why can't you greet?" and proceeded to ignore me. This proved my tip-off to the elaborate and complex cultural code of greetings so central to Nigerian social life. In other words, a personal relationship is like a "jump start" for business transactions.

LESSON THREE: EVERY CASE IS UNIQUE

Mrs. Ojo had succeeded in obtaining for me a three-month visa, but I planned to stay for over two years. Prerequisite for a "regularized" visa was university affiliation. This sounded deceptively simple. The following two months spent registering as an "occasional postgraduate student" took a terrible toll on my nervous stomach. The worst feeling was of an ever-receding target, an ever-thickening tangle of convoluted mazeways. No one could tell me what it took to register, for in fact, no one could possibly predict what I would confront farther down the road. Nothing was routinized, everything was personalized, and no two cases could possibly be alike.

This very unpredictability of the process forms a cybernetic system with the strength of personal ties, however initiated. "Dash" and "Long-leg" are the locally recognized means for cutting through red tape or confronting noncooperative personnel. "Dash" is local parlance for gift or bribe. "Long-leg" (sometimes called "L-L" or "L-squared") refers to petitioning a powerful person to help hack your way through the tangled overgrowth. To me, it evokes the image of something swooping down from on high to stomp on the petty bureaucrat causing the problem.

During my drawn-out tussle with the registrar's office, I recounted my problem to anyone who would listen. A friend's grown son, upon hearing of my difficulties, wrote a note on his business card to a Mr. Ade in the Exams Section. Amused by his attempt to act important, I thanked Ayo politely. When I next saw him at his mother's home, he took the offensive and accused me of shunning him. It came out that I had not seen Mr. Ade. But, I protested, I did not know the man. Moreover, he worked in exams, not the registry. That, I learned, was not the point. I was supposed to assume that Mr. Ade would have known someone in the registry. Not only had I denied Ayo the chance to further his link to Mr. Ade, but ignoring his help was tantamount to denying any connection to him or—more important for me—his mother.

This revelation was reinforced when I ran into a colleague. He accused me of not greeting him very well. I had greeted him adequately but apologized nonetheless. As the conversation progressed, he told me that he had heard I had had "some difficulty." He lamented the fact that I had not called on him, since as Assistant Dean of Social Science he could have helped me. His feelings were truly hurt, provoking his accusation of a lackluster greeting. Indeed, things were never the same between us again, for I had betrayed—or denied—our relationship.

LESSON FOUR: YOUR FRIENDS HAVE ENEMIES

Well, I did eventually obtain a regularized visa, and it came through "long-leg." But the problems inherent in its use derive from the highly politicized and factionalized nature of Nigerian organizations, where personal loyalty is everything.

Early on, I became friendly with a certain social scientist and his family. Thereby, I had unwittingly become his ally in a long drawn-out war between himself and his female colleagues. The disagreement had its origins ten years before in accusations of sex discrimination but had long since spilled over into every aspect of departmental functioning. Even the office workers had chosen sides. More significant, though, was the fact that my friend's chief antagonist and I had similar theoretical interests. Though in retrospect I regret the missed opportunity, I realize that I was in the thick of things before I could have known what was happening. Given the original complaint, my sympathies could have been with the other camp. But ambiguous loyalty is equivalent to none.

Once I had learned my lessons well, life became more pleasant. True, every case was unique and personal relationships were everything. But, as my friends and allies multiplied, I could more easily make "the system" work for me.

Most Nigerians develop finely honed interpersonal skills, which stand them in good stead when they arrive in the United States. They easily make friends with whomever they run across, and naturally, friends will grant them the benefit of the doubt if there is room to maneuver. The psychological need remains, even in our seemingly formalized, structured world, for a friendly, personable encounter.

On the other hand, as I was soon to learn for myself, anyone adept at working this way suffers tremendous pain and anxiety from the impersonal enforcement of seemingly arbitrary rules. For instance, a friend took it as a personal affront when his insurance agent refused to pay a claim because a renewal was past due.

As a result of my Nigerian experience, I am very sensitive to inflexible and impersonal treatment, the flip side of efficiency:

Leaving Nigeria to return to Boston after two and a half years, I stopped for a week in London. I arrived only to find that my old college friend, with whom I intended to stay, had recently moved. Playing detective, I tried neighbors, the superintendent, directory assistance. Tired and bedraggled, I thought of inquiring whether a forwarding address had been left with the post office. Acknowledging me from inside his cage, the small, graying man reached for his large, gray ledger, peered in, slapped it shut, and answered:

"Yes."

"But . . . what is it?" I asked, caught off guard.

He peered down at me and replied: "I cannot tell you. We are not allowed. We must protect him from creditors."

I was aghast. In no way did I resemble a creditor.

Noticing my reaction, he conceded: "But, if you send him a letter, I will forward it."

Bursting into tears of frustration, in my thickest American accent, displaying my luggage and my air ticket, I begged and cajoled him, to no avail. I spent my entire London week in a bed 'n breakfast, cursing petty bureaucrats as my bill piled up. *"That," I thought, "could never happen in Nigeria!"*

NOTE

1. The theoretical analysis from a lengthier essay has been deleted from this presentation. In the original version, great pains were taken to avoid any possible evolutionary interpretation of the relationship between patrimonial and bureaucratic authority. Over the millenia, bureaucracies have been invented and reinvented in Africa, Asia, and Europe. Moreover, patrimonial relationships exist everywhere bureaucracies exist.

   The suggested readings (below) provide the bases for most of my original analysis of aspects of interactional and bureaucratic organization discovered in my Nigerian fieldwork. For those interested, a more thorough analysis can be found in my original essay of the same title in L. Perman (ed.), *Work in Modern Society* (Dubuque, IA: Kendall/Hunt Publishing Company, 1986).

   I am grateful to Oladele Akinla, Paul Brodwin, Anne Hornsby, Dorinne Kondo, Anne Sweetser, and Jeong-Ro Yoon for helpful comments on an earlier version of this essay.

REFERENCE

MERTON, ROBERT K.
1968   Social Theory and Social Structure. New York: Free Press. Chapter VIII: Bureaucratic Structure and Personality.

SUGGESTED READINGS

BENDIX, REINHARD
1977   Max Weber: An Intellectual Portrait. Berkeley and Los Angeles: University of California Press (first publ. 1960).

BRITAN, GERALD M., AND RONALD COHEN, EDS.
1980   Heirarchy and Society: Anthropological Perspectives on Bureaucracy. Philadelphia: ISHI Publications.

FAGE, J. D., AND ROLAND OLIVER, EDS.
1982   The Cambridge History of Africa from the Earliest Times to c. 500 B.C. Cambridge: Cambridge University Press.

FAIRBANK, JOHN K., EDWIN O. REISCHAUER, AND ALBERT M. CRAIG
1973   East Asia: Tradition and Transformation. Boston: Houghton Mifflin.

FALLERS, LLOYD A.
1956   Bantu Bureaucracy: A Century of Political Evolution among the Basoga of Uganda. Chicago: University of Chicago Press.

GRANOVETTER, MARK S.
1973   The Strength of Weak Ties. American Journal of Sociology 78:1360–1380.

LLOYDD, P. C.
1974   Power and Independence: Urban Africans' Perception of Social Inequality. London: Routledge & Kegan Paul.

SMITH, M. G.
1960   Government in Zazzau 1800–1950. London: Oxford.
1974   Corporations & Society. London: Duckworth.

WEBER, MAX
1978   Economy and Society. Berkeley and Los Angeles: University of California Press.

🌺 Two Tales from the Trukese Taproom

MAC MARSHALL
University of Iowa

It was nearing sundown in Mwáán Village on Moen Island, Truk, as we bounced slowly along in the Datsun pickup. The landscape glowed, and the Pacific island blues and greens heightened in intensity as the shadows lengthened. The village's daily rhythm slowed, and the moist air was heavy with incompatible aromas: acrid smoke from cooking fires, sweet fragrance of plumeria blossoms, foul stench of the mangrove swamp, and the pleasant warm earth smells of a tropical island at dusk. All was peaceful, somnolent, even stuporous. And then the quiet was shattered by an ear-splitting shout out of nowhere: "Waaaaa Ho!" The horrible roar was repeated, and its source—a muscular young man clad only in blue jeans and zoris—materialized directly in the path of our truck, brandishing a two-foot-long machete.

The three of us in the pickup were all new to Truk. Bill, the driver, was an American anthropologist in his sixties traveling with his wife through Micronesia en route home from Asia, and he'd only been in Truk for a couple of days. Leslie and I, the passengers, had been there for approximately a month awaiting a field-trip ship to take us to our outer island research site on Namoluk Atoll. In the interim she and I were staying in a small guest facility on the grounds of a Protestant church–sponsored high school a couple miles from the town center. We had met Bill and his wife by chance the day before at a local restaurant. The four of us had spent this day voyaging by motorboat to another island in Truk Lagoon to explore the ruins of the former Japanese headquarters that had been destroyed in World War II. On our return we agreed to meet for dinner, and Bill had just come for us in his rented truck to drive back to town for supper. None of us had ever before heard the frightening yell, "Waaaaa Ho!" Nor had any of us been confronted by a young Trukese man built like a fullback and waving a machete over his head.

"What in the hell?" Bill asked, but before I could respond we were nearly upon the young man. Fortunately, the bumpiness of the dirt road limited our speed to perhaps five miles per hour, and Bill avoided hitting our challenger by swerving to the left just in time. As he did so, the young man brought the machete down with all the force he could muster on top of the cab, once again announcing his presence with a loud "Waaaaa Ho!" The machete cut into the edge of the cab approximately half an inch deep right where I had been holding on to the door frame a split second before. As steel bit steel, Bill panicked and floored the truck, but our attacker managed to strike another powerful blow with the knife on the edge of the truck bed before we escaped. We jolted along at fifteen miles per hour the rest of the way to town, the maximum we and the pickup could sustain given road conditions. We were completely shaken by what had just befallen us.

"Why in the hell did he do that?" Bill wanted to know. I was new to Truk, there to study and learn about Trukese society and culture. I had no answer to Bill's question. We literally did not know what had hit us, or more accurately, why we had been attacked. Over dinner we speculated on the possibilities. The young man might have been angry with foreigners and decided to take out his bad feelings on us. No, we rejected that hypothesis because it was clear that the young man would not have been able to tell who was in the truck when he burst out of the bushes and lunged at us. It all happened too fast. A second thought we had was that the young man had it in for someone who owned a blue Datsun pickup, saw our truck approaching, and mistook us for someone else. But this hypothesis failed for the same reason: Because of the dwindling light and the thick brush along the roadside it seemed unlikely our attacker could see the color and make of the truck before he leapt into its path. Finally, based on our collective experience as persons reared in American culture, the four of us concluded either that the young man was emotionally distraught over a recent major trauma in his life or that he was mentally ill and a clear danger to the general public.

We were puzzled and truly frightened. What made the incident all the more bizarre was that Leslie and I had been treated with unfailing kindness by all the Trukese we had met from the moment of our arrival. We had walked through Mwáán Village several times daily for four weeks, many times after dark, and always we had been greeted by warm smiles and a cheery *"Ran Annim!"* What could have provoked this attack? Why in the hell *did* he do that? Although I could not know it at the time, this incident presaged much of my later research involvement with the people of Truk and directed my attention to a series of questions and puzzles that I continue to pursue.

I can now, with some degree of confidence, provide an answer to why the young man did what he did: He was drunk. The fearsome yell announced that fact immediately to anyone who knew the code surrounding drunken behavior in Truk, but we were ignorant of this as outsiders and novices in the subtleties of Trukese life. When young Trukese men drink, they are perceived to become dangerous, explosive, unpredictably aggressive. Given the option, the received wisdom is to avoid Trukese drunks if at all possible. We, of course, did not have that option and we became yet one more target of the violence associated with alcohol consumption in contemporary Truk. In fact, we were lucky that no one was hurt. Quite often the aggression of Trukese drinkers results in injuries and occasionally deaths.

How long has alcohol been available in the islands? Why do young men drink in Truk and why do women almost uniformly abstain? Why do drinkers so often become violent after consuming alcohol? What happens to the perpetrators of such violence? Questions such as these surrounding the Trukese encounter with alcoholic beverages are legion, and when pursued they open myriad windows into Trukese personality, culture, history, and social organization. Before I came to understand this, however, I had another traumatic experience involving Trukese and alcohol.

By the time this second incident occurred, Leslie and I had been in Truk for four months. We had left the headquarters island of Moen and sailed 130 miles to the southeast to a tiny and remote coral atoll which was to be the focus of my dissertation research. Namoluk was idyllic, an emerald necklace of land surrounding a turquoise lagoon bounded by the deep sapphire blue of the open ocean. Namoluk was a close-knit kin community of 350 persons where people knew one another in terms of "total biography": All the details of one's life and the lives of one's relatives and ancestors were part of local lore and general public knowledge. Everyone had a particular role to play that in some senses seemed almost predestined from childhood onward. Namoluk was fascinating, an integrated yet intricate community with a long history of its own which had been studied only briefly half a century before by a German scholar. I became totally engrossed in my research and in trying to master the local language.

We had taken up residence in a comfortable new cement house with a corrugated iron roof located more or less in the center of the village area. Our house sat at the intersection of two main paths and in between the locations of two of the island's three licensed bingo games. Since bingo was played daily by a large part of the population, a steady stream of islanders strolled past our front door. The family on whose homestead we lived slept in a wooden house next door, but members of the family were in and out of our house continually.

Soon after our arrival on Namoluk I learned that alcohol use was the subject of considerable controversy. Technically the island was dry by local consensus, but the legality of the local prohibition ordinance was questionable because proper procedures for enacting such a law had not been followed. At the time we came on the scene an intergenerational struggle was under way between men over roughly the age of forty or forty-five and younger men for control of the elective municipal government. Alcohol became a central issue in this struggle, with older men supporting prohibition and younger men enthusiastically drinking booze whenever possible. Even so, drinking was certainly not a regular event on Namoluk and when it did take place it often led to nothing more than boisterous singing and loud laughter late at night in the canoe houses. I began to get the impression that drunkenness on Namoluk was categorically different from what we had experienced on Truk a few months before.

And then it happened. Late on a Sunday afternoon we were lolling about our house, just being lazy and chatting with our landlord, when suddenly a huge commotion arose in the distance. Sounds of anguish, anger, and anxiety swirled toward us and then, out of the milling mob of men, women, and noise, came that unforgettable yell: "Waaaaa Ho!"

I sprang to my feet, jumped into my zoris, and dashed out the door to find a crowd of twenty to thirty agitated people at the intersection of the two paths, yelling, shouting at one another, and keeping two persons separated. As I took in the pattern of what was happening, I realized that a fight was threatening between two men who had been drinking, Each was being upbraided by female relatives to refrain from fighting, while at the same time men were standing by to make sure that their own male kinsman was not injured. Before I could stop to cooly assess the situation and record it objectively in my data notebook I found myself next to the antagonists. The larger man suddenly jumped on his opponent, wrestling him to the ground. Instantly he began pummeling and pounding the smaller man with his fists. I acted almost instinctively. Before I fully realized what I was doing I had a full nelson on the larger man, had pulled him off of his victim, and was trying to convince him to desist from such behavior.

Though strong enough to protect myself from harm, it occurred to me as I stood there that I had made a terrible mistake. All through graduate school my professors had emphasized the importance of not taking sides or getting involved in local political or interpersonal squabbles in the research community, lest one make enemies, close off potential sources of information, or even get thrown out of the research site. All of those warnings flashed through my mind as I pressed the full nelson on the struggling man. I was convinced that I had blown it and that this whole sorry episode would have nothing but negative repercussions for my work—and just at a time when things seemed to be progressing so splendidly and Leslie and I were beginning to feel like we really fit into the community.

But, oh, how wrong I was.

In learning why I was wrong, I also learned an important lesson about masculinity and how masculinity relates to fighting and to alcohol use in Trukese culture. And I had taken a major step toward what has become the central focus of my research over the past fifteen years: the study of alcohol and culture.

Once tempers calmed and it was clear that the fighting was over I released my hold and returned to my house, shaken and chagrined. How could I have been so stupid as to get involved in a silly drunken brawl? As I sat there feeling sorry for myself, a knock on the door roused me from dejection. It was two of the teenagers on the island, boys of about fourteen years of age, who were among our most loyal and patient language teachers. They asked if they could come in and, though I didn't really feel like company, I said, "Sure." The three of us sat on the woven pandanus mat on the floor and one of them immediately commented, "Wow, you were really strong out there a few minutes ago!" I wasn't sure whether I was being flattered or mocked, but before I gave a snide response I glanced at the boys and recognized the earnestness in their faces. I made some uncommittal answer, and they elaborated. My behavior had been thought impressive and salutory by everyone present: They said it demonstrated strength and bravery or fearlessness. If they only knew, I thought, that it actually demonstrated nothing more than the ignorance of an interloper endeavoring to keep the peace according to the inappropriate canons of his own culture!

Later that evening the man I had restrained, who was among the most influential and important of the younger men in the community, and on whose bad side I could ill afford to be, knocked on my door, accompanied by an older male relative. My landlord was with me and, while he knew what was about to take place, I was completely in the dark. The older man spoke long and rapidly in the Namoluk language and I understood only a little of what he said. Then the younger man spoke directly to me in English, asking my forgiveness for any problems he may have caused and noting that he would not have acted the way he had if he hadn't been drinking. "It was the alcohol that made me do it," he said. "We Trukese just don't know how to drink like you Americans. We drink and drink until our supply is gone and then we often get into fights." I was enormously relieved that *he* wasn't angry with *me,* and we begged one another's pardon through a mixture of Trukese apology ritual and American-style making up after an unpleasantness.

What I didn't recognize at the time, and only later came to fully understand, was that this incident that upset me so for fear I had botched my community rapport not only *improved* my rapport (including with the man I had restrained!) but also contributed to the development of my personal reputation on Namoluk. I noted earlier that Namoluk persons know one another in terms of total biography. As a foreigner from outside the system, I was an unknown quantity. Initially, people didn't know whether I was a good or a bad person, whether I would prove disruptive or cooperative, whether I would flaunt local custom or abide by it. Like every Trukese young adult—but especially like young men—I had to prove myself by my actions and deeds. I had to create and sustain an impression, to develop a reputation. At the time I didn't know this. Luckily for me, and purely by accident, my actions that afternoon accorded closely with core Trukese values that contribute to the image of a good person: respectfulness, bravery, and the humble demonstration of nonbullying strength in thought and deed. What I first believed to have been a colossal blunder turned out to be a fortunate coincidence of impulsive action with deepseated cultural beliefs about desirable masculine behavior. Now I, the unknown outsider, had begun to develop a local biography. But this was something I came to understand only after several more years of fieldwork in Trukese society.

SUGGESTED   READINGS

MARSHALL, MAC

1975   The Politics of Prohibition on Namoluk Atoll. Journal of Studies on Alcohol 36(5):597–610.
1979   Weekend Warriors: Alcohol in a Micronesian Culture. Palo Alto, CA: Mayfield.

MARSHALL, MAC, AND LESLIE B. MARSHALL

1990   Silent Voices Speak: Women and Prohibition in Truk. Belmont, CA: Wadsworth.

SEVEN

🦋 Reflections of a Shy Ethnographer: Foot-in-the-Mouth Is Not Fatal

JULIANA FLINN

I am shy. This proclamation is nothing more than a simple indicative fact that under ordinary circumstances would mean little. However, preliminary to ethnographic fieldwork, the issue presented problems of an extraordinary nature. Before I went to the field in Micronesia, I fretted over my shyness—worried that it would severely interfere with my research. Completely convinced I would make a fool of myself, I nonetheless dug deeply in the commitment to play the role of the child in remote surroundings and to learn, explore, and mostly, test myself. By accident, through an incident with a Micronesian informant and friend, I grew. Surviving chastisement, I learned something of both shyness and friendship, and more importantly I was compelled to face my own ethnocentricity.

Preparing to leave for the field, I discovered a reference to an article titled "Memoirs of a Shy Ethnographer." I eagerly sought a reprint, anxious for any tips dealing with shyness in the field. Simply knowing that others had contended with this personal problem would itself be comforting. Anthropologists had, in print, discussed culture shock, adjustment problems, even anxiety, but nowhere had I uncovered a discussion of shyness in the ethnographic enterprise. After all, cultural anthropologists are by the nature of their profession nosy: They have to enter a society, build rapport, gain some appreciable degree of acceptance, observe, participate, and ask people questions. I was moderately confident that I could do all that, but I dreaded the trauma that was likely to result. I wanted some hints. I needed some hints. And I needed the comfort of knowing I was not alone in worrying about shyness in the field.

My shyness essentially manifested itself as a fear of making mistakes and appearing blatantly foolish in public. I was apprehensive—worried at not presenting myself as perfect, the results of which would find me neither acceptable nor likable. I probably also had a touch of what is today being called the "Imposter Syndrome," the conviction that I only appeared to be a good graduate student and professional candidate. I suspect that women may be more prone than men to this particular problem. I recall echoing the feelings of a colleague who described her reaction at passing her doctoral examinations: "I can't believe it! I fooled them again, and they passed me. They still haven't found out that I don't know anything!"

Shyness, especially in dealing with graduate faculty, had disturbed me. Suspicious that shyness was preventing me from learning the social and political skills necessary for survival in a university, I often considered quitting, once especially after an awkward meeting with an advisor who seemed to have no idea why I consulted him. Perhaps because of a stubborn streak that counters my shyness, I persisted. I had more or less quietly pursued my own course in school without actively seeking advice and I decided to continue my unobtrusive ways. In fact, I put them to the test. If I failed in graduate school as a result of my own personal attitudes and approaches, I would then receive some confirmation that I was unsuited for the academic life.

I was not at all certain, however, that I would continue to remain successful quietly pursuing my work in the field. Perhaps I could manage graduate school without lengthy and frequent consultations with faculty, but I could not keep to myself in the field forever. Even though I had already been in Micronesia for two years as a Peace Corps volunteer, I prepared for fieldwork with a lingering sense of dread. I worried about approaching and talking to people—strangers, many of whom would probably have minimal or misconceived ideas of why I was there.

I looked back nostalgically on those Peace Corps years. They seemed so easy and free of stress compared to what was now facing me. In the Peace Corps I had a specific job to do, a clear role to play with structure and expectations that at least provided some degree of comfort. In fieldwork I would have to build my own structure, my own relationships, my own role—all of which seemed daunting.

I devoured articles about field experiences, especially about gaining entry into the field, building rapport, and interviewing. None of these dealt with shyness. Trusting that I was not unique, I wanted to know how other people had dealt with the problem. So I eagerly searched the library for the "shy ethnographer" article.

I was disappointed. The article had absolutely nothing to do with shyness. In fact, I never did figure out exactly what the title had to do with the article. I was on my own. To this day I remember the sick feeling in my stomach as I stepped into the jetway in San Francisco. How had the adventurous and persistent half of me forced the terrified half of me into this situation? What in the world was I doing?

Even more vivid is the memory of a sea of eyes swooping down the beach when my boat came ashore at the atoll. A wave of curious children descended to see a white woman carrying a blond toddler. But it was that same blond toddler who helped me contend with my shyness. He made my fieldwork easier. In fact, while I was in the field, I vowed that one day I would write my own article and finally thoroughly address the issue of shyness in ethnography—"Memoirs of a Shy Ethnographer, II." I soon discovered I was managing to deal with my shyness and even felt I had a few tips to pass along. I also decided that my first recommendation would be to beg, borrow, or steal a two-year-old child, preferably a gregarious and outgoing one like mine, though how I ended up with such a self-possessed and friendly child is still a mystery.

I had deliberately selected a remote field site on a coral atoll in Micronesia, more remote even than my earlier Peace Corps assignment. Yet this remoteness had positive effects which somewhat alleviated the problem of shyness. For example, the islanders held different notions of privacy than Americans, so I could easily watch and participate in many daily activities. I could easily wander by a homesite without feeling as though I was intruding into someone's privacy. This was, for me, thankfully a more comfortable environment.

Furthermore, I already knew several of the residents. Many had been my students several years earlier. The island residents knew who I was, since students had returned from school with tales of their American teachers. Some were initially confused about why I had come to their island, assuming I was returning as a Peace Corps volunteer, but I explained as best I could about my new role. Most saw me as a woman interested in learning about their customs. More important than my reasons for coming to their island seemed to be the fact that I was returning to Micronesia and had chosen to live with them instead of on the neighboring atoll where I had been assigned by the Peace Corps. I felt as though I was being treated as a long-lost friend, and they were convinced I genuinely liked them because I had chosen their island for my return.

Even more convincing to them, however, was the fact that I had brought my son, who was then about nineteen months old. The islanders were familiar enough with Americans willing to live with them because of years of Peace Corps service, but the majority of volunteers had been single and male. For a woman to come—and to bring her child—was a new experience which they interpreted to mean that I not only liked them, but I trusted them and their way of life to be good and healthy for my son,

Having a child with me in the field offered other benefits. I was much more real a person and woman in the eyes of my hosts. At my age and married—but deliberately childless—while in the Peace Corps, I presented an enigma. Although I now discovered the island women were curious about why I had only one child in the field, it was easier for them to now understand and relate to me and my situation. They might have to struggle with the notion of "anthropologist" but they had little trouble with "mother." And with a small child, I also found it much easier to be casual with people; my son often accompanied me and eased awkward moments when I felt compelled to talk about something. Even without a particular research purpose in mind, I could wander the island with him and simply stop and visit when he seemed so inclined. And several issues came to light because people would tell me of dangers to him. I was warned, for example, about walking with him on the beach in the evening for fear of malevolent ghosts.

Yet I was, in effect, myself a child in the field—a foolish and unknowing child. Intent on learning but still fearful of mistakes, it was important to me that the islanders learn to develop a concerned willingness to correct my blunders and misunderstandings. Much of my learning and questioning had to be public. I well remember exploring the island feeling like the pied piper because of the trail of children I attracted. I had forgotten what it was like to be noticed all the time, no longer anonymous.

Nonetheless, I contended as best I could with my shyness as I began learning their way of life. For example, I had ambivalent feelings about a young girl in the family with whom I lived—a girl who was a bit more outspoken than most. She was personally valuable precisely because of her lack of tact. Old enough to notice and explain my mistakes, she was at the same time either not mature enough or not inclined to politely ignore them. Most of her remarks centered on my speech. I arrived speaking a different Micronesian dialect, that of another island. Whenever I slipped into a word form or expression from the other island, she was the first to publicly correct me. Perhaps this young girl understood earlier than others. She chided me when I used a word from my Peace Corps experiences, especially when the local word forms were quite different. With bluntness she told me to learn to use the language of her people. Adults, on the other hand, tended to switch to the dialect from the district center—another dialect in which I was not well versed—when I had difficulty understanding. It took time for me to convince people that I could understand better if they just tried again in their own language.

These were valuable lessons. Considering that I wanted to explore attitudes toward people from other islands and that my hosts disliked the people from my Peace Corps site, I realized I could easily be given misleading answers if I sounded like one of those other islanders. Nonetheless, I was not accustomed to being scolded by a twelve-year-old girl. I swallowed my pride, reminding myself how useful she was.

Another outspoken woman was Camilla, a friend and participant in one of my greatest blunders. She had been a student of mine when I taught as a Peace Corps volunteer. Since then she had finished high school, returned home, married, and become pregnant with her first child. I cultivated a relationship with her for a variety of reasons. First, she was typical of the sort of persons I had come to study, a woman who had gone away to school, graduated, formed ties with other islanders while away, and returned to her home island. She was articulate, witty, patient, and seemingly comfortable with me. She was also a bit more outspoken than most. Since she knew I wanted to learn the ways of her people, she graciously volunteered information and provided instructions about how I should behave in local events and ceremonies.

One of the other reasons I liked Camilla was that she felt free to ask me questions. I discovered that I was much more comfortable answering questions than asking them; perhaps she should have been conducting the ethnographic research. But I learned much from the questions people asked me, perhaps as much as I learned from the questions I asked. For example, one woman, convinced that one of us misunderstood the other, pumped me for information about adoption in the United States. She very carefully set up her case: "Come on now, Julie. If you had ten children, and your sister didn't have any at all, wouldn't you share at least some of them with her?" Americans were immensely selfish creatures in her eyes.

When I asked about clans, people sometimes seemed surprised. "Why? Don't you have clans?" I had to answer no. "Well, then how do you know who your relatives are?" I enjoyed their candor and gained insights into how they viewed kinship.

One day I had gone to see Camilla and we had finished discussing the particular subjects of interest. I stayed, as was my habit, to talk as friends. Since she was pregnant with her first child, we began sharing stories about our experiences. In the back of my mind, I realized we were having this discussion in part because I had a child of my own—again an example of the advantages of conducting fieldwork as a mother.

Curious about local beliefs, I asked if she had any sense of whether she was carrying a boy or a girl and if she had any preference for one or the other. She said, "Some women say they know if it's a boy or a girl, and maybe before, in older times, there were people who could tell." Like the American I was, I also asked about names, wondering which ones she was considering and what meaning the choices had. She couldn't understand my curiosity. "We pick names after a child is born. How can you know what name to give before that?"

We had also been talking about the possibility of my returning sometime to her island and whether or not I would have any more children. She, like others, couldn't understand why I had only one child—especially at my age. Here I thought, compared to my experiences in the Peace Corps, arriving with a child would make such a difference. It did, but people also wanted to know why I had only one. In fact, they felt sorry for my mother. Many women lamented her fate: "The poor woman, she had only five children."

Thinking of how often people asked if my son and I would come back and how often they said they would like to see him when he was older, I said, "Well, maybe you'll have a girl, and maybe my son will come back when he's twenty or so, fall in love with your daughter, and get married." Camilla was appalled at what I considered an innocent remark. In fact, I meant the remark as an indicator of my close feelings. She glared at me, taken aback. I began to get the sense that I had said something I shouldn't have.

"Julie, you shouldn't say things like that. What an awful idea!" It was small comfort right then that I valued Camilla for her slightly atypical bluntness.

Now I had done it! I blushed, inwardly cringed, convinced that I had indeed made a fool of myself and that she'd never again take me seriously but would continue to treat me like some silly child. I had obviously said something I shouldn't have. How stupid had I revealed myself to be?

"Our children could never marry. You shouldn't say such a thing."

There it was again. Why couldn't she just drop it? But on the other hand, I figured I should pursue the issue; after all, I didn't want to repeat my mistake.

"I didn't mean to insult you. What's wrong with what I said? I want to know, so I won't do it again."

"It would be incest," she said, with a tone I interpreted as disbelief that I was so dense and slow to understand.

"Incest?" I thought I knew about that.

"Yes. Incest. Our children can't marry each other—we're sisters!" she responded.

"Sisters!" I liked the sound of that. I knew that the islanders created sibling ties for relationships we label friendships. Here I had been so overwhelmingly concerned about having made a foolish mistake, the result of which was this discovery of how fond Camilla was of me.

"Since we're sisters, our children are brothers and sisters and shouldn't get married."

I understood her point, and I relaxed, no longer concerned about a mistake. But over time I have seen many other implications of what she said.

This is the single strongest memory of my fieldwork, a turning point in so many important ways. First, I was able to take a very close look at the sort of role I wanted to play while living on the island. In this regard, I was made aware of how much my own values affected my behavior. Second, the abstract ideas I had read concerning kinship and Micronesian culture, instead of being an intellectual exercise, became very real and personal. As a result, I gained explicit insights into their meanings of kinship. Finally, perhaps because this was a cross-cultural friendship, the incident with Camilla was the beginning of personal growth for me which led to the realization that I could do or say foolish things and still be valued and liked.

I considered making explicit the created sibling relationship, partly to show I had a certain understanding of the relationship (and to recover some wounded pride!), partly because I was so pleased. But then I found my own personal values coming into play. I immediately realized that by making the relationship explicit—even more explicit than she had—I would have to treat her brothers as she did, including showing all the customary patterns of respect. I was comfortable with general patterns of courtesy and respect, but I disliked the thought of crawling in the presence of all her brothers. I also considered the dangers of inadvertently alienating others. Where would I stop? Who might be insulted or hurt because I had not befriended them?

Another practical concern was relationships with men. I wanted to remain marginal enough to be free to talk easily with men, including Camilla's brothers. There were distinct advantages to my being an American woman. For personal and professional reasons, I recognized the limits of how comfortably "native" I might go.

In one other way I discovered how very American—and ethnocentric—I had been by commenting on our children being potential mates. All the theoretical alliance material I had studied became real: I was trying to validate our relationship, marking it by hinting at an alliance through marriage—a Western pattern. Yet adoption, common in the Pacific, may serve similar functions when marriage ties are not strong. Adoption validates and strengthens ties since the natal and adoptive parents are siblings and share a child. It would have been much more culturally appropriate for me to have suggested that I adopt her child in order to mark our closeness.

This incident made very real for me the islanders' views of kinship as sharing—as behavior, not just biology. Camilla was genuinely appalled at my suggestion, despite the absence of any blood ties.

Perhaps most valuable was the sense of friendship that allows mistakes. I'm not sure why this particular incident was so crucial in this regard. It may have been precisely because I was so consciously concerned with being accepted and not seeming foolish.

I have continued to learn from my experience—and to think seriously about quiet, shy, and unassuming behavior as a possible asset in the field. In later conversations with other anthropologists, especially women, I have found I was not the only one to enter the field thinking I should be actively doing something all the time, seeking people out, asking questions, interviewing, and asserting myself. One woman, for example, talked of initially feeling uncomfortable about just "hanging around." Another woman commented that informants eventually revealed that they came to trust her because instead of beginning with questions, she quietly joined them in activities. Less modest behavior, in this instance, would have resulted in alienation.

My own shyness in the field may have been painful, but it fit local expectations of how a women should behave and may, all things considered, have inadvertently been a productive and useful ethnographic tool. What I value most from the incident with Camilla, however, is what I learned of meaningful friendship.

*   *   *

Eighteen years later I returned to the island, eager to rekindle my relationship with Camilla, curious to get to know the little girl she'd given birth to during my first visit, and ready to meet her many other children. I easily recognized Camilla, especially since I'd met her on and off over the years on more accessible islands we both happened to be visiting, but I did not recognize the drop-dead gorgeous young woman with her. It took some work to convince me that this was the little girl named Melissa, who was my son's sister. Watching my son grow up over the years, I should have realized that she, too, would mature, but this article and my memories had somehow frozen her in time.

Furthermore, I was potentially facing the very situation I had fantasized about so many years before: my twenty-year-old son was scheduled to visit, and the islanders were eagerly plotting his marriage to a local girl. Even without thoughts of marriage, I could imagine his interest in Melissa, with her looks. I was going to need to explain to my very American son why she was off limits!

Melissa took the relationship as seriously as her mother had all those years go. In fact, she turned the tables and made a proposal to me which was as abhorrent to most Americans (including my son) as was my original one to Camilla. One day when casually talking about my son, Colin, and his life in the United States, Melissa wanted to convince me of her commitment to her role and calmly said to me, "Please remember that I want to raise Colin's child." My initial (and thankfully silent) reaction was, "Take my son's child away from him? My grandchild away from me? What kind of person are you?" But I realized she was reaffirming her role as Colin's sister, because Pollapese women commonly adopt a brother's child. That practice involves sharing parenthood, not replacing one set of parents for another, and it cements a relationship between children (such as my future grandchild) with their father's kin (such as Melissa and Camilla and me). In a society that traces descent through women, the ties through men (like my son) are valued but need to be consciously maintained. Just as I had tried to affirm my relationship with Camilla with the marriage proposal, Melissa in the next generation was affirming hers with me with the adoption proposal.

EIGHT

Greasy Hands and Smelly Clothes: Fieldworker or Fisherman? [1]

PHILIP DeVITA

Fieldwork should have been extremely simple. Even if stretching my imagination to the extremes, there was absolutely nothing to worry about. After so many years at sea, so many past preparations for lengthy ocean voyages, a single summer on a remote island off the coast of Atlantic Canada was approached as if it were a weekend cruise. I'd been to the island twice before. The last time, on a bitter cold evening in March 1976, I met the head of the fisherman's association, a fishing captain and lobsterman himself. We'd spent endless hours talking fishing and boats. After a bit too much Beefeater, he had agreed to let me spend the summer documenting the traditional life of Acadian lobster fishermen.

The island was, at reasonable speed, only fifteen hours from my home in the Adirondack Mountains. The entire project was worth a gamble. If I didn't like the people or the setting, I knew that after the summer I could continue writing grant proposals in hopes of returning to the warmer and more familiar islands of the South Pacific.

Now, however, with a small grant from the Canadian Embassy and a few dollars from a grant to study socioeconomic change in a rapidly changing environment, I had enough to cover expenses for the summer. I'd three times written to the head of the fisherman's association reminding him of my impending visit. I was explicit, informing him of the exact day that I'd arrive. Most important, each time I reminded him of his promise to locate a small house for me to rent for the summer. Not having received a reply, I remained confident that he'd keep his promise.

The Canadian lobster seasons are restricted by federal conservation rulings. In this particular area of maritime Canada, lobstering begins on the first day of May and ends on June 30th. I couldn't be there until the second week in May, after classes had ended, but I left as soon as possible, driving nonstop to the island. Recalling my last wintry session with the captain, with my own money I'd purchased two cases of Beefeater, a case of Scotch, and two cases of mixed French wines for his wife and, hopefully, to share over fresh fish dinners. Camera equipment, the tape recorder, my old sailing clothes, and the other professional baggage essential to the fieldwork enterprise were also crammed into the car along with my tools, since my mechanically sound, rusted out Datsun hatchback had seen well over a hundred thousand miles.

Once the small ferry had transported me to the island, I parked the car on the rocky bluff overlooking the wharf. The lobster boats motored up to the buyers' docks, unloaded their day's catch, and moved off to their permanent berths. The lobstermen were rushing to end the business of the fishing day. Squinting into the western sun, I strained, looking for some sign of the captain or his mate. I would have driven onto the pier, but from years at sea, I'd learned to leave fishermen alone and stay out of their way when they're working. Time passed slowly while I searched the dock for a familiar face. At the farthest end of the wharf, I thought I'd recognized the mate in the cockpit of one of the recently arrived lobsterboats, but I wasn't certain enough to approach. Then I recognized the captain in the same boat, and a sense of relief and excitement replaced the tiredness. The world was again in some comprehensible order. At last, there was someone not unknown, someone recognizable. The slight hint of the presence of friends from the earlier visit erased the uncertainty and aloneness in the strange, new environment.

The lobster were offloaded, weighed, and sold. The vessel motored around to the south side of the wharf, and I watched intently as the two men lashed the dock lines and secured the vessel. I walked down to the pier to approach the fishermen, both heading for an old pickup truck, each with a bottle of beer in hand. I called the captain's name. I didn't know if they recognized me. He stopped, stared, and responded with my name. We shook hands, and before I had time to shake hands with the mate, he informed me that he had bad news.

"Philip," he said, "I talk with the fishermen. We do not want you on the island."

I was, understandably, stunned. My immediate response was controlled. I composed myself, not even providing nonverbal clues to display the shock and sudden disappointment. After living most of my life either as a guest in someone else's home or as a guest in foreign countries, I'd learned by experience to deal with situations where you know that you're not welcome. You become sensitive to the most subtle hints of interpersonal conflict and know when it's time to pack your seabag. The unexpected pronouncement was far from a subtle hint. It was a simple and blatant declaration of their attitude toward my presence.

So much for the cottage. So much for the research and my well-developed plans for the summer.

That my immediate reactions to the initial events on the wharf were handled so calmly was, in reflection, primarily due to two facts. First,

I was too tired to respond immediately to a situation which I couldn't, at that moment, fully comprehend. Second, there was the manner in which the captain made the announcement. In the blunt, matter-of-factness of the statement, this five-foot-two package of vibrant Acadian friendliness and vitality, even after sixteen hours of lobstering, conveyed no sign of personal rejection or anger. He didn't apologize, didn't explain. There was no recourse.

Hell, the ethnographer is nothing more than an intruder anyway. Rarely is he or she *invited* to snoop around into the lives of total strangers. We make our own decisions on the fieldwork setting and then, most often, show up in unfamiliar places, fresh out of the sterile classrooms of graduate school, eager and naive but determined to conduct research in textbook fashion to satisfy absolutely no one connected with the research environment. Before I was ever an anthropologist, I'd had run-ins with every kind of intruder imaginable. From the many past experiences in the South Pacific and Central and South America, I still can't accurately rank the uninvited intruders whom I met on a personal "dislike" or "nerd" scale. True, the Peace Corps members, anthropologists, missionaries, and government officials most probably felt that same way about me. Except, however, on extremely rare occasions, memories of meetings with many of these neocolonial do-gooders still leave a bitter taste in my mouth.

I'd read Gerald Berreman's (1962) account of his own personal difficulties with initiating field research among members of a Himalayan village. I'd more recently read Jean Briggs's (1970) honest and insightful report on her ethnographic problems with the Utkuhik-halingmuit of the Canadian Northwest. In relation to their problems and my current situation, I might be well ahead of the game cut off from my research efforts at the very beginning.

From the moment he told me that I wasn't welcome, I realized that the captain was right. Not that he had the power to keep me from his island or that how he had acted was right. These weren't meaningful issues. He *had* the right to prohibit me from conducting research into his and his neighbors' lives. On my own, in the years that were to follow, I was able to learn of the motives for his initial action. However, at that moment, I had no problems reconciling the fact of that particular moment. I didn't know the facts and, in this case, the facts are unimportant. The fact of the matter was that he and his friends had, as the captain had informed me, decided against my presence as both an outsider and a researcher, not, as was the case, being aware of what my presence as an anthropologist meant.

In the next breath, after having informed me that I wasn't welcome on the island, the captain ordered me to follow him home for supper. This was not an invitation. It was an order! Without waiting for a response, he jumped into his truck. I stood watching as he jockeyed the battered pickup to turn around on the narrow dock. Passing where he'd left me standing, he waved, pointing inland toward the village. The option to drive directly to the mainland and take a room in the old hotel was, for the moment, rejected. The hotel and hot shower could wait until later that evening. The unexpected invitation, especially taken in the context of his earlier pronouncement, was offered as if he had never told me that I wasn't welcome on his island.

At his small home next to the Catholic cemetery, I again met the captain's wife and three children. After a handshake and an awkward hug, his wife asked a few questions about the trip. Obviously, she knew that my project was over before it ever began. It made no difference to her. She, as I remembered, and as she would always be, was all smiles and easy friendliness. Both she and her husband, and almost all of the Acadian fisherfolk had this disarming quality of genuine warmth and relaxed, natural openness.

"Ah Philip, we'll take a gin." The captain was on the porch pouring the last few ounces of an unknown brand into glasses for the mate, himself, and me. With a toast, each of us downed the booze. Returning the few feet to the car, I grabbed a forty-ounce jug of Beefeater, a bottle of Cabernet, and my corkscrew. He hadn't offered his wife a drink, and I suspected this was because the bottle was almost empty. I also recalled that his wife had, in our March meeting, spoken of how much she missed good wine. I handed the gin to the captain and offered the wine to his wife. Their surprise and pleasure was obvious. While thanking me, the captain opened the gin as I uncorked the wine for his wife.

We went into the house and sat in the small breakfast room adjoining the kitchen. Conversation was polite and unforced. No one discussed the decision announced at the wharf. His wife prepared supper while we drank and the children chased the dogs around the yard. I was tempted to return to the car for a bottle of Scotch but decided to remain and "take" the gin slowly. Knowing not to even ask for tonic or a lemon for fear of embarrassing my hosts, nor to cut the alcohol with water lest I embarrass myself, I nursed the gin. Well, I thought, I'll be gone before the evening's over. Why suffer for the sake of impression? Yet, I kept quiet and drank slowly as both lobstermen, smelling of fish, drank as if the Beefeater was water.

Over the meal of boiled chicken, potatoes, turnip, and green vegetables, they killed the forty-ounce jug. I brought in two more bottles and told them to enjoy and drink in good health. The conversation continued easily and remained warm and open. No questions about what I'd do now. They talked about the late winter thaw that didn't free the channel until a week after the beginning of the lobster season, problems with rough seas and bad weather when they finally were able to set the traps, how they had to hurry to get ready since they'd already lost valuable time. They complained about the price being paid for lobster by the merchants at the wharf—how the price was set by outsiders in Boston and Halifax and how they were being cheated from a decent wage.

Concerned about the lateness and the long drive back to the mainland village, I asked when the last ferry left from the island. Without hesitation, both the captain and his wife ordered, and it was another order, that tonight I was to remain with them.

Where would they put me up in this small house? There were three bedrooms, one for the parents, one for the son, and another for the two daughters. Arguing at the inconvenience, and soberly wanting to get into a hotel room with a hot shower, they, with their typical response of "No problem," insisted that I sleep on the small sofa near the kitchen entry.

The evening was filled with the same friendliness that I remembered from my winter visit in March. Visitors arrived frequently, each introduced to me, and each, like most every Acadian I'd ever met, was immediately open and congenial. That I was an outsider made little difference. Acadians have that remarkable quality of making a stranger feel instantly at home. A guest is naturally welcome and accepted—as family. Conversation begins without formality, without the feeling that you're being examined, more as if they'd always known you and that you'd just returned home from someplace else.

The mate had left before dinner and returned during the evening with photographs of his record tuna catch from the past summer. Like the captain and his mate, the other fishermen drank gin either straight from the bottle or from flowered jelly glasses filled to the top. Knowing that I wouldn't be driving because they had decided that I'd remain, I went to the car for another jug of gin and this time returned with the Scotch for myself.

I'd caught lobster before but not, however, in traps. I dove for them off Catalina and San Clemente islands and even snorkeled for them in the bays in the Galápagos. Late in the evening, I asked the captain if I could go lobstering with him the next day. Perhaps, because of the Beefeater, or in the spirit of the party, he agreed to take me with him.

Shortly before midnight, with the guests finally gone, the house quiet, I fell into a dead sleep on the small sofa. I was relatively sober but too tired for reflection, too exhausted to even attempt to analyze the events of the past few hours. In dirty clothes, in desperate need of a shower or at least a chance to brush my teeth, I slept for the first time in over twenty-four hours.

The captain shook me awake. "Hurry, Philip, time to go fishing." A light was on in the kitchen, but the rest of the house was dark.

I struggled to get up, wanting more than anything to go back to sleep. What time was it? Still dark outside. I focused on the kitchen clock. It was two in the morning. I'd gotten two hours of sleep. He wants to go fishing? Get me out of here! I need some sleep!

In the bathroom I searched for toothpaste and rubbed my teeth with my fingers. My shaving kit was in the car. I splashed some cold water on my face and dried myself with the first towel I saw. Returning to the kitchen, the captain handed me a cup of coffee. He was busy throwing food from the fridge into a paper sack. "We have to leave so we can pass through the Gully on the right tide."

Without giving me time to finish the coffee, he announced that we must leave. I followed into the cold, damp morning running to my car to find a jacket and a pair of deck shoes. I found a jacket but didn't even waste time searching for shoes in my packed seabags. The truck engine was running. We stopped a few houses away to collect the mate and raced down the unlit road to the wharf.

I don't remember much more of that first day. I was too tired, too cold. In the darkness, we powered out in line with other boats, through the narrow gully and out to the open sea. I'd stayed out of their way while they cast off and only when we were under way did I move from the corner of the cockpit. With the captain at the wheel, the mate went below to the fo'c'sle. From the wheelhouse, I looked below. The mate had lit the kerosene stove and put on the kettle. "Tea," he yelled up through the companionway. I didn't want tea. I wanted to go to sleep. I struggled to remain awake.

After tea, the mate fell asleep in the lower bunk. I couldn't tolerate the kerosene and gas smells below decks and returned to the open cockpit and curled out of the wind between the engine hatch and the bulwarks. In the noise and the dampness of the cold predawn, I fell asleep.

They reached the lobster traps as daylight broke. Both of them fished lobster all that first day. I just watched as they worked their traps. Neither gave any indication of having spent the night drinking and having gotten only two hours sleep. The work was repetitious. Locate a jig bouy, pull the ten traps, one at a time on the hauler, empty, clean and rebait each trap, reset the jig, and head off in search of the next set. Between the more distant hauls, the mate napped on the chest freezer in the open cockpit. I slept whenever I could while they worked through the morning and early afternoon. At two thirty, the captain opened the throttle and powered away from the ocean shelf, the course set for home. The mate took the wheel while the captain went below "to take a sleep."

Both men had worked together, each knowing what to do once they'd located the set lines. They joked continually in Acadian French while they hauled and cleaned traps. Once each jig was reset, the captain returned to the wheelhouse to search for the next marked bouy. They were too busy to pay much attention to their useless passenger. I didn't care. After watching them make the first few hauls, I'd seen all I wanted of lobstering. I'd once made a night trip with bait fishermen off the coast of California and had been a few days on a seiner in Mexico. The crews of these commercial boats work hard, but not nearly as hard as did these lobstermen. My many years on sportsfishing boats and sailing yachts had been a party compared to the day's work performed by the two Acadians.

Before we reached the narrow passage into the harbor, the mate woke the captain. The captain took the wheel while the mate busied himself on deck. I'd slept enough and was anxious to get ashore and away from the island. I joined the captain in the wheelhouse for the final leg to the wharf.

I didn't ask questions. Why? Once we got back to the captain's house, I had plans to instantly head for the mainland. The rest of the summer was ahead of me and whether they wanted me or not, I was gone. Just get off the island, shower, have a good meal, and then a long sleep.

In the calm of the bay, the captain talked while I tried to hear above the noise of the engine. He talked about the boat, a new vessel built along traditional lobsterman lines at a shipyard in Halifax. The Ford marine engine was also new, but he complained, reaching behind to grab the tech manual from a bulkhead compartment. "Look for the rpm's. Look for the rpm's at full throttle." Without my glasses, I couldn't read the spec sheet. "Thirty-five hundred rpm's at full throttle." He rammed the throttle forward and I watched as the tach crept to 2,700 rpm and held, going no higher. Other, older boats were passing us as we cut through the calm waters of the harbor. "I changed propellers two times to make more speed. We go too slow. Something is bad—no good."

Before tying up to the buyer's dock, I told the captain that I'd take a look at the engine. He sold the lobster and secured the vessel, and the three of us returned to his house. We drank a few 5.6 Alpine beers. I had to give the engine time to cool off. I'd burned myself too many times crawling around the hot manifolds and water jackets of marine engines.

Alone, with the keys to the boat, I drove to the wharf and, with my own tools, worked on the engine for over an hour. All I did was clean and regap the plugs, set the points, and adjust the carburetor and timing. Running in neutral, the eight cylinders sounded better than they had before I began. The proof was to be determined by how the boat ran in the water, not how the engine sounded tied up to the dock. I returned to the cottage, got the captain, and drove both of us back to the boat.

"Let's go!" This was just another of his impetuous command-invitations.

I cast off the dock lines, and he powered out into the harbor. Once into the open bay, without giving the engine time to warm up, he opened the throttle. The tach reached 3,900 rpm and the boat was planing over the smooth water. The captain screamed in excitement while the engine whined in perfect tune. "You made more rpm's than the book!"

"We go home and take a gin!" Of course we would. I had the Beef-eater.

"O.K., captain, we'll have a drink and then I have to be going."

"Going where? You stay. Tomorrow you come fishing and make sure the engine works."

I didn't go fishing the next day. That evening, after dinner, after two more bottles of my gin with the mate and his fishing friends, the captain told the other captains that I was an expert marine mechanic. He lent me out for the next day to work on his friend's engine.

In my same clothes, without a shower, I slept on the couch for a second night. I did manage to find my shaving kit from among the pile of gear in the back of the car and scrubbed my teeth before going to bed. At two in the morning, before he left for his lobster traps, the captain woke me. "You sleep. Later my friend will take you to his boat. Make his engine work."

Welcome to the island! Welcome to the impulsive, impetuous, unpredictable world of the Acadian lobstermen!

I spent the next day tuning up the old, greasy, rusted engine on another boat. Then I fished lobster for the remainder of the season. For the summer, working their schedule six days a week—there's no fishing on Sunday—I slept two hours each night on the small couch and made up the rest of my sleep at sea. On Sunday the village meets in the community center for dancing, drinking, and, more often than not, brawling. Occasionally there's a wedding, but that too is a time for dancing and drinking. There was no time for research, except for the data I could collect on the captain, his family, and the mate.

For the next five years, during my time off from teaching duties, I returned to the island whenever I could. After lobster season, they fish tuna. Other boats, with proper licenses, fish mackerel. I became accepted as a mechanic and fisherman, not as an anthropologist. The work left me little time for research. During the second year, arriving early to learn of preparations for lobstering, the captain welcomed me with, "Philip, I usually hire another fisherman for the summer, but I knew you were coming to help me fish. Did you bring the gin?"

There was a time when I needed to spend long hours with a 95-year-old resident recording oral history, but my unpaid duties as a fisherman and mechanic left little time for sleep, much less time for ethnographic endeavors. Neither the captain, the mate, nor any of the other fisherfolk understood that my purpose in their community was for reasons other than catching lobster or fishing or fixing someone's engines. This, indeed, was participant-observation of a severely demanding nature.

I haven't returned to the island for almost nine years. The research will never be written up. In the course of my visits with these Acadian islanders, I became accepted to the point that I learned of all of their illegal activities, even participating in some. The socioeconomic advantages derived from poaching, bootlegging, ripping off the federal and provincial bureaucracies such as unemployment, social assistance, and the fisherman's loan board, can never be reported.

We exchange Christmas cards, and I keep promising to return for a visit. But I am getting too old to work lobster, and I've never been partial to gin.

NOTE

1. The name of the island and those of my hosts and friends have been intentionally deleted. These are unique people, friendly, loving and caring people, who live life with exceptional vigor. That they accepted me and eventually told me of their illegal activities—games that they play against a system which overlegislates and exercises constraints upon their traditional ways of life—ethically prohibits me from writing about them. To all of my friends on the island, I offer thanks for some very personal lessons as to what it means to fully live life in a harsh environment.

REFERENCES

BERREMAN, GERALD D.
1962   Behind Many Masks: Ethnography and Impression Management in a Himalayan Village. Society for Applied Anthropology, Monograph 4.

BRIGGS, JEAN L.
1970   Never in Anger: Portrait of an Eskimo Family. Cambridge, MA: Harvard University Press.

NINE

🌿 Of Teamwork, Faith, and Trust in West Sumatra

CAROL J. COLFER

A VILLAGE CALLS

We'd lived less than ten minutes by car from Pulai village for over two years, and I'd driven within a stone's throw of it many times. That day, together astride my husband Dudley's yellow Suzuki trailbike, we were out for a joy ride. In truth, we were seeking a bit of ever-elusive privacy, an escape from the public nature of our home in nearby Piruko.

The September day was beautiful with blue sky and white puffy clouds overhead. The road was neither a morass of mud nor a mass of billowing dust, both conditions to which we'd become accustomed. We headed across the Batang Hari River to the forests. Driving through the cool shelter of the trees was our relaxation, our joy.

The last few months had been difficult. I was the anthropologist on a team of soil scientists; and one of them—a dedicated, hardworking, and bright one, at that—had been unjustly accused of doing Christian missionary work in the area. It was becoming clear at that time that Jim and his family might be asked to leave the country, meaning a huge loss to the project and to us personally. They had become good friends.

As we rode along, Dudley and I were discussing my need to do some research in a Minang community. I felt I knew a lot about transmigrants from Java, but I wanted a clearer picture of the differences between the transmigrants and the indigenous population of West Sumatra. Our project had worked only with transmigrants (because of governmental interest in them), and I felt we were neglecting an opportunity to make use of indigenous experience. It also seemed possible to me that the Minang people might have noticed the lack of benefits from our project for their own local agricultural system. This could have been the factor that led to the accusation about the Christian missionary work. There were obvious problems with interethnic equity and, having recently become Chief of Party, I wanted to rectify these problems if at all possible.

The gist of our conversation prompted my husband to veer toward Pulai at a fork in the road, leading us onto a narrow path exactly wide

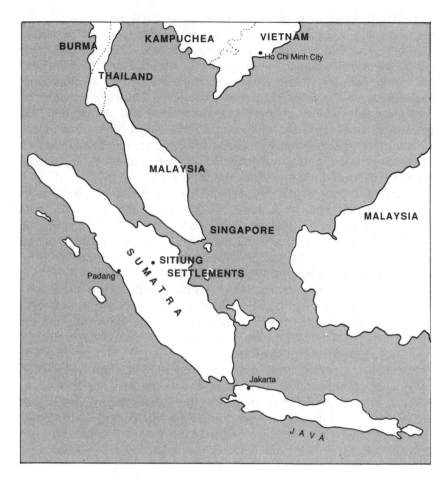

Sumatra, Indonesia

enough for a car. This turned out to be the axis along which the village was situated, paralleling the nearby river. We were greeted by a profusion of trees, hiding the community thoroughly from casual detection and also hiding the curious but friendly stares of children and a few adults in village yards.

Piruko, where we lived, was a planned transmigration community with every home replicated four times on every block, every yard exactly one-quarter ha in size. Although eight years of human occupancy had altered the once identical houses, the original square wooden structures were often still visible. Even the placement of trees in the yards attested to the standardization that characterizes such settlements.

Pulai was different. Brightly decorated concrete houses were interspersed with traditional wooden homes built on stilts, with Minang roofs, the outer peaks reaching skyward in the shape of a water buffalo's horns (or according to legend, a canoe). The houses were generally aligned along the road, but in a haphazard, natural fashion. They seemed a part of the surrounding forest, which gradually blended into the fruit trees and other greenery. Yellow flowers sprinkled the yards in abundance highlighting the brightly painted windows here and there, contrasting with the many shades of green that characterize the whole area. The profusion of trees gave the village a cool, refreshing air. I was enchanted.

We drove on across the river and proceeded into the forest in search of monkeys, boars, peace, and other natural phenomena. From that moment of discovery, I resolved to return to Pulai.

A few days later, Megan (my teenage daughter) and I decided to go for a similar joy ride. She'd been in Kalimantan with me some years earlier, working with Kenyah Dayaks who lived along a river. We wondered if the people of Pulai had the floating platforms that the Dayaks had used for bathing, sociability, and all functions requiring water. So she and I headed for Pulai.

This time, we stopped at a cluster of buildings that turned out to be a Muslim religious school and its dormitories. The dormitories were made of woven mats, strung together into human size boxes, and set up on stilts. Little did we know at that time that some of these "boxes" were occupied by entire families.

We were immediately surrounded by interested boys and young men, ranging in age from about ten to twenty—a common occurrence in Indonesia. They chattered away in Minang, their native language. We could understand only bits and pieces of their speech. Though we knew we were perfectly safe, we felt uncomfortable, closed in. As we resolutely moved toward the river, the circle broke, granting us freedom to go where we wanted.

Very steep steps had been carved out of the cool, damp banks of the river. Regular use kept the steps firm and grass-free, but on all sides lush vegetation surrounded us. Clamoring down the steps behind us was an entourage of the younger boys, grinning mischievously or smiling shyly.

At the bottom we found only a shallow side channel of the river between the shore and an island. We returned to our motorcycle, grateful to escape the persistent stares, the alien language, and occasional laughter of the boys.

I realized, as I contemplated working in Pulai, that the chance to conduct research on my own again was a powerful draw. I had worked for two years in a very collaborative mode, with soil scientists and agronomists. The decision to do so had been a conscious one: I wanted to use anthropological information to help determine research priorities on the project. To do that effectively, I had to work closely with the agricultural scientists. It had worked well.

Yet the enthnographic loss was significant. I had chosen—like my coworkers—to live in a comparatively comfortable home (with a generator, running water, fans), largely to enhance communication with my co-workers, recognizing that this would have a negative impact on my communication with villagers. I had accepted the driver that had been urged on me for the same reasons. We lived close enough to each other so that a significant amount of my leisure time was spent with co-workers, again reducing my contact with the local populations.

Some of our work involved designing and doing experiments collaboratively with farmers. Although this process provided some useful ethnographic information, I was always wondering what the farmers would be doing without our collaboration. That this close association with other team members presented a potential danger to my rapport with villagers (should they act, or be perceived to act, inappropriately) was also clear.

My co-workers were remarkably aware and culturally sensitive. But they were not anthropologists. The degree to which this religious controversy, for instance, might affect my work was troubling me. I'd lived and worked under the constraints of teamwork for two years and now relished the idea of returning to "real fieldwork." I was confident that my rapport with team members was sufficiently good to allow me to go it alone for a while.

GETTING PERMISSION TO WORK IN PULAI

I returned to Pulai one morning a few days later, driving through town more slowly, hoping someone might invite me in, trying to get a feel for the place, wondering how best to proceed. The people were friendly, but more guardedly so than the transmigrants. No one invited me in, but I noticed a small shed, outfitted on three sides with benches, full of men, apparently just sitting around. One thin man about my age (forty) gave me a particularly friendly smile, which cheered me in the difficult first moments when fieldwork actually begins.

I drove on to the river, lined with lush tropical growth, its beauty and breadth always a source of strength and inspiration to me. Coming back, as I reached the village edge, I saw the thin man again. Again he smiled, giving me courage to stop and ask him where the headman might be. I felt a surge of relief that he understood and spoke Indonesian, as well as Minang. I was self-conscious but grateful when he led me back to a little shop near the shed full of men and called the headman over to me.

The headman turned out to be a young man in his late twenties. He (and the toothless old shopkeeper) listened to the explanation of what I wanted—to learn about their agricultural system, about their way of life, so that our project could begin to do agricultural experiments that would be more appropriate for their own system. We also hoped this would help the government develop policies that were more appropriate for Sumatran conditions. He smiled shyly and nodded with what I took to be reserved approval. I could understand enough of the Minang language to pick up his occasional corroboration of something I had said, addressing himself to the older man, who seemed to speak little Indonesian.

Then the headman asked what exactly I wanted to do in Pulai. As I spoke of coming every day, spending time in the village and in the fields with families, interviewing people, he began to look more and more uncomfortable. His youth led me to suspect that he held the position of village headman because of educational certification requirements of the central or provincial government and that he might be headman in title only (or mainly). I could see that I was putting him in a difficult position. He looked enormously relieved and grateful when I asked if he'd need to discuss the issues with the village elders. Yes, one person shouldn't make a decision like this, he said. We agreed that I should return in a week's time.

The following week I got my first lesson in Pulai politics (and kinship). I learned that the "elders" the headman needed to consult were the clan leaders of Pulai's three major matrilineal clans (Tigoninik, Melayu Satu, and Melayu Dua) and the religious leader (who was also head of the religious school).

How fortunate that Pak Munir, one of the leaders of Melayu Satu, was the thin man who'd first smiled at me. The leader of Melayu Dua was a distinguished-looking middle-aged man who was also the head of the village elementary school. The religious leader was a member of the Melayu Satu clan. The leader of the Tigoninik clan, who I later learned was by far the most influential, never came to any of our meetings, though the young headman was also a member of this clan.

Each time I came to the village for a meeting, I lingered, hoping to meet some of the village women. On one such occasion, an old, but still strong, woman beckoned me into a room adjoining Pulai's grandest house. Large and new, this house was beautifully constructed of elaborately carved wood, with the traditional pointed roof and stilts.

The woman's lips and teeth were stained red and black from years of chewing betel nut. She struck me as forthright, curious, friendly, and self-confident. I was to learn that this was the clan home and meeting place for the Tigoninik clan and that she was the mother of the clan leader. She could not speak Indonesian and I could not speak Minang. But three women in their twenties and thirties translated for us.

Her message was that I had been talking with men of little import, that I needed to speak with and get permission from Pak Datok before proceeding. Pak Datok was her son. I promptly went to his home, and kept returning until I could explain to him my purpose in being there and request his permission to proceed.

I suspected that I had been accepted, at least provisionally, one day when these influential men invited me to accompany them the following week to a village rice-planting party. Pak Munir quickly assumed the role of my champion, explaining my agricultural, *not religious,* motivations to all of the villagers.

The process of getting permission to work in Pulai underscored an important Minang (and perhaps pan-Indonesian) value. Interpersonal relations should be cordial; conflict should be avoided. In all of these formal meetings with the men of Pulai (and with the head of the subdistrict), there was a strong undercurrent of concern. I could feel the distrust, the suspicion. They all asked me many questions and warned me, in polite, gentle terms, that they did not want any *politik* (political maneuvering) on my part.

They were, of course, referring to Jim's alleged religious activities. Missionary activity was strictly forbidden to our project by Indonesian law, and it was greatly feared by the devoutly Muslim Minangkabau of the area.

One of the rumors that seemed most absurd to us was that Jim had been paying a million rupiah (US $1,000) to anyone who would become a Christian. This was consistent with a common warning to children in West Sumatra to not take money from foreigners. Christians were reputed generally to pay people to convert. Pulai's inhabitants believed these rumors, and many feared that I had come to their village with similar intentions.

Despite these genuine suspicions and fears about my motives, no one ever brought up this subject directly. The villagers mentioned politics, they spoke generally against "carrying or bringing people from one group to another," but neither the alleged missionary work nor Jim was mentioned until I brought it up. I was then able to address their concerns directly, though it took months and a dramatic event before I truly won most people's trust.

ACCEPTANCE FINALLY COMES

By January, I was beginning to despair of ever getting beyond the villagers' suspicion that I had religious intentions. There seemed to be no end in sight. Pak Munir initiated almost every interchange, when we were together, with an explanation of my agricultural not religious interests, and he took every opportunity to point out the agricultural nature of my actions and questions—as did I. Yet the suspicion remained.

The people of Pulai brought up their own religion, Islam, continually. Pak Munir and I went out to Fahmuddin and Miryam's rain-fed rice field in early January. The rainy season was underway in earnest, and we had a difficult time getting through the many huge mud holes in the road. The same road we'd traversed so easily in October was now a quagmire, regularly entrapping the log trucks that moved between the highway and the settlements and forests.

There were three married women in their late twenties working together in the field—Miryam, Rukiyah, and Sam (all of the Peliang clan). They lived near each other and regularly traded labor. Sam was married to the influential Pak Datok.

I watched the women weeding, bent double over the sharply sloping hillside, and tried to copy them. The slope was so steep I regularly slid down a foot or two. Pak Munir, true to the local division of labor, sat on a log during the two hours we worked, fondling a weeding tool but never touching a weed.

The women asked about Christianity and circumcision. My explanation prompted a lesson in Islam. Pulai boys are circumcised between ages six and twelve and become real Muslims at that point. Girls are "circumcised" at six days after birth, though this involves only a light scraping of the clitoris, not its removal. People consider youth of both sexes under age fifteen to be too young to sin, not yet fully responsible.

Women are considered dirty during their menses and are forbidden to fast, to pray, or even to be touched by their husbands. Postmenopausal women are clean and pure, and for premenopausal women, menstruation has a purifying function.

This discussion led to concerns over family planning. The women knew something about and expressed interest in all kinds of contraception. We compared effects of the Pill in our respective countries. They said they were afraid of birth control. Sam told of a woman who'd gotten an IUD, which had worked its way up into her body and was approaching her heart. The woman had been taken to Padang for an operation the previous Tuesday. I was to hear more about IUDs in the near future.

They wondered why my husband had wanted to marry me, since I couldn't have any more children. Minang men, they all agreed, wouldn't want to take care of another man's children (though many, I'd noticed, do). How long was I divorced before I remarried? Islam required them to wait three and a half months before marrying again. Was adultery allowed in America? Prostitution? Premarital sex? I explained that, as in Pulai, none of these things was really allowed, but they all happened.

The next day we went to another upland field, this time accompanied by Pak Munir's wife, Niisah. This was my first chance to talk with her alone. Some twenty years ago, she had come from Sawahlunto, the district capital, about eighty kilometers from Pulai. But she was taken in by a family and the Melayu Dua clan after marrying Pak Munir, which was an exception to the usual matrilocal residence pattern. She rarely did agricultural work, partly because Pak Munir was successful at contract and other entrepreneurial work. They had no fields under cultivation, though he occasionally claimed partial ownership/interest in his clan's rubber orchards.

We went out the same slippery, muddy road to the area I'd watched the community plant in October. Niisah called to everyone we passed—a common practice—saying we were on our way to Nur's field. Nur was weeding her field with another woman, Yanti (both around forty years old). Yanti, like Nur's husband, is a Tigoninik, but the women consider themselves to be friends, not relatives. Nur is Melayu Satu. Their homes are quite close, their fields adjacent.

We talked about the "1001" names they knew for kinds of weeds. I was increasingly getting the impression that only the women weed. These women said the men fish and tap rubber and "look for money."

Again, family planning emerged as a topic of interest. Niisah had eight children, seven of whom survived; Nur had six children and one grand-child; and Yanti had three children (two boys and a girl). It's important in this matrilineal society to have at least one girl. They told me, wor-riedly, about a woman who'd become pregnant with an IUD in place, and they wondered what would happen. I promised to look in a book I had.

The next day I went out that wretched road again, with Niisah, this time to a field belonging to the headmaster of the religious school. There were almost thirty women weeding his field (no men, no children), many of whom were students. I learned to sharpen the weeding tools from Nur, who also lent me her head kerchief. The women worried that my "beautiful white skin" would darken in the blistering sun. Conversation, laughter, singing, all serve to lighten what is undeniably a dreary, hot, back-breaking task.

When Niisah and I returned to Pulai that afternoon, we received word that the woman with the IUD was not doing well. When I offered to go see her, Niisah accepted gratefully. The woman, Risani, lived in a small box in a row of similar boxes built on stilts between the regular houses on the road and the river. The entire dwelling was about two by three meters, and its walls were woven from forest fibers. The house, like the school's "dormitories," looked like a rice storage structure. I had thought that was what it was!

Risani and her husband and three children had come to Pulai from Solok (about one hundred kilometers to the west) in search of their for-tune. Risani was seven months pregnant, writhing on the floor in pain and hot as a firecracker. She had been passing blood and pus. Her young husband sat by, trying to look impassive, yet with anxiety etched deeply into his face. I too was afraid for her life.

I asked what had been done. Her abdomen had been smeared with charcoal, and the local healer had "read" over her. "To read," in this way, is to whisper magico-religious phrases over someone or something.

My own anxiety level was rising. I was doing fieldwork, and this was an opportunity to find out about how people made decisions regarding health care. From an academic standpoint, I knew that I shouldn't in-terfere. Yet it looked to me as though this woman might be dying.

I decided the pursuit of knowledge could wait for a more benign moment. I asked, "Has she been to a doctor?" No, not yet. I didn't know whether or not her husband approved of doctors. I said I thought she needed to go to the doctor. No response. "Is transportation the problem?" No response. "How about if I come and get her?" No response. Her husband stared unhappily and silently into space.

Finally I asked if the problem was money. His face riveted to mine— a strong yes. I offered to pay; and they gladly agreed for me to take her.

I went home to get my jeep and driver. After considerable maneuvering, we managed to get the vehicle through the narrow paths to her hut. Getting Risani's body, awkward with pregnancy and pain, into the jeep was another hurdle. She lay on the floor in the back, still moaning and writhing in pain, with her husband beside her. I sat in the front, twisted around, holding her hand.

The twenty-minute ride over bumpy roads to the health clinic seemed interminable. The tenor of her moaning informed us clearly that the bouncy ride was painful. I could monitor the depth of her discomfort by the pressure of her hand on mine. Her husband held her other hand. I saw him rearranging her sarong, but I wasn't sure what he was doing. My mind was on her struggle, her danger, and my own fear for her life.

As we drove into the clinic yard, I was surprised and dismayed to see a gaggle of foreigners (one of whom I knew) coming toward me with outstretched hands. I hated to leave the woman in my charge, but the clinic personnel were already opening the back door of the jeep to take care of her. Politeness seemed to dictate that I greet these people. I listened as patiently as I could to their reason for being there (they were in fact looking for me) and explained that I was in the midst of an emergency.

After extricating myself temporarily, I returned to the cluster of people behind my jeep. I was amazed to discover that Risani had given birth to a baby girl in the car on the way to the clinic! The baby, premature, was the tiniest I'd ever seen, though apparently perfectly formed. Mother and daughter were taken into the clinic, and I was required to turn back to the visitors.

Every effort was made to save the baby, within the capabilities of the small rural clinic. Risani's husband came to my home to fetch me three days later to bring her and the new baby home. I could hardly believe the baby was still alive, and I couldn't help noting sadly that her chances in that small crowded hut were rather slim. Indeed, a few days later I learned that the baby had died. But Risani was well. The IUD was never found.

This event, to my surprise and relief, brought to an abrupt end people's overt suspicion of my motives in the community. I was never again called on to explain my purposes in being in the village. The general concern for Risani, actually a stranger in Pulai, is reflective of a cultural ideal that strongly values human beings and welcomes them into the community wherever they come from. My concern for this unknown woman and my willingness to pay for her medical care (twenty-five dollars) seemed to demonstrate to the people that I shared this value. They were then responsive and able to accept and trust me as they could not before.

TEN

Some Consequences of a Fieldworker's Gender for Cross-Cultural Research

SUSAN DWYER-SHICK

When an anthropologist enters a community, he or she comes most likely as a stranger. And as a stranger, the anthropologist will be expected to occupy the status, displaying its associated behaviors, of similar individuals already known to community members. Initially, if not overtly cast as a potential enemy, the fieldworker might be identified as a missionary, teacher, tourist, or even "hippie," depending on the recalled earlier encounters between locals and foreigners (see e.g., Berreman 1962; Goldstein 1964). Social scientists, particularly anthropologists, have observed that people universally tend to interpret and misinterpret in light of their own experience, to cope with "unknowns" in light of apparently similar "knowns" (see e.g., Bohannan 1966). Obviously, the newly arrived fieldworker has an advantage if he or she comes equipped with knowledge of who the previous strangers were, even had they been other anthropologists. More importantly, as the anthropologist gradually moves from "outsider" to "insider" there must be corresponding insight into what will now be expected as appropriate behavior accompanying the insider or "friend" status.

This essay focuses on one such subjective attribute of the ethnographic enterprise: the gender identity and gender role of a woman conducting fieldwork within a largely sexually segregated society. Why gender identity and role? How come the experiences of a woman? What about sexual identification? Aren't women still only a minority of those in the field?

In the anthropological literature there has been a lack of consistent agreement on or treatment of sex and gender with respect to cross-cultural research. We need, however, to first distinguish between the two terms: while sex is designated as "male" or "female," gender, partly based on distinguishable characteristics such as sex, may have its source in culture and not biology.

But *is* sexual identity highly visible, even if it is unusual (e.g., the only woman faculty member at a departmental meeting)? And if visible (i.e., unequivocal recognition and accuracy), is sex a significant variable? In response to the first question, I don't think so. To be a man or a woman, a boy or a girl, is as much a function of dress, gesture, occupation, social network, and personality as it is of possessing a particular set of genitals, as at least one individual in an unfamiliar culture context learned with some humor.

In the early 1970s Wyn Sargent traveled in the highland area of Papua, New Guinea, dressing her lanky six-foot frame in safari hat, shirt, pants, and boots. Sargent, self-described journalist and media-dubbed anthropologist, wrote about what happened when she greeted the women of the compound as they were leaving for the fields one morning:

> The Dani women are full-hipped, big-bellied creatures. When they get together they are a robust, boisterous, rowdy bunch. Their energy is volcanic. . . .
>
> Aem [a Dani male] told the women in the courtyard that I was a woman, too. They viewed this idea with curiosity. Some of them shoved in a little closer to get a better look. One old woman with a runny nose knocked my hat off my head and ran her fingers through my hair. My blouse was opened and the women took turns peeking inside at my underclothing. Another woman squeezed my bosom. Then she turned to convince the others that I really was a woman. The announcement created a pandemonium so grand that even some of the men stepped outside of the *pilaito* to watch it.
>
> "Mamma Wyn! Mamma Wyn!" they screamed. And then they smacked the daylights out of me. I was jostled and hustled around in the dirt. They slapped me with big loving punches. The punches were repeated and improved upon with such elaboration that the breath was finally knocked out of me.
>
> The Dani women do not love men as much as they love one another. . . . The women are compulsively devoted to one another because they work, eat and sleep together. They spend what other time they have in drawing attention to themselves to acquire the love and admiration from one another which they need to be happy. (1974:49–50)

The second question addresses the significance of sex as a variable when biology is not in dispute. Again, the importance of sexual identity may be more apparent than real. For example, Kenneth Goldstein and others in the audience thoroughly enjoyed this anecdote about Sargent's sojourn among the Dani women when I included it in my paper at a session on methodology during the 1977 Annual Meeting of the American Folklore Society. Interestingly, Goldstein's hearing of this story prompted recall of a related incident from his own fieldwork in north-eastern Scotland.

In the early 1960s he was collecting items of folklore and their traditional contexts, paying close attention to variations in both. On one occasion he was collecting obscene riddles and stories from several members of a women's group. The group met weekly, but it was typically Goldstein's wife, Rochelle, who was the "collector" present, having been dispatched by her husband with instructions to "remember everything." When he inquired as to the possible reluctance of the women to share such things with a man (remember, Goldstein was interested in the potential alteration of an item as well as its natural context), one woman laughed heartily before responding: "We forget what is in your pants when you are here with us!" The meeting audience enjoyed this story, too.

Finally, in an experiment to investigate the expectancy effect in anthropological research, Gary Alan Fine and Beverly J. Crane concluded that "although the sex of the interviewers by itself did not have any significant effect on the collection of riddles, the interaction of interviewer's sex and expectancy proved to be highly significant" (1977:18). In other words, sex may be a significant variable, but then again, it may not. Moreover, Fine and Crane suggest that there are considerations beyond the visible biology of the interviewer which must be evaluated. For example, were the female interviewers particularly influenced by the presence of an expectancy (i.e., a bias that operates to produce results that conform to the expectations of the person in authority) because "women have been more culturally conditioned to respond to others' expectations since women have traditionally been dependent upon pleasing others as a means of deriving a positive self-image" (1977:18–19)? Might women be more "susceptible than men to any special attention by the experimenter to the task (i.e., the Hawthorne Effect), and could this have produced increased effort by the female interviewers in the experimental expectancy situations" (1977:19)?

Nonetheless, much of the preceding represents hindsight. It is an attempt to gain perspective from a field situation wherein I was frequently the only woman present, within a study community that tolerated—even encouraged—my crossing boundaries between same-sex groups and which included the collection of data not usually available to female members of the study culture. Clearly, I remain anxious about my acceptance (or even toleration) by women and men who are participants in a cultural tradition that recognizes social segregation based on sex. This apprehension was most acute when I perceived my presence to be in conflict with any usual status role in the community, that is, when certain areas of social life, or particular segments of the community, would have been expected to be closed to me because of my femaleness.

Upon reflection, however, I am convinced that the particular status I have been able to occupy at any given point in field research has had a significant influence on my access to, and the kinds of, data available for collection. More importantly, I now understand that my sexual identity as perceived by the community members is a variable which must be a conscious part of my own understanding for enactment of the appropriate behavior in the appropriate context. Of course, such role playing is often a prerequisite for acceptance within the community and for reducing the chances of making a culturally wrong move (see e.g., Goldstein 1964). It is also a valuable insight into the cultural definition of appropriate behavior of individuals within a specific social context (e.g., the approved behavior for adult women visitors in a private home). Quite aside from the admittedly emotional need for acceptance and the desire to be able to recount stories of a rewarding field experience, there is a very practical matter: acquisition of a public image which will encourage a flow of information that is frequent, in sufficient quantity, and scientifically valid for analysis and interpretation.

What are some of the possible consequences of sexual and gender identity when an anthropologist is in the field? There are at least three separate, yet intimately related, points: the personal and subjective; the ethonographic; and the theoretical and methodological (see Golde 1970). Undoubtedly, such reflective presentations provide the first-time fieldworker with a measure of comfort in undertaking that initial trip to the field. For the professional and experienced fieldworker, the subjective discussion of another's fieldwork provides a comparative framework in which to weigh his or her own experiences. Finally, anthropology as a social scientific discipline can profit from serious attempts "to understand the field experience in contexts consonant with current theories of human social behavior" (Hatfield 1973:15).

For illustrations and examples, I shall use the framework and events from my own life and fieldwork. During the summer of 1975 I traveled to Istanbul, Turkey, accompanied by my husband (Stephen) and our then not quite two-year-old daughter (Sarah). I had been invited to participate in the First International Turkish Folklore Congress, and I anticipated time for some preliminary fieldwork. However, the summer was planned primarily as a visit with Turkish family members and friends, most of whom I had not seen in more than ten years and none of whom had yet met my husband or daughter. I met able and helpful colleagues at the congress, I collected some interesting items of political folklore, and we three thrived within the warm hospitality of the Turkish extended family. The stay ended for all of us much, much too soon.

The following summer I returned to Turkey, but this time as a folklorist, and alone. In addition to the required preparations to leave for the field, I had spent considerable time during the intervening year preparing Sarah for my departure and absence. Since she had been jointly raised by her father and me sharing her care from birth—each of us remaining at home while the other assumed employment or research responsibilities outside on a mutually agreed to basis of approximately equal time—Sarah did not need to be prepared for change in caretakers. Of course, changes in the amount of time with one caretaker, and possible scheduling difficulties (e.g., we "rescheduled" her third birthday party for an afternoon before I left), were openly talked over, especially since Sarah appeared to enjoy such conversations. In fact, my departure and absence from Philadelphia were in many ways made easier for Sarah by her own travel to Istanbul the previous summer. She asked us often about the things she did and the people she met.

In fact, such conversations about Turkey very soon took on the feel of a storytelling session. "Tell me again, Mommy, about the time I wouldn't go to bed without the slippers Grammy [the term she used for the grandmother in the Turkish family] bought for me at the covered bazaar." "Do you remember when we took the ferry to the islands and we all rode donkeys?" "Did I really get to eat cookies for breakfast!" "Can't Togay and Anne come to visit us? I'd let them sleep in my room." "How come Dede [Grandfather] gave me sugar cubes and kissed my arm? Did I really give him my other arm to kiss, too?" During our shopping trips to purchase the several small items that I would take along as gifts for the children, Sarah was most insistent that we make the right choice: "But, Mommy, I would really like to have a Mickey Mouse puzzle. Remember how much Leyla [a three-year-old girl] wanted to meet Mickey Mouse? I know she'd like this!"

In anticipating fieldwork, a primary concern was how I as a single woman (i.e., being unaccompanied by, or absent from, my husband) would be evaluated within a cultural context having a strong emphasis on identification of a woman through some male relative—father, brother, husband, son. Furthermore, I was concerned about how a woman's separation from her young child would be judged, since Turkish women are the primary caretakers of children, particularly children as young as my own daughter. Among those Turkish friends who had met my husband and our daughter the previous summer, I encountered few, if any, problems. For these very cosmopolitan friends the reaction was most often amusement, as though my explanations of unaccompanied presence and father-caretaking were yet another strange American custom. There was neither a diminution in their welcome of me nor in their insistence that I spend more time than I was able with them. But, then, these were family and friends, not "informants," as both they and I unconsciously assumed. Unfortunately, their lack of reaction did not prepare me for what was to happen when I left Instanbul to live and work within areas of the country I had never been before and where I was largely unknown.

Many fieldworkers have learned that informants are likely to have as many, and sometimes a good deal more, inquiries of the fieldworker as he or she had posed during the formal or informal interview. Predictably, such questions related to the researcher's background. And although there is curiosity and genuine interest on the part of the inquiring informant, that individual is also securing needed information to assist in determining just where this "stranger" should be placed to "fit" within the community thereby allowing "predictability" of his or her behavior.

Inevitably, the first questions I was asked by women of all ages were about my age, marital status, and children. "How many children do you have?" These were quickly followed by inquiries about my family: "How sad your father is dead." "No brother? Too bad." Next, there were a few questions to learn my citizenship and nationality. "You come all the way from America?" "No Turkish relatives?! But you can speak Turkish; surely you must have some relatives who come from Turkey?" And, finally, the question asked of all fieldworkers: "What did you say you're doing here?" I answered each of their questions with the "truth." Self-righteous, I was not going to hide anything or distort my answers. I have never felt anything but a conscious respect for the reciprocal nature of any social interaction in the field. Unfortunately, it was only after a series of painful starts and stops that I finally understood my predicament: A basic contradiction existed between my own definition of self and that of those individuals who I hoped would become my informants. By answering questions about myself and my family "truthfully," I was hindering rapport establishment with all of the women and some of the men. Once I grasped that, I was able to determine the behavior appropriate for a Turkish woman and, therefore, by extension what the informants were expecting of me as a woman.

Interestingly, while I had been concerned with the "having left" part of the summer's arrangement, my potential women informants focused on the "with whom." When responding to inquiries about who was taking care of my daughter, I answered in Turkish (the language of the question) that the caretaker was my husband, Sarah's father. My explanation evoked puzzled expressions, muffled laughter, then a small grin on the face of the original questioner as the question was repeated, although this time more slowly and carefully so that I would not misunderstand the Turkish. In other words, my "inappropriate" response had been understood as a function of my unfamiliarity with the Turkish language.

Until I caught on to what was happening, we would go over the question again, first in Turkish, then in English (on one occasion, enlisting a young schoolboy who had an elementary knowledge of English), now back to Turkish. Finally, I realized that my reputation as a trustworthy person—a person to be trusted with information, tasks, confidences, and friendships—depended on my answering "correctly." So, I took a deep breath and lied. Ever after in response to the caretaking question, I answered that it was my mother who was looking after Sarah and, by implication, Stephen, too. Eventually, I confirmed that a Turkish woman quite often does travel in the accompaniment of some of her children, or with other women, or even alone. However, she has always made the appropriate arrangements before such a departure. These arrangements include the trusting of her children—and quite likely her husband as well—to an individual approved by the community. Such an appropriate person is most often the woman's mother; perhaps in her place it is the husband's mother, or frequently sisters or aunts if her own mother is not available. Under no circumstances, however, would a Turkish woman leave her child(ren) in the care of her husband, the(ir) father.

And there was the rub. I had answered each time carefully and truthfully, but I had only succeeded in making matters worse. While I had been concerned about the reaction of the community to my separation from my young daughter and to my temporary singleness, the community concern was directed at the arrangements that I had made for my absence. I even intercepted knowing glances from the older, married women, later confirmed in casual conversations as translating: "How nice to be without a husband. Husbands are a lot of work." When I returned to the United States, it was small gifts for my mother—and not for my husband—which some of these women entrusted to me as a token of their friendship with me and their appreciation of my mother's responsibility.

Admittedly, there were some raised eyebrows in my own family and community as I prepared to leave my husband and daughter to spend the summer doing fieldwork in Turkey, a thing and a place inadequately understood by many of them. But such misunderstandings, while at times unpleasant and uncomfortable when voiced by members of my own family or neighbors, could not be as important or as persuasive as they would be if they came from members of the study community. In Turkey I was not known, at times my work would appear abstract, and all I would have would be my explanation as to who I was, strengthened by some helpful introductions and written letters from Turkish and American colleagues.

The next examples come from time spent collecting folklore in northeastern Turkey. I was very interested in recording actual performances of traditional storytellers and singers which are still common in the coffee houses in that part of the country. The coffeehouse in traditional Turkish life is a male domain, that public area where men of all ages gather for congenial and animated conversation, enjoy music and story sessions by favorite performers, and drink cold liquids or hot tea, but rarely coffee. Whereas male community members dominate the public spaces of the community, females congregate in those which are private—behind the walls of the compound and inside the home, within special areas of the house that are defined as "female" and into which male family members do not go uninvited. In fact, when several women are visiting, particularly women outside the immediate family, men do not enter at all. In small villages where there is not a conveniently located coffeehouse, or for some other reason, a special room in the house itself may be set aside for strictly male use. Here, men entertain male family members and friends in the late afternoon and evening hours, serving refreshments, sponsoring a performance, welcoming the special guest.

In Kars, the largest city in northeastern Turkey, I was accompanied by a Turkish folklorist who had worked previously with several of the city's traditional folk musicians, or *ashiklar* (wandering or strolling minstrels). During the evening's performance in the coffeehouse owned by one of the minstrels, I felt most conspicuous. Assurances aside, I was extremely self-conscious being the only woman member of an audience that by eight o'clock had swelled to more than two hundred. However, to the three minstrels my presence was apparently without difficulty: I was a folklorist and a *hodja* (literally a religious teacher, but commonly used an an honorific). In fact, my introduction to the audience was in this formal capacity; I was consistently addressed by the performers and members of the audience as "hodja." On no occasion that evening, or during later visits to the coffeehouse, was I addressed using the common respectful greeting for women of my age (i.e., personal name plus *hanIm*). I was not perceived of as a woman, but consistently as a professional folklorist—a folklorist engaged in important folkloric research recording on tape and film the famous minstrels of Kars.

Did my presence alter the performance in any way? What about the material selected? Could audience participation have been muted? According to my informants, there had been no alterations in the performance because a woman was present. Nevertheless, they did not rule out the possibility that they had altered or modified their material, or their behavior as members of the audience, to reflect their "best" for the folklorist to record and photograph. A straightforward assessment, and one with which I essentially agree. Certainly, a trade-off. Had I not been recognized as a folklorist, I would not have been admitted as a woman.

And my own perception of this? I came to think of myself as an "honorary man." For the duration of my stay in Kars, and particularly in my work at the coffeehouse, I was "passing" as a man. Imagine my amusement when I read almost three years later a small *Newsweek* piece about Queen Elizabeth II being made an "honorary man" to permit her attendance at a banquet given in her honor by the government of Saudi Arabia during her state visit to that country.

Later, in the course of my fieldwork I stayed in a remote village a difficult day's journey by jeep from Kars, perhaps no more than five kilometers from Turkey's northeastern border with the Soviet Union. While in this village, I was received in turn by adult males who told me stories of the well-known minstrels their village had produced and by adult women and small children of both sexes who allowed me to participate in their round of daily activities (e.g., baking bread, washing clothes, preparing food for the men, caring for small children). No member of either group expressed curiosity about my time spent with the other; on no occasion was the Turkish folklorist (a man) asked to join me in the women's quarters, not even when it was obvious to everyone that I desperately needed his help in comprehending the village women's speech, and they mine!

To be sure, a "foreign" male fieldworker might have been permitted access to the folklore that I collected from the women in this secluded community, but I seriously doubt it. Instead, I think that it was perfectly clear to all members of the household, male and female, why I was there. However, the reasons each group recognized and, therefore, the data able to be collected, would depend on which of my ascribed statuses I was perceived to be occupying at any particular time.

Consequently, it is the social situation that defines gender, for gender is visible as a sum of qualities, including mannerism, way of speaking, dress, choice of topics in conversation, and so on. Gender is a visible fact most of the time; sex is not. We do not expect to see vagina or penis, breasts or hairy chest, before we react to an individual as male or female. Precisely because gender roles are very visible and most people feel competent to judge how others fill them, sanctions are likely to emanate from many sources (Oakley 1972:187–189).

During the summer of 1977 my mother traveled to Turkey to visit a Turkish family I had known for almost fifteen years. My mother had become very fond of the family's eldest daughter when, as a teenager, Zafer had been an exchange student in the local high school and had lived with our family for several months. While in Istanbul my mother met one of my Turkish colleagues, a professor who, sharing many of my own interests in folklore, had been most gracious in his encouragement and assistance while I was in the field. This is how my mother remembered that meeting with Ali Bey: "Professor Ali engaged me in a conversation, a long one, when Zafer introduced us. He told me he could understand how very worried I must have been when you traveled alone to Turkey, but that there was no reason for my worry. 'We could see Susan was from a good family. She was always polite to everyone, and she knew, understood, and showed respect for our customs. To Turkish people, these things are important. I watched out for her as I would for my own daughter, and I sent her to people who could help in her work. Susan was safe here with us.'"

So, I had passed after all; I had learned to act appropriately. And in turn this was rewarded, not only by a stimulating field experience in good company but also with the opportunity to observe traditional Turkish musicians and raconteurs and to participate in the daily social life of some Turkish men and women.

REFERENCES

BERREMAN, GERALD

1962   Behind Many Masks: Ethnography and Impression Management in a Himalayan Village. Society for Applied Anthropology Monographs 4:1–24.

BOHANNAN, LAURA

1966   Shakespeare in the Bush. Natural History 75 (7): 28–33.

FINE, GARY ALAN, AND BEVERLY J. CRANE

1977   The Expectancy Effect in Anthropological Research: An Experimental Study of Riddle Collection. American Ethnologist 3:517–524.

GOLDE, PEGGY, ED.

1970   Women in the Field. Chicago: Aldine.

GOLDSTEIN, KENNETH S.

1964   A Guide for Field Workers in Folklore. Memoirs of The American Folklore Society, vol. 52. Hatboro, PA: Folklore Associates.

HATFIELD, COLBY

1973   Fieldwork: Toward a Model of Mutual Exploitation. Anthropological Quarterly 46 (1): 15–29.

OAKLEY, ANN

1972   Sex, Gender and Society. New York: Harper & Row.

SARGENT, WYN

1974   People of the Valley: Life with a Cannibal Tribe in New Guinea. New York: Random House.

SUGGESTED READINGS

BOVEN, METTE

1966   The Significance of the Sex of the Fieldworker for Insights into the Male and Female Worlds. Ethnos 31:24–27 (supplement).

BOWEN, ELENORE (LAURA BOHANNAN)

1954   Return to Laughter. New York: Harper.

BUTLER, BARBARA, AND DIANE MICHALSKI TURNER, EDS.

1987   Children and Anthropological Research. New York: Plenum Press.

CASSELL, JOAN, ED.

1987   Children in the Field: Anthropological Experiences. Philadelphia: Temple University Press.

CESARA, MANDA

1982   Reflections of a Woman Anthropologist: No Hiding Place. New York: Academic Press.

FREILICH, MORRIS, ED.
1970   Marginal Natives: Anthropologists at Work. New York: Harper & Row.
1972   Sex and Culture. *In* The Meaning of Culture. M. Freilich, ed. Lexington, MA: Xerox College Publications.
1983   The Pleasures of Anthropology. New York: New American Library.

FRISBIE, CHARLOTTE
1975a   Fieldwork as a "Single Parent": To Be or Not to Be Accompanied by a Child. Theodore R. Frisbie, ed. Pp. 98–119. Collected Papers in Honor of Florence Hawley Ellis. Papers of the Archaeological Society of New Mexico, No. 2. Norman, OK: Hooper.
1975b   Observations on a Preschooler's First Experience with Cross-Cultural Living. Journal of Man 7 (1): 91–112.

GOLDE, PEGGY, ED.
1986   Women in the Field: Anthropological Experiences. 2d ed., expanded and updated. Berkeley: University of California Press.

KIMBALL, SOLON, AND JAMES WATSON, EDS.
1972   Crossing Cultural Boundaries: The Anthropological Experience. San Francisco: Chandler.

LAWLESS, ROBERT, VINSON H. SUTLIVE, JR., AND MARIO D. ZAMORA, EDS.
1983   Fieldwork: The Human Experience. New York: Gordon and Breach Science Publishers.

NUMEZ, THERON A.
1972   On Objectivity and Field Work. *In* Crossing Cultural Boundaries: The Anthropological Experience. Solon Kimball and James Watson, eds. Pp. 164–171. San Francisco: Chandler.

POWDERMAKER, HORTENSE
1966   Stranger and Friend: The Way of the Anthropologist. New York: Norton.

WAX, ROSALIE
1971   Doing Fieldwork: Warnings and Advice. Chicago: University of Chicago Press.

WHITEHEAD, TONY LARRY, AND MARY ELLEN CONAWAY, EDS.
1986   Self, Sex, and Gender in Cross-Cultural Fieldwork. Urbana: University of Illinois Press.

ACKNOLWEDGMENTS

I would like to acknowledge my debt and gratitude to several people, named and unnamed, who participated in and contributed to my fieldwork experience. To Kenneth S. Goldstein who first taught me, to Stephen and Sarah who went some times and some places with me, and to numerous Turkish and American women who nurtured me, I give thanks. Within these pages all personal names of Turkish friends and colleagues and those of some geographical locations have been fictionalized to afford anonymity.

ELEVEN

🦋 Fieldwork That Failed

LINDA L. KENT

Fieldwork is the hallmark of cultural anthropology. It is the way we explore and learn about the vast detailed intricacy of human culture and individual behavior and it is, importantly, the way in which most cultural anthropologists earn and maintain their professional standing.

Some of the early personal accounts of anthropologists in the field make fieldwork sound exciting, adventuresome, certainly exotic, sometimes easy. Margaret Mead, in a preface to *Coming of Age in Samoa* (1949), related her despair of ever learning the native language, only to find herself one day thinking those same thoughts *in* the native language. From there on it was, apparently, all downhill. Malinowski, the classic anthropological fieldworker, describes the early stages of fieldwork as "a strange, sometimes unpleasant, sometimes intensely interesting adventure [which] soon adopts quite a natural course" (1961:7). He goes on to describe his daily routine of strolling through the village observing the intimate details of family life, and as he tells it, such observations seem possible and accessible. The trick is in the stroll.

In more recent years there have been numerous realistic accounts of fieldwork (e.g., Cesara 1982, Golde 1986, Spindler 1970, Whitehead and Conaway 1986) which portray the difficult, dirty, depressing, discouraging conditions of fieldwork as well as the thrill of insight and discovery, and the challenge presented to the ethnographer's self-esteem and confidence. In a wonderful article in the *American Ethnologist*, Miles Richardson (1975:525) writes about the realities of his own fieldwork:

> Later that morning, I thought I would be like Malinowski and walk through the village, etc., so I got Tex and went out. The men had left for their work, the women were cleaning house behind closed doors and windows, and the kids were in school. But at least Tex enjoyed it. Being a Labrador, he couldn't resist jumping into a large spring boxed in with concrete. As I called him out, a man walking by muttered, "Gringos! Washing their dogs in water that people bathe in."

Hortense Powdermaker (1966:53) describes her reaction to being all alone at last in Lesu:

> A day or two later, my anthrolopogist friends left me to return to their own work. As I waved goodbye, I felt like Robinson Crusoe, but without a man Friday. That evening as I ate my dinner, I felt very low. I took a quinine pill to ward off malaria. Suddenly I saw myself at the edge of the world, and *alone*. I was scared and close to panic.

Despite both the glossing over and the gnashing of teeth, these accounts have in common the fact that the fieldwork, however romantic or scary, was, in some sense, successful. The anthropologist stuck it out, gained entry, established rapport, collected data, wrapped up, returned home, and published.

Less well documented are the fieldwork attempts that fizzled. These attempts may be instructive, both because they outline some of the pitfalls and because they show that there are some endeavors that just aren't going to be successful, and no fault to anyone. Discussion of fieldwork that failed, although there may not be the need to dwell on it, can also make the whole enterprise of ethnography a bit more human and accessible to new or aspiring anthropologists.

I have two stories to offer in the context of fieldwork that fizzled. The first took place when I was a student interested in studying Gypsies for my master's thesis. I was interested in how Gypsies use caricature as cultural camouflage, how they deliberately exaggerate *our* notions, or images, of them and thereby reinforce the stereotype and protect their "real" identity at the same time. It was of course their "real" identity I was after. Having identified the cleverness with which they fooled others, I never considered my own stereotypical notions about Gypsies. I certainly never thought I would be putty in their hands.

In 1974, toward the end of my first year of graduate study at Louisiana State University in Baton Rouge, I had decided to begin fieldwork for my thesis during the summer in New Orleans. From my reading, I knew that there was a strong possibility that New Orleans would have a sizeable Gypsy population, since Gypsies abound both in large cities and in the South. I also wanted to experience living in New Orleans, an exciting, romantic city, if only to enjoy the contrast with Baton Rouge. I was awarded a small research grant from the Student Government Association and I set upon my new adventure with a curious blend of confidence and fear.

It was odd that I had gone to Louisiana in the first place. A Massachusetts Yankee descended from generations of Massachusetts Yankees, I could certainly have found reason to stay in the northeast. But I had always found fascination in other peoples and places, a fascination that drew me to anthropology and ultimately to the study of traveling peoples, Gypsies and Tinkers. How I happened to find myself in Louisiana was the result of a comedy of circumstances, as much due to youthful confusion and lack of planning as to anything else.

In my first semester of graduate work, I experienced incredible isolation, loneliness, and an overwhelming lack of confidence. I had majored in history as an undergraduate and had very little preparation for the seminars and advanced courses I was taking. I struggled to understand new words like *nomothetic, emic,* and *etic,* and pushed my way through Marvin Harris's redoubtable tome, *The Rise of Anthropological Theory* (1968). Where were the people and places I had come to learn about?

Second semester I took a course in ethnographic methodology and a little cool breeze began to pierce the steamy humidity of Louisiana. I loved the course, I loved interviewing, I loved having constant feedback, support, and advice as I handed in my "fieldnotes." And I loved most of all the idea of myself as a fieldworker. With visions of Margaret Mead in my head, I set out for New Orleans that summer to find Gypsies, discover their secrets, and do great things. I had all the confidence of the unborn. But in my glow of optimism there was a small constant tick of dread. My major professor would be out of the country for the summer, and my small circle of new friends in Baton Rouge was likewise dispersing. I would be completely on my own.

Looking back across the years at this first adventure, I now see much more clearly the impact of personal circumstances on the choices and responses I made at that time. At that point in my mid-twenties, I was alienated from my family of origin, seriously introverted and self-isolating, and had great difficulty forming close relationships or initiating interaction with others. I don't know how I ever thought I could do fieldwork. I did not take any of these factors into account when I left for the field. I didn't consider how that may have influenced my selection of topic for study or my ability to carry out such a study. I never thought I was running away from anything nor did I imagine that my interest in Gypsies, or in anthropology, had anything to do with disenchantment with my own society and myself in it.

In New Orleans, I sublet a cockroach-riddled student apartment on the second floor of a house on a quiet street not far from Tulane University. I began what I thought was a systematic search for my study population. I interviewed people in organizations I thought might have contact with Gypsies: the New Orleans Police Department, state and city welfare, Board of Education, Salvation Army, Travelers' Aid. I read through news archives and history books. Through these efforts I did in fact compile a list of Gypsy addresses in the New Orleans area, but my efforts to contact these "elusive laughing vagabonds" (my own unquestioned stereotype) were futile.

I spent endless days walking or riding buses to places where Gypsies had just been, or used to be, but no longer were. Sometimes it seemed, from the material things left behind, that they had indeed "just left," and perhaps in a hurry. In other cases I found vacant lots, abandoned mobile homes, rundown apartment buildings. More than once I found myself in neighborhoods that felt decidedly unsafe. I frequently returned home through the incredible summer heat with a feeling of resignation and despair—how could I be a famous anthropologist if I couldn't even *find* my informants? But I also had very private, unacknowledged feelings of relief: If I couldn't find Gypsies I wouldn't have to talk to them, I wouldn't have to justify my inquiring presence, beg their acceptance of me. If I dutifully covered all of the bases, searched diligently, and genuinely couldn't contact them, then who could blame me if my fieldwork failed?

For weeks I wrestled between being a victim of, or taking charge of, my research. I eventually reached a point, the low point, where I dreaded actually meeting a Gypsy. It was then, of course, that I found Madame Ruby.

Madame Ruby and her family lived in a small house on a rural highway leading into New Orleans. A large sign outside the house showed the palm of a hand, with the lines of fortune emphasized. Almost resentfully, I went up and knocked on the door. A dark-haired woman in a headscarf and a long colorful dress invited me in and asked what I wanted. My memory obscures my exact words, but I stumbled through some sort of introduction, saying I was interested in Gypsies and that I was a student. She responded by telling me her fortune telling rates (three different prices depending on how much detail I wanted) and then said she wasn't a Gypsy so she couldn't tell me anything about them.

I looked at her in disbelief. Not a Gypsy? Of course she was a Gypsy—she fit everything I had read about them. Her occupation, her dress, her features, her accent, everything seemed "Gypsy." And as sure as I was about it, I was equally sure from her direct, slightly amused denial that I had come to an ethnographic dead-end. I told her, a bit insistently, that I thought she was a Gypsy. She denied it again (yes you are, no I'm not) and wouldn't entertain any more discussion about it. Did I want my fortune told or not? Numbed, I took the five-dollar version. "You will have good luck in the future." Sure I would.

No one had ever told me, nor had it occurred to me, that I would run into such an impasse. (I never doubted then, and do not now, that she was a Gypsy.) I see now how naive I was to try to "gain entry" into a group whose existence depends on camouflage and who had every reason to suspect my motives. Without someone to serve as an intermediary, someone trusted by the Gypsies, to introduce me and explain what I wanted to do, my efforts were doomed from the start. In all of my reading about how Gypsies exaggerate some of their stereotypical characteristics in order to protect their identity, I never realized that they also rely on denying their identity to achieve the same purpose. Madame Ruby told me she was Mexican; Gypsies frequently claim a nationality rather than an ethnicity when it seems advantageous to do so.

After six weeks of heat, complete isolation, and cockroaches, this was the last straw. I gave up and went to Boston. There, in the company of friends and with the pain of this first lesson in fieldwork fresh in my mind, I set about studying Gypsies again. And the "good luck" foretold by Madame Ruby came to pass, resulting in a master's thesis on the life history of a Gypsy headman (Kent 1975).

There are many "lessons" to be learned from this experience: Some of them I am still learning, others probably have yet to be realized. The lesson I stress here is that the fieldworker is a person as well as a scholar, with attitudes, emotions, habits, fears, and experiences that trot right along beside the scholar and indeed inform the scholarship. A second lesson is that "good" fieldwork is not, as Rosalie Wax (1986) points out, the result of any one person alone. The fieldworker, even if deliberately alone in the field, must have someone with whom to communicate and consult about the work. In my often self-imposed isolation and my efforts to do it all myself, yet disregarding myself in the process, I lost both my focus and my spirit.

In the course of my research on Gypsies, I came across the sparse but fascinating literature on the Traveling People, or Tinkers, of Ireland. I also learned that there were Irish Travelers living in the United States (see, for example, Harper 1971). Although my first choice was to do my doctoral fieldwork in Ireland, I determined in the fall of 1977 to carry out a preliminary study in Mississippi. Earlier that year I had been admitted to candidacy for the Ph.D. at the University of Oregon and had spent the spring semester teaching at Idaho State University. I approached my new adventure with optimism and confidence.

My first step was to contact the anthropology department at Memphis State University. I explained what I wanted to do and asked about sharing an apartment with graduate students. The response was reassuringly warm. The faculty offered suggestions, ideas, and interest in my project, and I received an offer from a young graduate student couple who were willing to let me stay in a spare room. I moved to Memphis, found my way around, talked to faculty and other people who knew about the Travelers, gave a student lecture on Gypsies, and became a volunteer at the Southern Folklore Center. Within a few days I had identified a mobile home park, just across the border in Mississippi, which was home to several Traveler families.

Again, without the critical trusted intermediary person to introduce me, my entry into the Traveler encampment would be virtually impossible. The only person who really knew and was respected by these Travelers was a priest named Father Mike. Father Mike agreed to host a meeting with some of the Traveler elders whose approval I would need before I could go further. The meeting was arranged but was continuously called off, first due to the death and funeral of a respected Traveler, then canceled or postponed for a variety of reasons. I sensed that Father

Mike was reluctant to share "his" Travelers with me. When I finally suggested that I would try to make contact on my own, he agreed to let me use his name. I began visiting the park cautiously, respectfully, talking to women as they worked outside in their yards, hanging laundry or looking after their children and gardens. I felt uncomfortable walking through the park, doing the Malinowski stroll, observing the intimate details of family life. I hung around the edges of the park, trying my best to be innocuous, hoping for some sign of welcome. I "succeeded" to the point where I was invited inside one of the mobile homes and was introduced by a woman to her family and neighbors. A small, precious, precarious beginning.

Then an odd thing happened. Some Gypsies passed through Memphis and were accused of petty theft and vandalism. The local television station decided to do a human-interest news feature on Gypsies and called the anthropology department at the university to inquire whether anyone there knew about them. I had just given my Gypsy lecture to an undergraduate class and my name was mentioned to reporters. Without thinking about the Travelers, I said yes to the request for an interview, parts of which were aired on the five o'clock news. To my great surprise I was introduced as an "expert who had come to Memphis to devote her life to the study of Gypsies"!

Two days later Father Mike called to inform me that the Travelers had met to discuss the news interview and had decided not to meet with me anymore. Didn't I know, Father Mike added parenthetically, that Gypsies and Travelers are archenemies? The one is always being blamed for what the other does and vice versa. And they compete for some of the same economic territory, such as paving driveways and selling used cars. If I had indeed come to the area to study Gypsies, then why was I hanging around the Travelers? The Travelers were suspicious, and I was no longer welcome.

In panic I drove to the mobile home park and tried to talk with one of the elders. I explained the inaccuracy of the news reporter's statements about me. I swore (truthfully) that I hadn't seen or spoken to any Gypsies in the area at all, that I was interested in the Travelers. I found myself trying to convince him not only that I was sincere but also that I was a good person, as if *that* were somehow the issue at stake.

During this encounter, the Traveler elder's statements and questions revealed to me in short order the enormity of the task I had set upon myself in trying to gain entry into this community. What was my religion? (The Travelers are virtually all Roman Catholic; I have a Protestant background.) Why did I come down here from the north? Why was I, a single female, traveling around alone? Why did I want to study the Travelers? He said he had seen me on television and that he didn't think the Travelers would do me any good and that I certainly wouldn't do them any good. He asked me to leave and, as his parting shot, told me to "be sweet."

I crept away, humiliated and angry. I was angry at the injustice of this Traveler, judging me in terms of my religion, marital status, gender, and geography. (Yet certainly some of those same categories were of significance to my interest in the Travelers.) I was angry at Father Mike for not helping me, at the news reporter for making inaccurate statements. I was angry because I had invested considerable time, travel, money, and energy in this project and because I really believed I was ready, professionally, to do it (something I hadn't felt in New Orleans). I left Memphis feeling frustrated and sorry for myself.

What I only began to learn from this experience at the time was how important it was to me to be seen as a "good person," how much I was seeking approval from my informants or potential informants. I realized that I had wanted the same approval from the Gypsies and, in the course of my master's fieldwork in Boston, felt I had indeed attained a measure of it. This need continued even after the debacle in Mississippi and played itself out again in my more successful doctoral fieldwork in Ireland the following year (Kent 1980).

The need for approval at least partly results from the reality that the fieldworker comes uninvited and, no matter how skilled, is bound to be intrusive. She offers little or nothing in return for the privilege of entry into her informants' lives and may receive rewards and recognition back home, even financial profit, which her informants do not share. Somehow, if the people she studies can at least like her—that is, find her pleasant, amusing, interesting—then perhaps these qualities will constitute a form of repayment for all she takes and learns from them. For me, wanting to be seen as a good person was also a need for acceptance and wanting to belong, obviously something I didn't feel among my own people. I suspect this may be an unspoken motive for many anthropologists, especially those who have not yet found professional acceptance within the discipline. I know it was true for me. The paradox is that my fieldwork failed in part *because* I needly so badly for it to succeed. The importance of being accepted clouded my ability to look at and plan the most advantageous course of action. In both cases, among Gypsies and Travelers, I presented myself as a puppy in the rain, pleading to be taken in, hoping I would be seen as pitiable and harmless enough to be accepted. It has been a long, hard lesson to realize that this is not the road to acceptance, either in the field or at home.

Richardson's "myth teller" (1975) is still an inspirational piece. It speaks eloquently of the magic, wonder, and mystery of this most human of enterprises: the challenge of understanding other humans. In recent years, with the emergence of interpretive and then reflexive anthropology (Wilson 1988), the challenge of understanding oneself in the process of understanding others has earned our attention. It is through failures as well as successes, both our own and those of others, that we learn about being human.

REFERENCES

CESARA, MANDA
1982   Reflections of a Woman Anthropologist: No Hiding Place. New York: Academic Press.

GOLDE, PEGGY, ED.
1986   Women in the Field: Anthropological Experiences. 2d ed. Berkeley: University of California Press.

HARPER, JARED
1971   "Gypsy" Research in the South. *In* The Not So Solid South. J. Kenneth Morland, ed. Pp. 16–24. Southern Anthropological Society Proceedings No. 4.

HARRIS, MARVIN
1968   The Rise of Anthropological Theory. New York: Thomas Y. Crowell.

KENT, LINDA
1975   The End of the Road: The Life History of the Gypsy Headman in Boston, Massachusetts. Master's thesis, Department of Geography and Anthrolopogy, Louisiana State University, Baton Rouge.
1980   "In the Houses of Strangers": The Impact of Government Policy on the Irish Travellers. Doctoral dissertation, Department of Anthropology, University of Oregon, Eugene.

MALINOWSKI, BRONISLAW
1922   Argonauts of the Western Pacific. New York: E. P. Dutton. Reissued Prospect Heights, IL: Waveland Press, 1984.

MEAD, MARGARET
1949   Coming of Age in Samoa. New York: Mentor Books (first publ. 1928).

POWDERMAKER, HORTENSE
1966   Stranger and Friend: The Way of an Anthropologist. New York: W. W. Norton.

RICHARDSON, MILES
1975   Anthropologist—The Myth Teller. American Ethnologist 2(3):517–533.

SPINDLER, GEORGE
1970   Being an Anthropologist: Fieldwork in Eleven Cultures. New York: Holt, Rinehart & Winston.

WAX, ROSALIE
1986   Gender and Age in Fieldwork and Fieldwork Education: "Not Any Good Thing Is Done by One Man Alone." *In* Self, Sex, and Gender in Cross-Cultural Fieldwork. Tony Larry Whitehead and Mary Ellen Conaway, eds. Urbana: University of Illinois Press.

WHITEHEAD, TONY LARRY, AND MARY ELLEN CONAWAY, EDS.
1986   Self, Sex, and Gender in Cross-Cultural Fieldwork. Urbana: University of Illinois Press.

WILSON, LYNN
1988   Epistemology and Power: Rethinking Ethnography at Greenham. *In* Anthropology for the Nineties: Introductory Readings. Johnnetta Cole, ed. Pp. 42–48. New York: Free Press.

PART TWO

Other Worlds, Other Cultural Logics and Realities

TWELVE

Not a Real Fish: The Ethnographer as Inside Outsider

ROGER M. KEESING

It was to be my first night in a Solomon Island village. . . . At Bina, on the west Malaita coast, where I had been dropped by a government ship, I unpacked my two backpacks before the gaze of all the village children and many of the adults. Out came the mosquito netting, then the Abercrombie and Fitch air mattress and its foot pump. I spread the mattress on the ground, screwed the pump into the valve, and pumped, but nothing happened, in front of the expectant crowd as the sweating white stranger pumped away. Finally, after endless fiddling with the valve and sotto voce cursing, Western technology at last unfolded its mysteries.

Awakening on the thatched verandah to find a steady rain, I watched where the locals were going off, along the beach and around the point, bent under pandanus leaf umbrellas, for morning pees. I followed the same path. I discovered only by later observation that it was the women's latrine; the men's latrine, separated (as I was to learn) even in such Christian villages by strict rules of gender segregation, was a structure built over the water. My hosts were too polite to comment on—or claim compensation for—what I later realized had been a massive breach of propriety.

There had been no way to learn any Pidgin in advance, and after less than a week in the Solomons I could scarcely communicate at all with the villagers (although a couple spoke a bit of English). By midmorning, the carriers arranged by the district officer to guide me across the middle of the island had not arrived. Eventually, in late morning I succeeded in persuading two young men to carry my bags and lead the way; but after an hour and a half of walking into the foothills they announced that they would take me no further. Not until I had spent another reluctant night in a Christian village could I persuade anyone to take me further.

The still pagan Kwaio of the mountains above Sinalagu on the east coast, who had perpetrated the 1927 massacre of a district officer and his

entourage,[1] were feared by the colonial government as wild and dangerous. Their hostility to outsiders, especially missionaries and government,
was legendary in the Solomons. Yet the lure of the mist-shrouded Kwaio
mountains had been reinforced a few days earlier as I had traveled down
the coast on a small ship with a Malaitan government clerk. "You
wouldn't want to go up *there*!" he advised me. "The people live in houses
on the bare ground, like pigs, and they don't wear any clothes!"

After conferring with the district officer, who claimed to know the
Kwaio and their mountain fastnesses well, it seemed that their potential hostility might best be defused if I approached their heartland from
a different direction than Europeans usually did: by land rather than
by sea. But with no maps, little information, and no way of communicating effectively, I was relatively helpless in seeking to enlist
cooperation and explain my intentions. All I knew was that I was supposed to get to a place called 'Aenaafou, which the district officer had
told me was the key midpoint on the path to "Sinerango."[2]

My guides the next morning set off, but not toward 'Aenaafou. "You
can't get there from here," an English-speaking Christian man had explained, translating for me. "The river is up." I had been in no position to
argue, and at least I was moving inland—and upward. For the next nine
hours, I struggled and sweated up and down precipitous paths: an hour
and a half of climbing straight upward to a long-deserted mountaintop
settlement site, then a plunge down the other side, on slippery red clay,
into the gorge below. Looking back at the maps (which in 1962 did not
exist), the maze of elevation lines shows this to be the steepest, most
broken terrain in the Solomons, almost vertical in many places. Rather
than following the contours, the path zigzagged from peak tops to water-
ing places a thousand or more feet below.

We did not pass a settlement all day. But exotic it was, not least of
all because my tour guides were two cheerful and pretty teenage girls,
smoking pipes and stark naked. They bounded up and down the path
like mountain goats; my fifty-pound packs were a trifle. At the end of
the afternoon, exhausted, I was led into a mountaintop clearing with
several thatch buildings. It was clear from the response of the men
gathered there, surly-looking and carrying long machetes, bows and
arrows, and clubs, that I was neither expected nor particularly welcome.
Trying to explain my presence through linguistic filters, I learned that
this was a marriage feast. I was told I would have to stay inside one of
the houses, from which I could only peek through narrow gaps in the
thatch. Having been warned by the government that I might well be
killed by Kwaio warriors, who had dispatched a dozen Europeans
through the years (and were to dispatch another, a New Zealand missionary, three years later), I was less than relaxed.

What followed through most of the night was uninterpretable and
often terrifying. Perhaps two hundred people, the women and many of
the men naked except for shell ornaments and woven pouches, streamed

into the clearing as dusk fell. Several times, a warrior clutching a machete or club ran screaming around the house from which I was peering, shouting with what seemed hostility; one chopped down a banana tree beside the house with fierce whacks. Shouts and speeches, then falsetto screams echoing out on all sides, naked bodies back and fro in the flickering firelight. Eventually, persuaded by the sheer lapse of time that I was not to be the main course and numbed by physical exhaustion, I strung my mosquito net in a corner of the house and collapsed into sleep, only to be awakened in terror when someone stumbled into my net and he and it collapsed on top of me.

In late 1964, after almost two years of fieldwork, I could look back and smile at my early anxieties and innocence. I had been to a dozen wedding feasts, had helped to finance some with my own strung shell valuables, and knew now about the conventionalized mock threats and food distributions that had terrified me that first time. I spoke Kwaio fluently and had been received by these fiercely conservative mountaineers with a warmth and enthusiasm that had been amazing. (Only later did I more clearly understand the extent to which I had, through accidents of history, been incorporated into their historic project of anti-colonial struggle; when I arrived they were trying to write down their customs in emulation of colonial legal statutes, and I was to be their scribe.)[3] Taking part in feasting prestations, incorporated into kinship and neighborhood networks, allowed into shrines to take part in rituals,[4] I felt like a comfortable "insider."

But of course, I wasn't. I could never leave my own cultural world despite my partial successes in entering theirs. In fact, the lonely isolation, after ten months with scarcely a word of English (and mail service only once a month), was taking me near the edge of psychological balance. I choose two small episodes late in my fieldwork to illustrate both my precarious state and the unbridged and unbridgeable gulf between their world and mine. Both began while I was sitting in my thatch house typing field notes (I was very good about that in those days and have been degenerating every since).

As I sat typing one day, a wizened little man I hadn't seen before— he turned out to be from the mountains ten miles down the coast— slipped rather furtively beside me and whispered, "Come outside, I want to tell you something important." I put him off several times while I finished my journal entry, but eventually I followed as he led us secretively into a dark corner of an empty adjoining house. He leaned over to me and asked me portentously, in a hoarse voice scarcely loud enough to be heard, "Do you know where we all come from?" "What do you mean?" I asked. "Do you know where we Malaita people came from?" "Not exactly," I said, "but we're finding out something about that." "We all come from the same place, you Americans and we Malaita people. Do you know that?" Aha, I thought. A visionary glimpse of the human past. . . . I shifted into lecturing mode, and for five minutes or so I gave him a condensed explanation of the evolution of humankind and the prehistory of the Pacific. He heard me out politely. "I didn't think you knew," he said. "I'll tell you. You know that mountain at Iofana, beyond 'Ubuni—that's where we all came from. We Malaita people and you Americans." And then he gave *his* five-minute lecture, about the snake ancestress 'Oi'oifi'ona from whose eight human children the Malaitans—and Americans, by way of a migration to and beyond Tulagi—are descended. He was right. I didn't know.[5]

A few weeks later, I was again at my typewriter. I heard a commotion in the harbor a thousand feet below and went out to look. Loud voices, splashing of human—and other—bodies in the water. "They're driving *kirio* [dolphins] onto the beach and killing them," explained a local lad. A couple of minutes later, some young men from a settlement just up the hill came bounding down. "We're going down to kill a dolphin!" they announced. I was horrified: I had just been reading Lilly's early accounts of dolphin intelligence and had spent hours with my former teacher Gregory Bateson before I left California, discussing his plans for dolphin research. "Don't kill a dolphin! They're intelligent! They're like people!" I called out. But they paid no heed and went bounding down the precipitous path to the harbor.

Two hours later, they were back, carrying a huge leaf package. "We got one!" they called cheerfully. I was still horrified. Although Malaitans eat dolphins, that is a fringe benefit; they kill them for the teeth, which are used as exchange valuables and ornamentation. The young men unwrapped their package, to display a big butchered dolphin. I confess to a moment of ambivalence at the sight of red mammalian steaks—I had had no meat but an occasional strip of pork fat for months. But my outrage on behalf of a fellow sentient being far outweighed my urge for steak, and I abandoned my typewriter in favor of rhetoric.

"Don't eat that thing! You shouldn't eat *kirio*. They're not fish [*i'a*, in Kwaio]! They're like people, not fish! Look at its blood—it's red, and warm, like ours!" My friends went on cutting logs and building up a fire to heat the stones for a leaf oven, oblivious to my rhetoric (but giving me odd glances). My rhetoric was impeded somewhat by language problems. Dolphins may not be fish, but they are *i'a*. "But they're not *i'a to'ofunga'a*, 'real *i'a*,' I insisted (but they are: The category includes dolphins and whales as well as fish). The locals were unimpressed, so I reiterated the argument about warm, red blood. "And look," I said, "they can talk. *Kirio* can talk, they way we do."

This was too much, and they stopped building the fire. "What do you mean, they can talk?" I remembered that in the *Life* magazines in my house, there was an issue with a Lockheed ad showing a scuba diver tape-recording dolphin squeaks; and I bounded into the house to look for it. A few minutes later, I returned in triumph to the fire-builders, who had returned to the task and were heating stones. The ad was perfect. Fortuitously, the microphone the scuba diver was holding looked exactly like my tape-recorder microphone. "Look at this," I said. "The *kirio* is talking onto the tape recorder. They talk just the way humans do. That's why you shouldn't eat them."

At last, I had their interest. "We didn't know they could talk! How do you talk to them? What language do they speak? How can they talk under water?" I explained as best I could about dolphin bleeps and the efforts to decode them. But they went on with their stone-heating and then put the tasty-looking meat into a leaf oven. "You shouldn't eat them," I pressed again. "They're not like fish, they're like us. They're intelligent. They talk." But after the possibility of humans talking with dolphins had faded, so had their interest. But not their appetites. Eventually I went back to my typewriter, wondering why my logic and rhetorical force hadn't persuaded them to bury the poor kindred spirit rather than eating it.

Only after typing fretfully at my notes for another fifteen minutes did it dawn on me that until 1927, when the government imposed the *Pax Britannica* after the massacre, the Kwaio ate *people*. . . . .

Last year, a quarter of a century later, on my eighth fieldwork trip into Kwaio country, chewing betel and squatting around a fire reflecting with Maenaa'adi about the outcome of the divination he had just performed and the ritual about to be staged, I was still all I will ever be: an outsider who knows something of what it is to be an insider.

NOTES

1. See Keesing and Corris 1980.
2. The government had been getting all the place names wrong for fifty years.
3. See Keesing 1978, 1988; and Fifi'i 1989.
4. In the category of small-boy-who-doesn't-know-any-better, a status into which I was inducted after my wife's return to the United States at the end of 1963.
5. This episode was brought back to mind in 1989 during a session taping stories of ancient ancestors and human origins with the brilliant young pagan priest Maenaa'adi and my longtime Kwaio collaborator, the late Jonathan Fifi'i. During a pause, Fifi'i turned to me and said, "When I was in California with you [in 1966–67], I met some people who said they were descended from apes and monkeys. I thought that was really interesting. I'm descended from a snake."

REFERENCES

FIFI'I, J.
1989   From Pig-Theft to Parliament: My Life Between Two Worlds. R. M. Keesing, trans. and ed. Honiara: University of the South Pacific and Solomon Islands College of Higher Education.

KEESING, R. M.

1978   'Elota's Story: The Life and Times of a Solomon Island Big Man. St. Lucia: University of Queensland Press (2d ed. 1983, New York: Holt, Rinehart & Winston).

1988   The Anthropologist as Messiah. Etnofoor 1:78–81.

KEESING, R. M., AND P. CORRIS

1980   Lightning Meets the West Wind: The Malaita Massacre. Melbourne: Oxford University Press.

THIRTEEN

Ethnocentrism and the Abelam

RICHARD SCAGLION

Ethnocentrism is the belief that one's own culture is superior to all others. Anthropologists have found that virtually all cultures, and indeed nearly all individuals, are ethnocentric to a greater or lesser extent. In its worst forms, of course, ethnocentrism emerges as racism or ethnic prejudice and provides justification for the persecution of others who are "different." In introductory anthropology courses, anthropologists usually introduce the notion of ethnocentrism by explaining that anthropologists try not to be ethnocentric or judgmental in studying, describing, or analyzing other cultures.

Ethnocentrism can take very subtle forms, however, and one cannot easily put aside one's cultural prejudices. In illustrating the concept of ethnocentrism to my introductory anthropology classes, I often tell a story of an argument I once had with one of my friends of the Abelam tribe. The Abelam, a group of horticulturalists living in the foothills of the Prince Alexander Mountains of the East Sepik Province in Papua New Guinea, are the people with whom I have done most of my fieldwork. Abelam men traditionally pierced their nasal septa and wore ornaments in their noses for certain ceremonial occasions. On one such occasion, a friend of mine, dressed for a ceremony, came to see me at my field house. As I was temporarily occupied inside, I shouted out for him to rest on my veranda, and I would be out to see him shortly.

Earlier in the day, I had been reading several months' worth of *Sports Illustrated* magazines, which had been sent to me by sea mail, and which I had left on the veranda. I could hear my friend leafing through the magazines (obviously looking at the pictures, since he couldn't read). Suddenly he burst into uproarious laughter. Remembering the general hilarity that a trick photograph of a two-headed man had once occasioned in the village, I expected something similar. I rushed out to see what was so funny. My friend was laughing so hard that he couldn't speak; he merely pointed down at the page. I didn't get the joke. I saw a very elegantly dressed woman in what I think was a liquor advertisement, looking quite properly attired for the opera. She wore a black strapless evening gown with beautiful diamond jewelry, including a necklace and tiara, and had elaborate diamond pendant earrings. I would have thought he would consider her to be finely decorated. I asked him why he was laughing.

For a while he was still laughing so hard that he couldn't speak, but finally he managed to gasp out, "This white woman has made holes in her ears and stuck things in them." I looked at him, sitting there with an ornament in his nose, and pointed out that he had made a hole in his nose and stuck something in it. "That's different," he said. "That's for beauty, and has ceremonial significance. But I didn't know that white people mutilated themselves!" I pointed out that on the streets of Pittsburgh, where I live, women with pierced ears are fairly common, but that if he walked around with that feather in his nose, people might think it was pretty funny. We argued for a while about where it might be proper to make holes in one's body, and for what purposes, and I finally ended the discussion by dogmatically asserting that I thought it equally odd to have any sorts of holes in one's body other than those present at birth.

This incident illustrates the fact that the Abelam are just as ethnocentric as the members of other healthy cultures. As an anthropologist I was prepared for this, of course. What I was not prepared for was that the Abelam would teach me how really ethnocentric I was myself, and that they would fundamentally change the way I view the world. None of this happened overnight, however. There was no single great revelation, but rather a series of small incidents in which, in the words of Ed Cook, "I made an ass of myself in the field." It has been a humbling experience.

In 1974 all this was yet to come, however, for when I first met the Abelam, I was a smug young anthropologist who "knew it all." I had come to Abelam territory to study the introduction of a court of law, based on a European model, which had been set up by government officials in the preceding year. I was curious to learn how the Abelam were reacting to the Western law which had been introduced to keep peace in the villages. I quickly learned that they were not using the court at all, that they totally rejected this imposition of a foreign government. Having relatively little to do in "town," I decided to move into Neligum Village, in the northernmost part of Abelam territory. My education was about to begin.

It didn't take me long to see why the Abelam weren't using the introduced courts. Very simply, they had their own methods for resolving disputes, which were very effective. Whenever an argument broke out in the village, respected elders were quick to arrive on the scene and cool down the parties involved. The elders immediately mediated in the dispute and were generally successful in reaching a solution that was satisfactory to all. A communal meal usually followed, which further smoothed things over and served to underline the fact that peace had been restored.

The longer I stayed with the Abelam, the more I began to respect their traditional way of life, and the better I came to appreciate why they did the things they did. The Abelam are a horticultural people whose staple foods are yams, bananas, taro, and sago, which they supplement by hunting wild pigs and small game in the forest. They are famous for their artwork and for their majestic, towering men's houses which dominate the village skylines. They have a fairly comfortable life by any standards. Famine was unknown in Neligum Village. Abelam have a rich and fulfilling ceremonial life. Their knowledge of the local ecology is truly remarkable. They have names for all the local plants and animals and know all of their characteristics and uses. Once, early in my fieldwork, I foolishly stumbled into a patch of stinging nettles and my leg immediately reddened with an accompanying sharp pain. My Abelam companion searched for a few moments in the forest, while I sat in severe pain, feeling sorry for myself. In short order he produced an herb, which he applied to my leg, almost magically eliminating the pain. Hmm, I thought, these people know what they're doing.

With my general respect for their way of life firmly established, the Abelam began the next step in my education: giving me a good dose of much-needed humility. The incident that most vividly sticks in my mind occurred the second time I went hunting for wild pigs. The first time out was very interesting and enjoyable for me. I observed the Abelam's hunting techniques and took photographs of what turned out to be a very successful hunt. The Abelam set up nets in a semicircular arrangement wherever there were breaks in the forest undergrowth. Men then hid just beyond the nets, sending women and children out to make lots of noise and drive the game into the nets. When the game became entangled in a net, the men hiding nearby then dashed out and secured or dispatched the animal. As soon as the men dashed out, I dashed out with my camera, and we all had a good time.

About two weeks after my first successful hunt, a group of Abelam men came to my house and asked if I'd like to go out hunting with them again the next day. In my anticipation, I hardly slept that night. Anthropologists are very concerned with rapport, or getting along with people in the study community. They want to be accepted. Here, I thought, is a big breakthrough. This is the first time they have asked me to do something with them. Always before I had intruded myself into their activities, and they had let me go along. Wow! I thought, They *like* me! They *accept* me.

The next day a large party set out, and I helped the men carry the pig nets. After the nets were all set up, I started to take my place with the men behind the nets. "Nah," they said, "we want you to go with the women and children and beat the bush. We've never seen anyone who makes as much noise in the jungle as you!" I was crushed, but had to admit to myself that they were probably right, since, in 1967, a sergeant in the U.S. Army had made essentially the same observation more than once.

For a while, the Abelam continued to have a good laugh at my expense, as I gradually achieved some measure of competence at their tasks and understood their way of life more fully. They smiled when I got lost in the jungle, they laughed at my misuse of their language, and their amusement knew no bounds when I slipped and fell on my rear end in the mud. This last was a fairly common occurrence, and to the credit of the Abelam, they usually held their uproarious laughter until they were sure I was un-injured. Sitting there covered with mud and surrounded by Abelam friends doubled up with glee, it was very hard to maintain an attitude of cultural superiority.

Despite their own ethnocentrism, the Abelam were smart enough to realize that many items of Western technology were useful for them, and they were always willing to try new things. I finally got to the point where I began to think I knew enough to help them. While steel tools (mainly axes and machetes) had been used by the Abelam for many years, I had noticed that they were still using digging sticks for making holes in which to plant their root crops. These instruments were heavy, pointed sticks which were thrust repeatedly into the ground at an angle in the same hole. Once they had penetrated deeply, they were used as a lever. The hard-packed earth exploded out of the ground, leaving a hole suitable for planting. I thought I might introduce a shovel to make their task easier.

A large crowd gathered to watch the crazy anthropologist dig a demon-stration hole with a shovel. After watching me struggle for several minutes trying to sink my shovel into the hard-packed soil, someone handed me a digging stick, asking me to "try this." I was amazed to see how easy it was to use, and how quickly even my own inexperienced hands could dig the hole. Later that day, several people mentioned to me that everyone knew about shovels, and various people in the village owned them, but they were rarely used for garden planting because they didn't work well.

I like to think that at this point certain of my Abelam friends and I were beginning to learn from one another. It had taken me fully six months of living in Neligum Village to learn enough even to talk to people in their own terms. I was now beginning to sense a real change in many people's attitudes. Whereas, to be honest, I was originally seen as a somewhat bizarre and curious oddity, I now felt I was beginning to be taken more seriously and people were more likely to listen to my ideas.

Throughout the period of my "initiation," one of the individuals most understanding of my ignorance was an elder named Moll Apulala, who subsequently adopted me as his son. He never faulted me for not knowing or understanding something in the first place, but was completely in-tolerant when I misunderstood or misapplied something he himself had taught me. Illiterate himself, he believed (and probably still believes) that reading and writing have turned my own brain to mush and totally ruined any ability for memorization and analytical thinking that I may once have had. Of course, his own powers of memory are uncanny.

After I became his son, my education became more intense, and I began to rethink certain ideas. For example, Pacific scholars believe that dogs have been present in New Guinea for a very long time, probably arriving with early Melanesian migrants, whereas cats are a more recent European introduction. I expressed this idea, which was immediately contradicted by my Abelam father, who asserted that both had been present in Abelam territory since "the time of the ancestors." I thought I could offer him some linguistic evidence to convince him he was wrong. "What is the Abelam word for *dog?*" I asked him in Tok Pisin, the lingua franca of the area. "*Waasa,* as you know perfectly well," he replied. "Okay," I said, "and what is the Tok Pisin word?" "*Dok,*" he replied. I pointed out that "now we have a pattern. The English word for dog is *dog.* So you can see what happened. When Europeans arrived, you had dogs and had your own word for dogs, so you didn't need to borrow the pidgin English term for them. But what is the Abelam word for *cat?*" I asked. "*Pusi,*" he replied. "Well, there you have it," I said. "As you know, the Tok Pisin word for cat is also *pusi,* and in English we often call cats *pussies.* So what has happened is obvious. Unlike the case with dogs, where you had your own word, since you didn't have cats before we brought them to you, you had to borrow our word for them."

"There's where your logic is faulty," he countered. "Clearly, it was you who borrowed the word from us!"

I never did believe him, nor did he believe me, but I confess that this discussion made me think much more clearly about what I think I know, and what evidence I have or should accept about certain "facts." But as yet I had not begun my fundamental rethinking of the natural world. It all started innocently enough. I had been asking the usual questions about Abelam conceptions of natural phenomena, such as the moon, sun, rain, night, and day. Being generally courteous people, my Abelam friends asked about Americans' beliefs in these areas. Having been well trained in science and technology, I felt on safe ground here. I gave them the usual lecture that all of us have had in the second or third grade. I picked up a coconut and explained that the earth wasn't really flat, as it appeared, but was actually a large sphere. I showed them where we were in New Guinea, and where the United States, Australia, Japan, and other places were. I could sense that they were willing to accept this idea, since they live in a mountainous region that doesn't apear very flat anyway. I then waxed eloquent, picking up a flashlight (the sun) and a citrus fruit (the moon), and demonstrating how the earth moves around the sun, and the moon around the earth, creating the phases of the moon and such. My friends listened politely, and I thought everything was fine. Everything *was* fine until the next week, when I overheard some elders discussing how it was that the Americans all walked upside down!

I of course tried to disabuse them of this notion. I picked up another coconut and showed them how New Guinea could be on top and the United States on the bottom, as I had originally portrayed them, but if the earth rotated (here I inverted the coconut), the United States would be upright and they themselves would be upside down. They argued that this couldn't be correct. They were here now, and they could see that they were standing straight up. Furthermore, they were old men who had lived for many years, and they had *never* been upside down. Now they had me, although I didn't know it yet. I thought about this problem (in English, of course). I had taken several physics courses in college, and a statement of Newton's law of universal gravitation came to mind: "Every body in the universe attracts every other body with a force that is directly proportional to their masses and inversely proportional to the square of the distance between their centers." Unfortunately, I couldn't rely on this English jargon. I had to explain "grabity" (as my friends pronounced *gravity*) in real, concrete terms in either the Abelam language or in Tok Pisin. I quickly became so confused, speaking in these other languages, that I began to realize that I didn't understand "grabity" either. It was just something that I had accepted since the third grade. Why *don't* those people on the other side of the earth walk around upside down? I still don't *really* understand.

I think I now believe that "grabity" is merely a model of the natural world, and is not necessarily "real." It is just a heuristic device, something that is useful for organizing and predicting natural phenomena. I also think that certain beliefs held by the Abelam—things regarding ancestral ghosts or water spirits, for example—may not be any more real than "grabity," in that none of these things can be tangibly verified. But they are no less accurate predictors and organizers of the observable world, and as such are just as valid. In short, I don't know what I believe anymore, but I do know that Western culture doesn't have a lock on knowledge.

I stayed with the Abelam for a little more than a year on that first field trip. Since that time, I've revisited them often. As I write this paper, I'm preparing to visit them yet again, for the first time in several years. I first lived with them as a young man; now I'm firmly established in middle age. What will they think of me? I remember once, after an absence of three years, I arrived in the village to be greeted with the observation that "Oh, you're bald now!" (Actually a bit of an exaggeration, in my opinion.) The humbling of the anthropologist will be ongoing, no doubt, and I'm sure my education will continue. I still have a lot to learn from them. I can only hope that, in some small way, they are also learning something from me. But if nothing else, at least I know I am contributing to the village by being an almost endless source of amusement.

FOURTEEN

What Drives the Birds?
Molting Ducks, Freshman Essays,
and Cultural Logic

PHYLLIS MORROW

I once heard a rather succinct statement about differences in cultural logic from a Yupik Eskimo: "Before the white man came, we used to build our houses underground and bury our dead above the ground. After he came, we built our houses above ground and buried our dead below. We haven't been warm since." After a dozen years in the Arctic, I increasingly appreciate his observation, as I see more and more ways that each culture's assumptions about the way life "ought to be organized" create disorganization cross-culturally. What follows is a story not so much about unraveling the logic of another culture, which is never fully possible, as about discovering its pervasive, entangling presence.

But let me back up. I need to tell you how I came to be here, physically and philosophically, in the first place. I have vivid childhood memories of a favorite series of books about people around the world. I must have been very small when I first became fascinated with them, for their texture—a tactile, coated cloth—is as strong in my recollections as their content. Two, in particular, I studied over and over again. One showed pictures of classical Egypt, and the other "Eskimos of the Far North." Some days I imagined myself slaving away over a hot pyramid. Other days I wrapped myself in my mother's old fur coat and pretended to mush my dog team. I spent a lot of time wondering what life was like in such contrasting places. When my father returned from a business trip to Alaska in 1956, I was six years old. He brought me a seal-fur belt, adding more layers to my associations with the North, for I loved the distinctive smell of the leather, as well as the sleek, honey-colored fur. Although I never thought of going to Alaska myself, the place certainly had pleasant associations from the beginning.

Looking back at that childhood, it is no surprise that I chose to major in cultural anthropology when I entered college, but it was not until I was in graduate school, five years later, that I rediscovered the North. That summer, a trip to southwestern Alaska rekindled memories of the

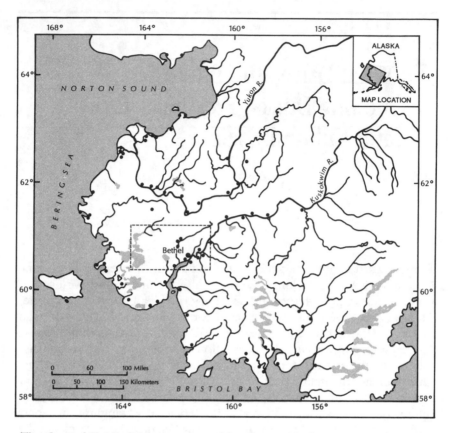

The Central Yupik Eskimo region of Southwest Alaska

ripe, oceany small of seal oil, introduced me to real people—Yupik Eskimos—and taught me that cultures are very complicated when met outside the pages of a textbook. I realized that this was where I wanted to do my fieldwork. I had no premonition that "the Bush" would be my home for the next decade and that I would soon marry and settle in Alaska permanently, although a friend of mine, accurately sensing that I might never return, begged me not to go. As I learned the Yupik language, I gained a deep respect for a group of people seeking a healthy integration of tradition and change and very tired of trying to explain themselves to "outsiders." This explaining seemed to take a lot of time when people would rather be out hunting or fishing. After a year in a village, I found myself enmeshed in language issues and particularly concerned with improving the interface between cultures through improved translation and cross-cultural communications. I took a job there, and I stayed, wrenching myself away only briefly ten years later to finish my Ph.D.

Now, as I reread my "field notes" (a motley collection of carbon-copied letters to friends, journal entries, maps, and errata) from that first

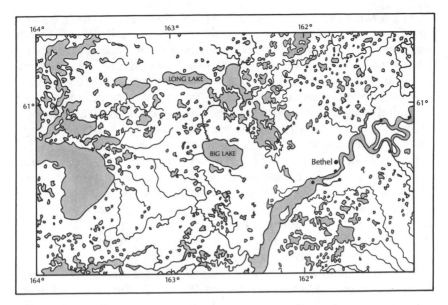

Big Lake and the "Tundra Villages"

year of living in a Yupik village, I feel a mixture of nostalgia and empathy for the hesitant outsider who tried so hard to make sense of what was happening to and around her. My training in anthropology had prepared me to look for the cultural patterns inherent in everything people do, yet my own patterns and those of the people with whom I lived were so subtle as to defy notice. Often, they just didn't seem to be there, until—but that's what my story is about.

It was our last day in the village, and we were packing to leave. Among our friends were John and Anna, a young couple who were still childless, like my husband and I, and who lived nearby. Anna and I frequently picked berries together, jigged for fish, and took long sociable steambaths in the evening with her sisters and cousins. She was not a talkative person, but we had grown close simply through this companionship, and now she lingered around our disordered house, watching me sort possessions with an expression of regret. At one point she had gone home for a while and then returned to tell us that she and John were going on the communal drive for molting birds, out on Big Lake. This was the first we had heard of the drive, and by then familiar enough with communication styles to recognize an invitation, we decided to forget the packing and join the expedition. Soon we heard Gregory, a man of about fifty, announce the drive to the neighboring villages over CB radio, and another neighbor, having heard that we planned to go, had sent their young son over to accompany us. As we were to find out later, this was a standard way of assuring his family a share of the catch.

In a few hours we set out in a caravan of four skiffs: ours, John and Anna's, and several younger members of Anna's family. We were not going far as the crow flies, but the tundra is a flat expanse of marshes and tortuous sloughs, doubling back upon themselves so often that you seem to spend as much time facing your point of departure as your destination. We corkscrewed endlessly up the river, stopping our boat frequently to help John repair his eternally broken engine (at one point he had to hand-fashion a new pin with his pocket knife), to pole through shallow spots, and to wait there for others who would need our help. Whenever we pushed one of the heavy wooden boats through the shallows, we expected someone to act as the leader, to give us some audible cues—counting, grunting, or heave-hos—which would concentrate all of our efforts at the same moment. Either we missed these cues, or coordinated labor was not really critical, because somehow we all made it across. This should have given us faith in the apparent disorder to come, but at the time it just seemed curious.

Toward evening, we made a final bend in the river and found ourselves facing a vast expanse of water. It loomed like a gray inland sea, the bushes on the closest shores mere blips on the horizon. The far shore was invisible; we stared out over the curvature of the earth. For the first of many times we began to wonder exactly how the bird drive would be managed. A century-old account had told us that, on the marshes:

> Salmon nets are arranged by means of stout braces and stakes to form a pound with wings on one side; the people form a long line across the marsh and, by shouting and striking the ground with sticks as they advance, drive the birds before them toward the pound. As they approach it, the line of people converge until they reach the wings, and the birds, thus inclosed, are driven in and killed with sticks. (Nelson 1983:135)

We had no idea how this would translate into motorboats on this large lake.

We stopped, got out of the boat to stretch, and then hitched our craft to John and Anna's. We fired up our Coleman stoves in the boat, ate dried fish and drank tea, and then headed out to the middle of the lake, where we waited for the drive to begin. Eventually, from the lack of concerted effort, it became obvious that the drive would not happen that night, and John pointed out a spot across the lake where we would camp with several other boatloads of people about our age. A standard eight-by-twelve-foot canvas wall tent was set up with a tundra "tree" serving as a pole at one end and an oar, which was somewhat taller than the tallest available tree, at the other. Some people hooped other trees over their boats, lashed them to the sides, and covered them with tarps to make quonset-shaped shelters. Our little backpacking tent was viewed with interest but some skepticism by the younger boys. A smoldering fire of tundra moss set upwind from the wall tent provided a dense cloud

of smoke, which gave some relief from the mosquitoes if you were willing to sit in the middle of it; the men quickly monopolized the tent,
the only other spot that was relatively mosquito-free. After we tired of
donating blood to the insects, one of the women decided to smoke the
men out of the tent, which we did by discreet but assiduous applica-
tions of damp moss and waving of jackets. After they moved out, one
by one, thinking that the wind had changed direction, we occupied the
tent. At around eleven P.M., a young boy waved a freshly shot duck in
the tent door, and we toyed with the idea of eating again, but decided
that we should get some sleep before the drive. The boys, however, had
figured out our earlier trick and decided to smoke us out of the tent,
so we emerged, only to find a pile of feathers and six ducks in various
stages of nakedness and disembowelment. The message was clear: We
sat down to finish the job that the boys had decided was "women's
work." After finishing the ducks in total darkness, a brief commodity
in August, we fell into our sleeping bags, only to be awakened by daylight
at four A.M.

Tired, but eager to begin, we broke camp and motored back out on
the lake. By six A.M. we had not figured out what, if anything, was being organized and where the other boats were. We scanned the horizon
with binoculars and pulled up broadside to other boats to ask people.
"*Naamell*" ("I don't know"), they would shrug unconcernedly. When
Gregory, who had originally announced the drive, passed, John asked
if he was going to be the leader. Gregory said no.

John finally spotted boats some distance from us, and we decided
to join them. Half an hour later we were sitting in midlake on a sicken-
ingly pitching boat. It was a nasty windy day, with big swells and white-
caps. For a while we stayed with John, then stationed ourselves between
some boats that seemed to be lining up across the vast expanse of water.
And then we waited for something to happen. One hour. Two. Who
was calling the shots here?

It was chill and the wind stiff. By 10:30 we were craving some familiar
sign of action, rank, organization, command. We began to feel lonely.
We had long since separated from John's boat, and the boats nearest
us—still at some distance—were filled with strangers from other villages.
At eleven o'clock, Gregory's boat plowed over to us, and he shouted
that our end of the line was too slow and that when he passed again
we should advance some distance. This was a great revelation, since we
did not know that we were supposed to be moving.

Across the lake's great diameter, we could just barely make out boats,
stationed at intervals of up to a quarter of a mile, stretching all of the
way to the horizon. Wet and cold, we began a process whose end and
progress we could not gauge. Most puzzling of all was the absence of
birds. We had seen only four ducks all day, and they were flying, not
being docilely herded across the water. It was only later that we learned
that the number of birds in molt follows a bell-shaped curve and that

it is possible to sweep the same lake three times over the course of a few days to maximize the catch.

Fighting the waves, which sometimes washed over the stern, and my stiffening fingers, I spent the hours trying to convince myself that the horizon was really horizontal, as it pitched and rolled rhythmically with the boat. Totally disoriented, I struggled to find the pattern to it all. What would this look like from the air? Why did everyone else still seem as uninformed as we? Like us, the occupants of others boats seemed to be just passing the time, hunkering under tarps trying to keep warm or dry.

For the next four hours we continued to sweep slowly over the lake. By four P.M., in an excess of fatigue and near-hypothermia, we pulled over to shore to rest and make tea. There, we discovered that others had dropped out for lunch much earlier; in fact, many had simply slept until noon. Others had just arrived that day; they had not camped. Discouraged, we realized that we had maximized all of the possible discomforts of this operation, including positioning ourselves on the roughest part of the lake.

Having seen a few other boats zipping toward the far shore and back, we decided, for lack of a better plan, to try that for a while. I had some fears that we were about to drive into the middle of the ducks, but since we had not seen any ducks that seemed vaguely unreasonable. Giddy with fatigue, I began to enjoy what had become an exercise in meaninglessness.

As we powered into the center of the group, we suddenly saw a thousand black, bobbing heads ranging across the bay and clearly moving toward a cliffed shoreline. Excitedly, we returned to our position in the line. This was obviously not the time to quit!

Over the next hour, boats began to converge. We counted seventeen craft. The apparently aimless boats moving across the front of the line and darting in and out of the center turned out to be "runners," whose job, we now saw, was to scare up the birds and to keep the boats moving in a uniform pattern. There had been difficulty in maintaining an unbroken line, we realized, because we were about the only ones dumb enough to stay in the midlake waves for long.

As we began to close in, more and more boats appeared, and there was a rush of excitement. Suddenly, from formless anarchy, sprang a precisely orchestrated structure. As we converged on the ducks, the runners began to shout and beat on the bows of their boats, drumming with taut wet anchor lines. Others joined in, a few at a time, beating on pots and pans. Now there were more than seventeen boats in a fairly tight arrangement across the end of the lake. It didn't seem cold to me any more, but I was reminded of the intensity of the wind by the fact that I could only hear the shouts and beating of sticks of those quite close to us. We drew in closer and closer, dropping anchor for a few minutes and then hoisting it to move in a few yards at a time. At long last we spotted John and Anna; John's motor had given out again, and this time we supplied him with fresh sparkplugs. It was good to be surrounded by familiar faces.

As we moved within about 150 yards of shore, I saw young boys picking up ducks that had escaped from the water and wringing their necks. The shouting and excitement increased. Now other boats began to dart in and out and around the swimming birds. The frightened animals dove and resurfaced, popping up and down in some confusion but still moving in a concerted pattern. By now we were in the shallows, and as we fought the water weeds tangled in our prop I understood why their Yupik name meant "imitation hair." The roaring outboards and the exuberant shouts made a great joyous din. This productivity, after twelve hours of suspense, this hungry anticipation of ducks in the cooking pot, excited us all.

Quickly, those who had brought salmon nets—six or eight boats—began to feed them out into the water. The other boats parked around the perimeter, and the occupants held the nets a few feet out of the water or tied the floatlines to their own boats. Yet others drove the birds into the one end left open. Then, in one swift move, the gap was closed and the nets encircled the prey. The rest of the boats moved in and ranged themselves broadside, and suddenly the boats and people, nets and ducks, seemed choreographed. The women and children held up the nets, facing in, low to the center, wringing the necks of trapped birds. Two men fired shots into the center from both sides, which frightened me since we were all facing each other. But this was merely to start the ducks diving into the nets, in a frantic effort to escape, for immediately we were wringing necks and disentangling ducks and tossing them rapidly into the boats, while the men stood facing out from the net in all directions, shooting at the escapees in a mad free-for-all of shotguns and whooping. The men were having a carnival time, the little birds popping up for a fraction of a second, while everybody fired at once, many at the same duck, and then immediately firing at some other bobbing head as they simultaneously teased each other about who had hit the previous one or who had hit it first. They shot again over and over, as fast as they could reload, their shotgun barrels heating up from the rapid fire.

After all of the netted ducks had been caught, several boats ranged off to catch, shoot, and retrieve missing ducks, while the boys continued to snatch those that had made it to shore at the base of the cliffs. We disengaged the final birds from the nets, and the net owners pulled them in. In each boat, there was now a random assortment of ducks, whatever the occupants had managed to grab.

I was totally fatigued, and gray from motion sickness. It had been twelve hours since I had been on land. Still, there was only a brief respite, for the ducks had to be distributed. We all sped back to the mouth of the river. Surprisingly, we were not far from where the drive had begun.

Disoriented by the apparent randomness of our long drift and by the enormity of the lake, we had not realized how systematically we had swept the lake's surface in the course of that long day.

Where we had stopped to eat the night before, people lounged on the ground near five piles of ducks. As each boat arrived, people tossed their ducks on shore, where two men rapidly sorted them according to species. Although we could tell that they were distinguishable, we did not know the species names in any language. For an hour, boats continued to pull into shore. When everyone had assembled, Gregory, whom Anna now pointed out with a slightly deprecating tone as "the boss," instructed one representative from each household to come forward. At first, only men approached, forming a big semicircle. Again, Gregory asked people to come forth, and the more reticent women and girls there as sole representatives of their households moved into the ring. Anna and I, represented by our husbands, sat back to watch. Near the end of the drive, I had counted thirty-eight boats; now there were over fifty people from seven different villages waiting for their shares.

Gregory directed three men from different villages to pass out the ducks. There was absolute equality of distribution, each family representative receiving the same number of each species, a total of eight, regardless of age or work contribution. Near the end of the distribution, when there were not enough to go around evenly, the lucky people who happened to be at one end of the semicircle got an extra bird, but it was clear that the goal was equality. Some people stayed afterwards to cook a communal feast, while others dispersed into smaller kin groups to camp another night or to drive back to their village. There were stories of earlier bird drives, of a lake now abandoned for drives because the supernatural humanlike beings called *issinrat* always spirited the birds away at the last minute, and speculation about why this drive had been less successful than others. Some drives yielded as many as fifty birds per household. Perhaps, people thought, it had been the combined effect of large waves, gaps in the line, and the earlier indecisions. Drives on Big Lake were often problematic, it seemed, when the wind came up. There was talk of doing another drive, on a longer, narrower lake, the following week. Exhausted, we went home to bed.

Later, I was to spend a great deal of time puzzling about how the bird drive had all come together in the end. Obviously, there were certain minimum requirements in my mental model for organizing a large number of people into a working group: acknowledged authority or leadership, efficient use of time, and a means for disseminating information and dividing tasks. Yet in the bird drive, the "leader" had denied being a leader, time had seemed irrelevant until the last hour or so, and everyone was about equally uninformed. On the other hand, none of this bothered anyone else, so the problem was clearly with my model.

The key seemed to lie in the characteristic tension in Yupik society between an egalitarian and consensus-based ideal and the need for leadership in many situations. On the one hand, experienced individuals are respected and emerge as situational leaders. On the other hand, putting oneself ahead of others is socially unacceptable, and anyone who professes leadership borders on hubris. In short, at the same time that individuals are pushed forward as leaders, simply because the need for structured organization is appropriate in some situations, those people are discouraged from acting like leaders. In this way, Gregory became both the leader and not the leader.

Second, a critical mass of people with the same goal in mind, enough of whom have done a similar task in the past to be familiar with it, is necessary to do the job. Each participant freely uses his/her own judgment (e.g., joining the bird drive at various points in the process, dropping out temporarily when the waves become too rough, and so on). If conditions are such as to permit the task to "happen," enough people will stay committed to the job to accomplish it. If not, they will vote with their feet. This amounts to an effective form of consensus decision making. There is no need for the group to gather, discuss and overtly plan a course of action; in fact, given the need for a flexible adjustment to wind, weather, geography, and equipment, such plans and discussions would be either impossible or counterproductive.

Emotionally, there was general acceptance of the assumption that things would happen when it was time for them to happen. In short, there was no frustration, because there was no arbitrarily imposed notion that the drive should happen within particular time limits. No wait was "too long," no conditions "too frustrating." One always had the options of leaving, of joining the process late in the day, or of simply sticking it out until the time was ripe. The bird drive, as random as it had appeared, was as orderly as it could be under the physical and social circumstances.

Not all visitors to the Kuskokwim region, however, come to appreciate the effectiveness of local ways. Over my year in the village, for example, I had heard villagers privately express innumerable frustrations at the insistence of various visiting bureaucrats that people commit themselves to attending meetings and making binding decisions about everything from school policies to land management.

This was, of course, simply not an appropriate way to decide important issues. People generally preferred to make decisions using a more time-consuming, but more participatory, process analogous to the one I have described. Even when this fact is explained to the bureaucrats, which it rarely is, being quite taken for granted, the bureaucrats have a difficult time adjusting their system to facilitate local control. Often, the outsiders go ahead and make decisions based on limited input and then draw mistaken conclusions about why more villagers do not participate in their forums. Meanwhile, the villagers feel that their opinions have not been solicited.

It is not just the process of decision making that makes me recall the bird drive, though. Oddly enough, I think of it in connection with the papers that Yupik Eskimo freshmen write when they enter the university. When I hear other instructors condemn their writing as illogical, I wish I could send my colleagues out on that bird drive, to give them some faith in the internal logic of systems other than their own.

For the principles of essay organization are as implicit in their "correctness" as are the principles of work organization. And, in order to appreciate that fact, you have to be willing to make the a priori assumption that the illogic may be in the mind of the beholder. How is it possible to develop such an appreciation? In addition to participating in such events as the bird drive and discovering that there is a happy ending despite your suspicions, one way is to become sensitive to the way stories are used in the culture. These oral forms give clues to the ways words may be used in written texts, at least by students who have not yet learned their professors' expectations.

Two simple examples may serve to illustrate this potentially complex point. One relates to the fact that many Yupik stories rely on an "if the shoe fits, wear it" sort of impact. Eating dried pike at a respected elder's house, I was once regaled with the story of how her sister came into a room where her children were eating and scolded them for not finishing everything except the scales. The story was not overtly addressed to me, but then again, I was the one person present who was not eating my fish skins. Remembering that fish and game return to be caught again only if humans show them respect by, among other things, using them fully, I dutifully peeled off the scales so that I could chew up and swallow the skins. Similarly, student papers often contain stories that, to the non-native reader, seem only tangentially related to the topic. The writer assumes that the connection will be clear; in a culture that honors individual autonomy by allowing people to either acknowledge or ignore a message, stating the point explicitly would be culturally equivalent to bludgeoning the reader. An added problem is, of course, that even if a non-Yupik reader realizes that he is being told to eat his fishskins, he is not likely to know why. The answers to this sort of question are in the broad context of cultural knowledge that the writer assumes, incorrectly in this case, to be shared. The answers are not in the text.

Having been surrounded by books all of my life, this lesson was a hard one for me to learn. It was brought home to me the day our outboard engine refused to stay in gear. Neither my husband nor I are mechanical wizards, but we have faith in our ability to figure things out, at whatever plodding pace might be required. So we did the logical thing.

We sat down in the boat, opened our owner's manual carefully on top of the covered engine, and were beginning to make some headway in identifying the problem on the trouble-shooting page when a Yupik friend walked by. "Maybe I should help," he offered, using a standard polite phrasing in no way meant to imply that we obviously needed it. He came over, moved the book, removed the engine cover, and revealed, to our immediate embarrassment, a broken part lying in lame isolation from the rest of the machine. "Maybe this is the problem," he said helpfully, with a pleasant smile. The incident certainly taught me something about mechanics—and about Yupik communication styles (we were thankful that he had spared us humiliation). It also made our differing orientations toward literacy quite clear.

The way that students corroborate objectively stated facts is another case in point. The analogous case in the oral tradition is illustrated by the story of a woman and her baby who were turned into rocks by a shaman: "This is true because I saw the rocks and they are indeed shaped like a woman with her child on her back." In the academic context, I have read papers that say such things as this: "Uayaran was a great warrior who lived a long time ago. He was trained to drink only the water which dropped from a feather dipped in it. When I was little, my grandmother never let me drink water when I wanted to." The apparent non sequitur is intended to explain Uayaran's training in the context of Yupik methods of toughening young boys. The writer saw no need to explain how the two thoughts connected; culturally, this is a straightforward juxtaposition and needs no elaboration. Furthermore, in this context, the traditional justification for the water restriction—"Too much water will make the flesh soft instead of firm," or couched in more obviously pragmatic terms, "A person must be self-disciplined in order to survive times of hardship"—may not be stated at all. To the writer and his presumed audience, these reasons are, in some ways, less important than the fact that the teaching itself is so time-honored. The message is: "It was done in Uayaran's day, and in my day, too. We have perpetuated this tradition, and therefore it is valuable." In this telling, too, the tradition is passed on.

If, at this juncture, you are beginning to feel that you could walk into an Eskimo village and interact with people, showing some understanding of Yupik ways, then perhaps I have done both you and Yupik culture a disservice. I began this essay with the statement that it is never fully possible to unravel another culture's logic, and I conclude with a repetition of that warning. In fact, there are layers upon layers of possible explanation here. The density of reality is always much greater than even the most subtle exegesis, and mine has been quite superficial. Just to add perspective to this statement, let me add that it is part of my cultural tradition, and not the Yupik one, to attempt such an analysis in the first place. "What drives the birds?" is not a Yupik question.

My point, too, is not that I can answer that question but that the question and my need to ask it are important things to ponder. This essay is not merely an interesting description of somebody else's way of thinking: Implicit differences in cultural logic make explicit differences in the way people are treated. If my colleagues see chaos where there is merely a different sort of order, then Yupik students get low grades. If bureaucrats see indifference to public issues where there is actually a preference for a different decision-making process, then public policy does not reflect public input. Try substituting the name of another ethnic group for "Yupik," and the point becomes a general one.

Fortunately, even a partial understanding of differences, such as the one I have sketched, helps me to understand my students' papers and to show them ways to structure their writing for non-native audiences. Perhaps it will make my readers, too, suspect that books—and essays like this—cannot sufficiently explain cultural systems. It always helps to try a different strategy, such as taking the engine cover off. At the moment you notice that something works for the participants although it seems to defy your logic, it may be time to look for another logic.

REFERENCE

NELSON, EDWARD
1983   The Eskimo About Bering Strait. Smithsonian Institution reprint.

FIFTEEN

🐚 What Did the Earthquake Mean?

ALICE POMPONIO

On February 9, 1987, the Vitiaz Strait off the northeast coast of New Guinea was rocked out of its predawn somnolence by an earthquake that measured 7.4 on the Richter scale. The epicenter was eventually determined to lie under the sea off the west coast of Umboi, the volcanic island which is the focal geographical feature of the Siassi Archipelago. Tiny Mandok, a ten-acre coral islet off the southern tip of Umboi, was not spared.

The earthquake struck at a time when the villagers of Mandok and I were already physically and spiritually depleted by a series of sorrowful and confusing events. Then without respite we were shocked by the terrible earthquake. Each tremor compounded our confusion. Fear of a possible tidal wave added terror to our sorrow. I was scared. It is most difficult to maintain scientific perspective and objectivity when one's own tiny speck of the cosmos seems about to be obliterated.

The people of Mandok kept asking me, "Ali, what did the earthquake mean? Why did it come? Was it sent to punish us?" Each question was followed by an interpretation reflecting their shared concerns regarding this new catastrophe. I was reminded of E. E. Evans-Pritchard's classic account of Azande witchcraft. In it, the major factor requiring explanation was not why a dilapidated silo fell, but why it did so at the exact moment in which a man happened to be sitting under it. We all needed reassurance badly. Many Mandok expected me to supply some. I couldn't, really, but felt obligated by the bonds of friendship and loyalty to people who had taken me into their confidence and trust to at least try.

This was my second trip to Mandok, in the Siassi Archipelago. On my first, six years before, I was adopted into the family of a village bigman, and thence into the village. This permitted me to live with the people on Mandok, learn their language, and participate in their daily life to the extent to which I was able. I lived on Mandok for some fifteen months and, using Mutu, the local vernacular, did an extensive study of the impact of Western education on this rural island community. My family and my village relationships were real and most rewarding. We got along fine, for the most part. I asked, they answered. They asked, I answered. They were very patient with me in my struggles for clarity in their language and my awkwardness as an outsider trying to live among them. When I returned to Mandok in October 1986, I was treated to a real homecoming and seemed to pick up more or less where I had left off before. My Mutu was rusty, but my linguistic recovery was swift.

When the earthquake struck, however, I was humbled to learn that in times of severe duress, the usual gaps in the multidimensional process of cross-cultural communication can become almost unbridgeable chasms. Explanations of any sort suddenly become most difficult to convey.

What did the earthquake mean to me, coming when it did? As I mentioned, just prior to the earthquake we of Mandok suffered a most disheartening series of personal and village disasters. During the entire time I was suffering from a back injury I sustained in the process of getting to Mandok. This caused me constant pain. Just as I was again becoming mobile after three months of virtual immobility, there was a sudden and unexplained death in my village family that threw the whole village into sorrowful turmoil. The attendant frustrations of the death, the funeral, and the general malaise of the whole village had me depressed. Then came the *coupe de grace,* the last straw—a 7.4 earthquake, unheralded, full-blown, and terrifying. I didn't need it at all—really I didn't.

I was beginning to feel that perhaps some local spirits were angry with me. Maintain objectivity, indeed! What about sanity? What about life? I really was down in the depths of a blue funk.

And yet a little voice inside me, outside myself yet from somewhere inside, kept insisting that I had to record these events, and the Mandok's reactions to them. After all, how often has an anthropologist been so fortuitously positioned to record this kind of a disaster as it happened? (And lived to tell about it? asks a cynical voice from another side.) There was just one problem: I could not hold a pen steadily enough even to start writing. In time I decided to write a letter. But to whom? Not my family, for sure, because I hoped they never even heard about the earthquake. (They had, as it turned out.) I had friends in Lae who I knew would know about the earthquake and be worried about me, so I decided to write to them. I thought that if I could focus my attention on informing them of the state of Siassi as I knew it, I could unwind enough to do the necessary. The decision itself lifted my spirits and calmed me down.

I present the letter here in edited form, expanding it to include subsequent events.

Thursday, 12 Feb.
Mandok

Dear Rae and John,

The sky is cloudy, the air leaden. The sea is in a flat, dead calm. There is only the barest occasional breeze to ease the smoke from a smouldering fire past my nose. On Monday night this village was a real ghost town of only fourteen die-hards, too stubborn (or stupid) to leave. Today, Thursday, the village is still virtually deserted—we now number about forty-odd. An occasional staccato whirring announces the arrival of yet another helicopter or plane. Short of another *guria* (Tok Pisin for "tremor, earthquake"), these are the only events that cause anyone to move from the apathetic stupor that grips us all. The sagging, deserted houses hang indifferently, their sad slump the constant reminders that jolt one's senses from an otherwise almost euphoric calm. The proverbial lull-before-the-storm effect is all-enveloping.

If I were a superstitious type (famous last words!), I would by now be resigned to the fear that the gods were not entirely well disposed toward my research. My back injury causes me constant, unrelieved pain, despite the medication I am taking. Doing fieldwork upside down is *not* fun. Thanks again for the sun lounger, it helps immensely. At least now I have some mobility to move around in the village and take my "therapeutic bed" with me. (Aren't euphemisms wonderful?) The teens are very good about carrying it and setting it up for me. Just as I was beginning to believe I was coping with all of this, we were struck with an unmitigated sequence of events, disastrous to all concerned.

My village brother, son of a bigman and a bigman in his own right both on Mandok and in town, died suddenly. Incredible—there was no apparent cause or reason to expect it. He had finished off his feasting cycle for the masked figures on Mandok just two days before. All of us were whisked to Finschhafen (the seat of his authority) in a state of frenzied disbelief and shock. It was true, despite our secret hopes to the contrary. Pandemonium erupted. I am getting ahead of myself. Let me backtrack a bit and explain. Bear with me.

On Saturday, January 24, a speedboat came racing into Mandok, just ahead of the *M. V. Salamander* (the boat that services Siassi between Finschhafen and Lae). The messengers delivered a letter to our compound which was marked URGENT in red ink. This was the incredible report of my brother's death, which I had the dubious honor of reading aloud to my village father and family. We all packed small bags hastily and boarded the *Salamander* for Finschhafen.

Once there, and at the family's request, I called the attending doctor for the cause of death. His diagnosis: "asymptomatic natural death" (isn't that an oxymoron?) that was either a heart attack or an embolism. The family rejected the diagnosis as inadequate to explain the death of a seemingly robust forty-one-year-old man who they had seen just days earlier. They requested an autopsy. Since there is no embalming in PNG and the body had been frozen, there had to be a thirty-six-hour delay for the body to thaw. The order was given on Monday for the autopsy to be performed on Wednesday. Meanwhile, my brother's second-in-command (and very close friend) and I cleaned out his desk. He had been executive officer of the local development authority.

Siassi mourning custom forbids a bereaved family to speak out in public. In any case, they were much too grief-stricken to do so, hence they asked me to represent them in the funeral arrangements. This honor was fraught with emotional trauma on many levels. As a result, I was afforded an inside look at Melanesian reasoning. It was not always very logical or reassuring to my Western culture–oriented thinking.

There was much debate over the burial site. Because my brother and his family were very important Siassi, the family won this one: Their son would be buried on Mandok. A second debate ensued which almost nullified the first. My brother must be honored in a Finschhafen funeral service before the body was shipped back to Mandok. The Finschhafen bigmen set Friday as the date for their service. There was only one thing wrong with this plan: The family was leaving on the prior Wednesday night's boat! That tug-of-war was squared away in time, but not without a lot of talking and much aggravation. It was just one of *many* examples of the week's frustrations. There is much to tell that really isn't renderable in writing, without sounding picayune, paranoid, or ethnocentric. Suffice it to say the entire affair was an emotionally grueling week of shock, horror, frustration, and confusion.

The autopsy, which was inconclusive, added to the malaise. The surgeon who performed it was a nice man, well known and liked by the Mandok. His surgical skills were obvious, but his communicative skills left something to be desired. He did not speak Tok Pisin well, and this fact added much confusion to his report for the Mandok. The autopsy revealed that, for a bigman, my brother had extraordinarily small blood vessels. Other than that, nothing pertinent to the cause of death was found. My brother's wife had explicitly requested that his head remain untouched. However, when examination of the torso revealed nothing conclusive, she was prevailed upon to sign a release permitting examination of the brain. It was done, but to no avail. Nothing definitive indicating possible cause of death was revealed. The doctor concluded that some sort of (bodily?) electrical disturbance interrupted the rhythm of his heartbeat and caused his heart to stop. It just *stopped.* Lights out. The blood samples have been sent to Port Moresby for analysis. We await the final report.

The Mandok, however, have a different explanation for the death. Also present at the autopsy was a policeman friend of the deceased. Sometime near the end of the autopsy he asked the doctor if *poison* could have been the cause of death. As you probably know, *poison* here, is a polysemous term which also means "sorcery." The doctor apparently did not know this. He answered that it could be poison, it could still be a heart attack, or something in the brain—it could be anything. We simply do not know yet. To a Westerner, this kind of an explanation seems fair enough, cautious, and reasonable in light of the available evidence (or lack thereof, in this case). In PNG, however, translated through vernacular categories and local worldview, this response engendered an entirely different conclusion. Utilizing their own concepts of what *poison* means to them, the Mandok who were present at the autopsy (in PNG, family members have the right to view it—in fact, so does virtually anyone else who happens to stroll by the room at the appropriate time, but I am getting ahead of myself again) jumped instantly to the conclusion that the cause of my brother's death was sorcery.

It was a simple bridge that the doctor unwittingly provided. It all stems from this incident. Some months ago (May 1986), my brother was involved in a tragic accident at sea. It started out to be a happy family outing of related men and their sons. A "brother" from Aronaimutu, wearing his work overalls and boots, was one of them. They had all been drinking heavily. As they were coming into the harbor, not far from one of its encircling islets, suddenly the boat flipped over and went down. My brother and all of the Mandok on board somehow managed to swim safely to shore. The Aronaimutu man did not. He was never seen again.

One day, this man's brother was in Finschhafen. With my brother present, he publicly declared that my brother would pay for his brother's death and follow his brother to the grave. In Melanesia this constitutes a direct sorcery threat. To the Mandok, it was now a threat fulfilled. This Aronaimutu man cemented that notion in the Mandok's minds by his subsequent, very strange behavior. He was here on Mandok when the messengers came in by speedboat (or he came with them, I'm not sure now which). As soon as he read the letter he let out a cry and gave it to me to read aloud. He then took off. At the time, I thought he ran to the men's area or some other private place to grieve. I learned later that instead he ran for the speedboat and fled to Aronaimutu. Upon arrival at Aronaimutu, without mentioning the Mandok death to a soul, he went to sleep. Odd. To the Mandok, this behavior provided conclusive proof of his guilt. The reason he did not speak, according to my Mandok relatives, is that his great guilt silenced him. If he admitted to the "murder," then he would know that his own death would soon follow.

As far as the Mandok are concerned, the case is closed. The death is viewed as a sorcery payback. Some people have attributed the earthquake to my brother's spirit. They are convinced he is angry and lashing out at the world at large to destroy all of his personal worldly works, etc. Since this last interpretation was offered for the first time just one hour ago, I can't say yet how seriously it will be taken.

Papa hasn't mentioned anything of the sort. Two priests who were visiting the Mandok mission came by to view the damage and to console the few people left. One asked Papa why he hadn't gone to Umboi with the others. He looked at them, shifting his direct gaze from one to the other, and said; "If a man tries to shoot us, or throw a bomb at us, all right, we must run away and hide. But this is an act of God. How can you hide? Where can you run? No way. No. There is no running or hiding from the hand of God."

I can still hear the ever-so-faint smugness in Papa's voice as he delivered these lines—I guess it isn't often that an old Papua New Guinean man gets to lecture a pair of white priests on theology.

As for me, I feel generally numb inside. This death bore many similarities to the death of my own brother less than two years ago. That death also was sudden, shocking, and remains unexplicable to this day. (Since I started to write this letter, aftershock number two just trembled—we get a lurch about every hour or so.) The faces kept changing in my mind, back and forth, back and forth. Don't ask me how or why, I had *no* intention of being there, but events occurred in such a way that before I realized it I was standing behind his head, watching the autopsy. Actually, it was quite interesting, when I could (force myself to) "forget" who it was on the table being dissected. It wasn't as much of an ordeal as I had anticipated. In case you were wondering, that is how I know so much about what happened and what was said. I was there.

After the family members left the room I did point out the doctor's error (regarding "poison") to him. He did what he could to amend it in his later more formal and public statement, but it was too late.

So at the moment I guess I have some problems, eh? We still don't know (1) if this is a simple earthquake or volcanic activity, (2) if it is over, (3) if it is just cranking up for a biggy (8.0 is classified on the Richter scale as "major"—7.4 is "major" enough for me), or (4) how or why my brother died. Back to square one and no moves visible. I have this uncanny feeling that at any moment Rod Serling is going to peer out from under one of the sagging houses and welcome me to the *Twilight Zone*. Someday I should write a movie script entitled, "The Day the Earth *Wouldn't* Stand Still." Oh, to have Michael Rennie's pal Gor, the gigantic robot, and say to him, "*Gor, klatu barata nikto!*" (which in loose translation means "Get me the hell out of here!"). The air does have that quality to it that suggests that I am in the middle of a movie. The only problem is, none of us has a script! Eeesh. However, the plot continues, even though many of us would have walked out on this film days ago.

One week after the burial, just as the folks were settling into quiet, subdued mourning, the earthquake ripped us all out of our sorrow and dumped us into terror. As it is, I am starting to think, just because I'm getting paranoid doesn't mean they are not out to get me. This will certainly be a research period that will live long and vivid in my memory, provided of course I do live to tell the stories over again!

Well, on to the earthquake. Saturday night I was not feeling too well. Something got my gut in Finschhafen and had not yet let go. I fell asleep in the now-open half of the big house. It is the same house in which I lived on my first field trip. It was "open" because they tore down the walls to make a large clear space for the funerary vigil. It must have been about ten P.M. I was awakened from my "nap" by a low rumbling noise. The house trembled, then began to shake violently. Mama, who was sleeping beside me, started screaming, over and over. We were stunned, too stunned to move. But it was soon over, ending just as suddenly as it had begun. We all sprang from a deep, tired sleep and ended up rattled and wide awake. After talking about it a bit and calming each other down, we all went to bed. I had to get up several times that night, due to my own gastrointestinal *gurias*, so I didn't get much sleep. I did sleep Sunday afternoon a bit during siesta time. There were several aftershocks, but nothing serious. By Sunday afternoon, we were all inured to them. This was a big mistake.

Sunday night. I went to bed ready and virtually desperate for a good night's sleep. I had not yet recovered from the grueling ordeal of the *week*-long funeral. I needed a good, long, full night's sleep. I didn't get it. Once again I was awakened from a dead sleep by the shaking and rumbling. But this time, unlike the night before, it did not stop in an instant. It kept on getting more and more violent. I sat straight up in bed—a feat in itself when the whole house is shaking against one's own bodily movements. I swung my legs to the floor and groped in the almost total darkness for my flashlight with one hand, my netbag with the other. I found neither. During that time the hurricane lamp on the veranda was swinging insanely. It either fell or was taken by my "brother-in-law" as he fled from the house. Now it was pitch dark. In the blackness I sensed more than saw one of my bookshelves topple over. Things from the other bookshelf on the opposite wall went flying. The tremors ran in a north-south direction, so everything fell straight out from the walls, which ran east-west. Things fell all around me and blocked my way. I ripped the chair out from under the table (adjacent to the bed) and tried to dive under it. No dice. Fallen objects wedged the chair, so I could only fit my head and shoulders under it. (This was a real scene from the Three Stooges—too ridiculous to be plausible.) Brief moment—no rumble, no rock—I decided to escape from the house rather than hide under the table.

I scraped, crawled, and clawed my way out of the house. The distance is only two or three meters but it seemed endless at the time, what with the rocking, rolling, and dodging of catapulted books and things. (It was almost like the film sequences in horror movies in which, at the climactic moment, the action is viewed in slow motion. I was moving as quickly as I could with my stiff back, but however quickly I moved, it wasn't quite fast enough to avoid "the monster.") I got to the top of the ladder, and things calmed as suddenly as they started. I got an adrenaline afterrush and felt my head lighten and legs weaken. I was shaking, so I sat down. My butt did not hit the step before the rumbling and shaking started again. Without even thinking about it, I bounced off the ladder and flew down the stairs. Fear, the motivator par excellence, evaporated all weakness *wan-tu* (Tok Pisin for "one-two," "in an instant").

Free of the house, I called to my "brother-in-law." No response. My father appeared about three meters away, so I called him. He came and grabbed my hand and pulled me out of our yard. I resisted and tried to insist that *under* the house was the best place to be. He yelled at me, in loose translation, "Are you mad? Don't you see that the houses are all falling down around us? You come!" He then yanked my arm and led me to the clearing next to the church. Here, Mama took me in tow. She led me by the hand to the *maran,* the ceremonial clear space in the center of the village. Well, I was certainly not the paradigm of the objective scientist at this undignified moment, but frankly I didn't much care. Besides, I had plenty of company. The whole village emptied into this center. All were as shaken as I, but no one was really hurt.

Whoever gave the advice that during an earthquake you should stay inside and duck under a table or bed did not live in a bush hut on stilts, I can tell you that! Nor did this person store Siassi bowls on elevated shelves. These houses rock at the slightest bodily movement, let along a full-blown earth tremor. And kwila is a very heavy wood. Carved into the oblong shape of a ceremonial bowl (over a meter in length), it can be deadly if it falls on you. Thank goodness no one got seriously injured. Some people did get crowned with clay pots and flying Siassi bowls (the big ones), but no serious injuries were sustained.

We retreated back to the church clearing which sits on the edge of our compound. Some teenage boys were sent to watch the sea for signs of a tidal wave. None, thank goodness, but they still feared one. (What anyone would or could do if they saw one coming, I don't know. Disappear in a swoosh, I guess. The thought was too horrible to contemplate at that moment.) We all just sat glued to our places and waited for the sun to rise. It eventually did as, of course, it always does. I don't think a sunrise ever looked so beautiful to me, though, I can tell you that.

When word came that Aromot Island was cracked and many houses were down, most Mandok cleared out and went to the Muru garden area on Umboi. Here on Mandok our count was four houses demolished or fallen, and about eleven more tilted because of stilts that were knocked out from underneath. I have already taken some pictures—I'll take more and get double prints made.

Malai Island is supposed to have several houses down and a large crack that admits the sea, or water up from the lens. FKC sent a scouting team out yesterday. Lablab has some bush huts down, and a demolished wharf. The Kovai side (northwest) of Umboi seems to have borne the worst. The government station at Semo is *flattened.* All of its toilets and water tanks are demolished. Some people saw smoke coming from the mountain (Tarave) and we can see reddish brown landslide scars from Mandok. Our wharf, too, is down. A couple of teachers' houses on Por are tilting or destroyed.

I thought of calling you on Monday but Father Ansgaar told me it took two hours to get through to Lae on the radio, so I didn't. I sent chloroquine to the Muru refugees to be taken as a prophylactic, because by next week they will all be down with malaria. We have had rain and thunderstorms for the three nights they have been there, and most have only worn tarpaulins for protection. Every news bulletin we have managed to receive on our radios is dominated by news of cyclone Uma in Vanuatu. So a lot of people are really scared by the rain. The Siassi earthquake gets only the briefest mention, one to two lines at best. The first report, on Monday morning, put the epicenter on West New Britain. A number of people conflated the two events into one traveling maelstrom: They feared that whatever the "cyclone" was that hit Vanuatu was moving quickly toward us. I tried to explain the difference in the reports as best I could, but have to admit I was stuck on one very perceptive question. Can an earthquake cause that kind of a disruption in weather patterns? This seemed a logical question to some of the more educated younger people. If an earthquake can cause a tidal wave, why not a cyclone? The moon causes higher tides when it is full, and also, according to the Mandok, calms the seas. Knowing all of this, and given my own terror and lack of sleep, it sounded good at the time.

We have aftershocks *still*—day and night. But people are slowing dribbling back to Mandok. The Pindiu Road is down, Lablab and Mandok wharves are down, and the Semo/Gomlonggon Road is also buried under a landslide. Some people are saying that my brother's spirit is lashing out, since these were all "his" projects through the development authority. Is it true? At this point, even I am willing to say, *"Husat save?"* (Tok Pisin for "Who knows?").

Once the mundane details of finding and cooking food were taken care of, once some people started trickling back into the village, all were consumed with the question of what the earthquake meant. What exactly was it, and what did it mean? they asked me. I tried to explain plate tectonics by using a punctured soccer ball and enamel-coated tin plates.

Picture the following scene. We are sitting around a hip-high veranda. There is a fire. I am on the veranda because I still can't sit for very long or be up at all for more than forty minutes maximum. But there I am, like a gawky stork, balancing this deflated soccer ball and three enamel plates of different sizes, in between my two hands and my raised knee (ugh!). "You see," I say, "the earth is round like this soccer ball—when it is filled with air, that is. We see land, mountains, and sea (pointing with my chin), but we don't see that there is land underneath the sea, with mountains and valleys just like on the surface."

A hiss of wide-eyed amazement ripples around the fire, all eyes glued to the soccer ball and my clumsy hands and knees straining to keep the plates on it and my lap-lap discreetly tucked.

"The problem is," I continue, "that the formations of land cover the earth's surface sort of like these plates are covering this ball. As you can see, they do not fit too well." I break out into a sweat, trying doggedly to reclaim the knowledge of introductory geology that was once mine. I grimace at the thought of my brother Al's reaction to my rendition of his chosen field. But the trouper in me says, "The show must go on, the mail must get through." The stress of knowing that my adoptive family and friends are depending on me to say something plausible (and understandable to them) translates into, "Just *do it*." With my back now screaming for relief, I continue.

"Now, these plates don't fit, you see? And underneath them the earth is very hot, like a *mumu* (Tok Pison for "stone oven") that is so hot it melts the stones and starts boiling."

"Ah," someone says, "underneath the ground the earth is hot—so hot it melts the stones in a mumu? *Xoraa!*" (Mutu for "Wow!")

"Ye-es," I say tentatively, "and sometimes it breaks through the surface, sort of like when a boil breaks—like a volcano."

Eager noises of assent—I think they've got it now!

"But sometimes the stuff doesn't come out of a volcano. Sometimes it just sort of ripples these plates a bit, like a wave moves a floating canoe"—maybe a maritime metaphor will cinch it—"and they bump together," I say, shifting two plates together until they clang to illustrate the point. On cue, Mother Earth, as if to nod assent, shakes a little in silent aftershock. A few bottles rattle, house posts creak. We all stiffen and hold our breaths.

My father, who has been silent until now, wags his head from side to side, emitting a low, noiseless whistle, and concludes, "God surely does work in strange ways."

So much for science. Setting down my show-and-tell props, I accede to the querulous demands of my aching back and stretch it flat on the veranda. The lively chatter that ensues is encouraging. I think I gave them something to chew on, at least.

Well, that's it from here. You asked for a long letter, and you got it. Take care, *write soon*—with some good news, please, if there is any.

Cheers from the rock
and roll capital of PNG

Ali

So there I was, stuck in a dilapidated and deserted village, with no place to go and no way to get there, anyway. After the earthquake I got Papa to tell me the story of the Great Gitua Shipwreck, another in which *he* was involved, and of course past tidal waves, earthquakes, and other cataclysms in Mandok history. I also got two-thirds the way through *Grant's Guide to Fishes* with him. Showing him the pictures, he recited the Mutu terms for each, the conditions of fishing, etc., that I would eventually use to create a taxonomy of fish and other sea creatures. I also finished my lexis, *finally,* the day before the earthquake. Funny, it seems every time I did a full day of linguistics a disaster struck. Were these omens?

We all have our ways of dealing with trauma, however it comes packaged at any particular moment. My own behavioral response, to the extent to which my aching back allowed, was to record the Mandok's feelings, reactions, and above all their explanations for the series of cataclysms that hit them, their village, and the entire area. I was already behind in recording their reactions to the tragic death and funeral. Part of this was due to the fact that for so long I was genuinely in mourning with the family in Finschhafen. I felt it was appropriate to allow an intervening period to diminish the emotional charge pervading the entire village. Before any of us could recover from that trauma, however, the earthquake gave us all something new to worry about.

My emotional response was to try, as much as my shattered nerves allowed, to keep calm. My attempts to explain my brother's death and the earthquake as best I could were genuine. The people's responses to my explanations, and to the events surrounding them, were equally genuine. Each of us tried our best to communicate—really we did. But, as the old adage goes, some things get lost in the translation. In this case, much got lost, but other things got added. I did have the sense that I was in a movie. There was something surrealistic about the entire sequence of events and relentless trauma that encouraged that sense. The alternative sense was to insist to myself that just because I was getting paranoid did not mean they (whoever "they" are) were not out to get me.

Now, after the fact, it almost seems as if it was only a movie. But it wasn't. Oh no, not quite. That much I do know. I *lived* through this one.

SIXTEEN

Centering: Lessons Learned from Mescalero Apaches

CLAIRE R. FARRER

INTRODUCTION

In 1974 my daughter, Suzanne, and I moved to the Mescalero Apache Indian Reservation in southern New Mexico where I was, with Tribal Council approval and partial living support, to do dissertation fieldwork for a Ph.D. in anthropology and folklore. The reservation is largely mountainous, although there are some high plains; elevation varies from 3,400 feet to just over 12,000 feet. The area was familiar to us: From 1961 through 1971 my former husband and I had lived in Alamogordo, a small town about thirty-five miles from the reservation, and our daughter had been born there in 1962.

The reservation covers roughly 720 square miles and is the homeland of approximately 2,500 people, of whom about 85 percent reside there at any one time. Three ethnic/linguistic groups (Mescalero, Chiricahua, and Lipan) live at Mescalero; they are self-consciously separated by speech and designs used on clothing. But, in truth, the languages spoken are mutually intelligible and the design differences function as markers of family pride. These Eastern Apaches are matrilineal but have no clans, as do their Western Apache and Navajo "cousins." Fathers' lines are important and remembered, too, especially if one has a famous warrior or head man in one's lineage. But it is to the matrilineage that one owes primary allegiance and where the majority of affective ties are reported.

While there are a few wealthy people on the reservation, most people work at wage-labor jobs in nearby towns or at Holloman Air Force Base near Alamogordo. The Tribe has the goal of providing jobs for everyone who needs one, but that is not yet reality. Many do, however, work for the Tribe directly: in the Tribal administrative offices or in Tribal enterprises such as the cattle industry, sawmill, or fish hatchery. But most who work for the Tribe are involved in tourism. The Tribe owns and operates a large, elegant resort, the Inn of the Mountain Gods, and a very popular ski area, Ski Sierra Bianca. Additionally, some people work as conservation officers or big game guides with a few also working for the Bureau of Indian Affairs (BIA) or other federal agencies, such as the Bureau of Land Management (BLM). Preferred jobs, however, are with the Tribe.

My first contact with the Mescalero came through my former husband, who had employed a reservation man in his lab. The man invited us, in 1964, to the reservation for a summer ceremonial where I met his wife. That contact began what was to become the focus of my anthropological work. I still return to the reservation each year and, in between visits, maintain contacts with our adoptive family as well as with friends.

"Centering: Lessons Learned from Mescalero Apaches" is taken from my field notebooks and personal journals over a twenty-five-year period,[1] for I do not always learn quickly.[2] At the request of the individuals, all names have been fictionalized except Chino, as well as Second and Evans, respectively the then-president of the Tribe and the surnames of the family that adopted my daughter and me in 1975.

1964: THE FAMILY AND THE CENTER

Annie Brownfeather had told me to meet her after lunch the next day when we parted the night before, as my little family left the ceremonial grounds to comply with the Anglo curfew. She didn't tell me where to meet her or what I was supposed to be doing. Yet my curiosity had been piqued sufficiently during that girls' puberty ceremony as we watched the spectacular Mountain God dancers, with their tall headdresses and bodies completely covered with paint, masks, kilts, and moccasins. So, with Suzanne on my hip, I showed up the next afternoon looking for Annie. One of the women cooking in the long, oak-boughed cooking arbor directed me to a camp just to the south and east of the ceremonial mesa.

Camps, erected for the summer ceremonial, consist of tipis, tents, and arbors oriented toward the ceremonial mesa. Although the mesa is over 6,000 feet, still it gets hot during the day and everyone appreciates the coolness of an arbor, with the ever-present winds from the desert below blowing through the freshly applied oak boughs. Those same boughs keep one from seeing inside the arbors so that they become quiet and cool family refuges. Tents and tipis, with their canvas walls impervious to vision, are used for sleeping or storage.

As I entered the indicated camp, there seemed to be no one present, save a group of toddlers sitting in the dirt passing around a much gummed and chewed piece of fry bread. A man emerged from a large tent. "I'm looking for Annie. She said to meet her here," I said to him rather tentatively.

"Come in; I'm her uncle. She said you were coming."

I walked toward the the tent, Suzanne still on my hip but looking longingly at the other children. The uncle barred my way with arms folded and looked directly at Suzanne. In what I was later to learn was *'inch'indi'*, communication without words, he indicated I might go into the tent but Suzanne would have to stay outside. The only place to leave her was in the dirt with the other children, roughly in the center of the family camp area. As soon as I placed her in the dirt, with much foreboding I admit, a child handed her the communal fry bread, which she quickly pronounced "Good!" A woman who came out of the tipi said, "*shił łika*," ("it tastes good to me") to Suzanne before addressing me, "I'm Annie's sister; I'm watching them. She will be all right."

(As indeed she was; when I emerged from the tent several hours later, I was met by another woman who came out of the tipi with my sleeping daughter in her arms; Suzanne had been fed, washed, and dressed in warm clothes, for cold comes with the setting of the sun in desert country.)

Entering the tent behind Uncle, I watched the painting of the Mountain God dancers, a ritual that women are usually forbidden to see.[3] At the time, I did not appreciate the significance of my being there or the honor being bestowed in my being allowed to watch the body painting. But I did learn that almost everyone in the camp was related to each other and that the area where the children sat with their fry bread was the joint responsibility of all who camped there. It was the center of the family, occupied by those upon whom the family centered: the children.

1974: LIVING AT THE CENTER

Parking the U-Haul truck in the Indian Health Service Hospital lot, I got into the car with Suzanne and the dog to look for someone who could tell us which house was to be ours for the next year. At the Tribal Offices in the Community Center, I learned that a disliked Public Health Service physician was being evicted and that we were to have his house. The only trouble was that he was fighting the eviction and the Tribe had not yet solidified the contract with the Public Health Service (PHS) so that they, the Tribe, would pay PHS for the house Suzanne and I were to occupy. From graduate school to the center of a controversy: I wasn't sure I was prepared for that. So I announced I would be in Alamogordo at a friend's house. Leaving the telephone number to be called when things settled down, we went back to the U-Haul to get a couple of things and check the lock before heading down the mountains and into Alamogordo.

A woman's voice startled me as I closed the doors to the U-Haul; I'd not heard her approach and, anyway, my mind was on eviction notices and controversy and starting off on the wrong foot and on my plants dying in the back of the truck before I'd be able to unpack them. The woman said, "I remember you. You put her (with a lip gesture toward

Suzanne) with our babies; you trust us. You respect us. We will take care of you. No one will bother your things. You will live in the center of us."

And so we did. We lived in the first (easternmost) PHS house; ours was the one intended for the head of the hospital and, as such, was the only single-family house among duplexes. We were quite visible, perched on the north face of the precipitous canyon and were in a direct line with the home of the president of the Tribe. But our house was on a terrace below his home. Symbolic statements were being made by our living place: We were in the administrative center of the reservation, centered below but within eyesight of the leader of the Tribe, yet also centered in an Anglo enclave with PHS physicians, nurses, and dentists as our immediate neighbors. Across the street, in the BIA houses, there were both Indians and Anglos with the latter predominating. The choice was to be ours, whether we would maintain our center with the Anglos or with Apaches. We chose the latter, and our center became $^n d\acute{e}$, The People, as the Apaches call themselves.

1975: DREAMING FROM THE CENTER

I'd been trying to find Bernard Second for almost four months; everyone said I should work with him to learn the language and the other things I needed to know. Bernard was a young man who was reputed, as a Singer of Ceremonies, to be a Tribal resource, the one to whom people turned to learn the old ways, hear the old stories, learn the old ways of saying or doing things. Everyone said he was central, not only to the running of ceremonies but also to my work. But finding him was difficult, especially, as it turned out, because he did not wish to be found by me.

One day, when my planned activities at the elementary school had been postponed, I walked into the Tribal Museum, where Bernard's wife was director and curator. She and I chatted for a few minutes, for we'd become friends during the months I was trying to find her husband. She startled me by saying, "He's waiting for you in there," with a lip gesture indicating her office.

"You're late," he chided me when I walked into the office.

"How can I be late when I didn't know I was coming here?" I queried.

His only response was, "You are here because I called you."

I, thinking only of telephones, denied having been called. He shrugged and repeated that I was there because he had called me. (So much for my understanding of synchronicity!)

Bernard, whose own family later adopted us, said he had dreamed me before I arrived on the reservation but that his dream had been only that someone was coming with whom he should work to record some of the things he knew about his people, their history, and their language. He had been disappointed to find I was a woman for he had assumed his dream referred to a man; his knowledge was men's knowledge, not to be shared with women. As a consequence of matrilinearity, almost everything at Mescalero belongs to women, save religious and ritual knowledge. The men jealously guard the religion, its associated ritual, and the ritual language in which religious activities must be conducted. Bernard had decided not to be found until he was sure I was the one he had dreamed, for that person was to become a central point for him for some time to come. While he made no pretense of knowing why Power would chose a woman for what he believed to be a man's job, he nonetheless was finally convinced that he should work with me. And so he did. My center became Bernard, the center of the Tribe's ritual knowledge.

1978: CIRCLES AND CENTERS

ⁿda'i bijuuł, the circle of life, is formed by a quartered circle:

The visual metaphor it presents is a rich one for Mescalero people (Farrer 1980, 1990). It is simultaneously many things: the universe and its forces; the world and its four primary directions; the proper way to speak and construct speeches; the balance and harmony inherent in the universe and that which *ⁿdé,* The People, are pledged to maintain; the four stages of life (infancy, childhood, adulthood, old age); the four seasons enclosed by a year, measuring from one summer solstice to the next. The visual metaphor is all of this and more.

"Hmmmm. It looks like a floor plan for the girls' ceremonial tipi," I mused.

"It's the same thing! Pay attention!" Bernard responded.

The center crossing point, what I (Farrer 1987, 1988, 1991) call a chiasm (from the Greek chi symbol [χ]), represents the balance point of the universe, the firepit in the girls' tipi, and the girls' puberty ceremonial in the life of The People, as well as life in general within the created universe.[4] The center point is the metaphysical place where the Mescalero Apaches are no matter where they physically may be located. For they believe that their actions, both individually and as a group, are essential to the continued maintenance of the inherent harmony of the universe, as conceived and given genesis by *Bik'egudindé,* According to Whom There Is Life, Creator. As long as they maintain their own centeredness, they generate the energy required to center the universe. The arms of the chi, as in chiasm, are hooked so action and thought can capture processes and essences from wherever and through whatever is encountered. By this means, the visual metaphor is transformed into the proper way to conduct formal speeches or the appropriate way to sprinkle salt on food or the four stages of people's lives or the four seasons. In all things, however, it is the center that is crucial.

Maintaining the center is a job that requires all people, Anglo or Indian or one of any other ethnicity, to be mindful of their assigned place and responsibility. The Mescalero Apaches believe that our human minds are too puny to comprehend Creator. Thus Creator, neither male nor female but both and neither, gave to each people in the world a set of responsibilities. Hopi must be true to the Hopi prophetic vision; Christians must be true to the Christian vision; Moslems must be true to the Islamic vision; Apaches must be true to the Apachean vision: Each vision, and the plethora of others in the world, is necessary to sustain the whole as set in motion and place by Creator.

It is both a comforting and truly an awesome responsibility that Creator has placed upon us. The primary responsibility of each person is the maintenance of the center that is within so that as we each live our life's circle we will contribute properly to the universe's center.

1984: COSMOS AND CENTER

"If our religion goes, we go as a people," Bernard had told me some years before. The more I learned of the religion, especially that focused around the girls' puberty ceremony of which Bernard was Head Singer, the more I was forced to learn to pay attention to the sky, as well as to the rest of the natural universe. This summer I'd brought an astronomer to the field with me, as my own training in astronomy was minimal and I was not sure enough of our own Western European scientific dogma to feel on comfortable ground with comparisons and contrasts with the Apachean version.

We sat around the dining table at Lorraine Evans's, Bernard's youngest sister and my youngest adopted sister. The star charts were spread on the table, but they turned out to be useful only to the children, who delighted in exposing them to sunlight and then dashing into a closet to watch them phosphoresce in the darkness. Bernard sees the sky in its natural shape and colors and could not relate to the flat charts with their skewed perspective nor to the arbitrary lines we use to define constellations. Where we see Auriga, a six-star constellation (and also use it as a part of Taurus), Bernard talks of The-Three-Who-Went-Together (meaning three who died at the same time), a three-star constellation that includes Capella as well as Beta and Iota Auriga. Comparing knowledge systems is much more difficult than I had originally imagined.

Gene Ammarell, then the education officer of the Fiske Planetarium at the University of Colorado, Boulder, was with me thanks to a grant from the American Council of Learned Societies. He and Bernard could talk man-to-man about men's knowledge and their contrasting views of what constituted proper science. Yet, always before beginning, Bernard said to me, "Are you ready? Is it [tape recorder] on? Do you have your notebook?" And, then, bragging on me as though I was not there, he would say to Gene, "She takes notes in the dark, too. Now, what does she want to know?" Finally, I had provided him with a way in which he could directly teach me men's knowledge without violating his own cultural canons against instructing women in the esoteric knowledge of men. Why, I wonder, did it take me so many years to think to bring a man to the field with me?

In the beginning, Bernard relates, there was only Creator, who in four days brought the universe into being. On the last day people were created, for we are the weakest link in the chain of being and are dependent on all of the rest of Creation for our own sustenance. This genesis is made visible to people through the natural workings of the universe. It is seen in the four seasons, the circularity of the stars, the circles described by the motion of the universe around us, the stages of life through which we all should pass—unless we die prematurely. It is all there for us to see, if only we will open our eyes and pay attention, if only we remain centered. *$^{n}da^{\gamma}i\ bijuu\prime$*, life's living circle, provides both template and center for each of us.

1986: GENERATING THE CENTER

Again an astronomer came with me to Mescalero; this time it was Ray A. Williamson of the Office of Technology Assessment in Washington, D.C. We had a specific protocol and particular things to check from my previous work. Bernard was very ill and, as it turned out, was unable to finish singing the ceremony. We were able to work together only a couple of nights. But, perhaps, there were more important things to learn than specific star and constellation names and how they are used to time the ceremonial and life itself.

Each girl having a puberty ceremony has her own Singer, in the ideal at least. The Mescalero number fewer than 3,000 now and there are not always enough Singers to go around; oftentimes, two girls, usually sisters or matrilineal cousins, will share a Singer. All Singers follow the Head Singer, who is still Bernard Second. Even if a Singer learned a different version of a particular song or ritual sequence, he will follow the lead of the Head Singer during ceremonial time. When the Head Singer does not perform, or cannot do so, there is movement toward entropy and a threat of chaos.

Lorraine and I, and other women in the extended family, took turns caring for Bernard, who insisted upon staying in the tipi on the ceremonial mesa rather than going to a hospital where we women all felt he belonged. He had started the ceremonial, had sung for three of the four nights, but could not sing on the fourth, and most important, night when Singers and girls stay up all night performing various rituals. Bernard, the center of the year's ceremonial, was missing, and the re-creation of the universe that the Singers recapitulate during the four nights' singing was going to be missing its final time—the time when people assume responsibility for maintaining their own individual centers and, thus, the universe's center.

The last night moved toward ten P.M., the latest beginning time if all is to work out correctly the next morning with *haigha*, the pulling of the sun; still Bernard did not appear. Three of the other Singers came to me, as I sat just outside the tipi entrance, close enough to hear calls for assistance but far enough away to allow Bernard to rest. As they approached, I was silently screaming, "I'm an Anglo, an outsider, a woman; don't ask me anything!" But the Singers approached me as a woman of Bernard's family, since I was obviously barring the entrance to the tipi where he lay.

"Can he sing?" one asked.

"No," I said emphatically.

"Will he sing?" they persisted.

"Perhaps in the morning, if he can rest," I responded.

I wanted to run and hide so they would have to ask real family members, not a fictitious adopted one like me, what to do. But it was my turn to stay with Bernard. Then came the realization that perhaps this, too, was a lesson for me if only I'd pay attention, as Bernard had so often chided me to do.

The center is where the person assumes responsibility for the ongoingness of whatever may be in progress. It is not necessarily entrusted to the most able, the most knowledgeable, the most wise, the most deserving. It may well be given to the least among us. As Bernard had told me, in each generation there is one who carries the weight of the world; no one ever knows who it is, so it is wise to help all to the extent of our own ability for we never know if it is the fool, the crazy, the leader, or the everyday person who has been chosen in that generation. Only Creator knows who the person is. As long as each of us performs our assigned task, no matter how trivial it may seem, we are contributing to the centeredness of the universe. The balance begins, and ends, with each of us.

1988: ASSUMING THE CENTER

It was particularly warm for a November day, as perhaps two hundred of us trudged up the side of the canyon deep in the mountains of the reservation. We, Lorraine and I, were being led by cousins who cautioned us of slippery places and who formed a phalanx around us. She and I were holding hands and trying to talk of everyday things so that neither of us would cry any more. As we came into the clearing, with its mound of dirt from the very deep and narrow hole that had been dug, the lump in my throat made it impossible to breathe until the tears started to flow. Now that we were there, Bernard's funeral service and burial could begin.

Although I have over forty pages of notes on the next little while, what I remember most are the sky as screen for memories; the eagle who flew over, almost as a salute; statements Bernard made when I first met him that he would die before me, although he was ten years younger than I; the tall body, dressed in his Indian clothes and wrapped in a tipi cover, lying on a board—no elaborate coffin, for Bernard had outlined the elegant simplicity that was to be his funeral.

What I hear is the voice of Wendell Chino, longtime President of the Tribe, in an impromptu eulogy saying, ". . . Claire Farrer, a good friend to Bernard for many years. Now it is time to write all those things you two talked about for now they are important to my people."

In addition to fighting grief, I had to fight fear—fear of perhaps not being able to do what was expected of me; fear for being sure I did not know half as much as they thought I knew; fear of dying myself before I could write what little I did know; fear of not being able to fulfill, or even wanting, the role of being custodian of a portion of Tribal history and memory.

Then, I "saw" in my mind's eye a time when I was talking with a Mescalero woman my age who wanted to know what would happen to my notes, tapes, and photographs when I died. She had just introduced her granddaughter to me with the words, "This is the white lady I told you about. When your grandma can't remember, you ask her." I told her then of the instructions in my will concerning my professional material and reiterated that my material really belonged to the Mescalero Apache people. That same woman had been one of those consoling me just before we began the climb up the mountain side to the gravesite. And I realized my center had shifted yet again and now I must also husband the core of knowledge with which I'd been entrusted through the years. I felt as though I was the center of a Tribal round dance, but while it was my body in the center of the dance, the persona was much larger than, and different from, the personal me. I had finally joined others in securing a center.

1989: THE CENTERING PROCESS

At various times in our lives, our centers move. As infants we are centered on our own needs and desires—even if the fry bread is much gummed when it comes to us, it still tastes sweetly. As we mature, our center switches to our relatives, to our own children, and to outside others for some of us. We always live at the center of our own little universe; sometimes we can see it in spatial terms as we draw cognitive maps centered on our own egocentric perspective: *I* am here—everything else is out there.

Our dreams can shift our center from one awareness to another.[5] And some of us get lost in the chasm and chaos as we try to inaugurate a new center through a chiasm. Shamans, intuitive dreamers, healers, and maybe even me: All are chiasms effecting a movement from one reality to another, sometimes consciously and sometimes serendipitously. Perhaps our own consciousness is but a speck in the center of the cosmos; perhaps it doesn't exist unless it is consciously created and re-created in each encounter.

In reflecting I have found it strange that I, born in New York City and reared in a thoroughly Anglo way, should learn a tenet of my own Quaker faith in the mountains of New Mexico under a brilliant night sky marred only by the haze of the Milky Way and smoke from camp and cooking fires while sitting in the dark in front of a tipi worrying about an Indian man ill inside. But perhaps not so strange after all: If I am to believe what I have been taught and have learned through observation during the years I have spent at Mescalero, then I must allow that the balance and harmony each of us desires must begin in our own beings. I am the center, and so are you. Each Mescalero Apache who is properly attentive contributes to the essential and inherent balance and harmony of the universe. Each Anglo who is properly attentive has the same potential. Quaker or Mescalero Apache or layperson or Jungian analyst: Each begins the universal connection through a centering of one's own self. Some choose to begin by meditation; others choose to begin by drawing *$^{n}da^{\gamma}i$ bijuuł*, life's living circle, and in so doing, drawing their own center. It really is the same thing, as Bernard averred, and as he insisted, I would learn as soon as I could properly pay attention.

The center is always with us. And, if we reach out as in the arms of a chiasm, we have the potential to merge with another's center. By so doing, we *become* the process of centering.

ACKNOWLEDGMENTS

I sincerely thank the members of the Mescalero Apache Tribe for their forebearance through the years. Particular thanks are due my daughter, Suzanne, who shared many of the field experiences with me.

This article was first presented as a slide lecture at the C. G. Jung Institute of Chicago on November 22, 1987. An earlier, shorter version of it was published in *Friends Bulletin,* a monthly journal of the Quakers.

A NOTE ON ORTHOGRAPHY

I follow a simplified Roman alphabetization of Apachean words. Low tone is not marked on vowels, while *é*, for example, indicates a high tone *e*. Nasalized vowels are represented with a hook under them: *ą*. *ⁿ* indicates syllabic *n*. Fricative *l* is represented as *ł*. The glottal stop, which is sometimes phonemic and sometimes attached to consonants, is ʔ.

NOTES

1. Fieldwork has been supported by several agencies: The Whitney M. Young, Jr., Memorial Foundation, Inc.; The Mescalero Apache Tribe; the American Council of Learned Societies; the Phillips Fund of the American Philosophical Society; the Research Board of the University of Illinois, Urbana/Champaign; the Graduate School of the California State University, Chico. Grateful acknowledgment is tendered to each. Obviously, in so personal an article, I am solely responsible for its content.

2. See my *Living Life's Circle: Mescalero Apache Cosmovision*, Chapter 4, for extended examples of my slowness in learning.

3. See Opler's *An Apache Life-Way* (1965:100) for a brief discussion of the reason for the prohibition against women and children watching the painting of the Mountain God dancers.

4. While I have only recently published on the notion of chiasm, I have presented it in professional meetings on a number of occasions, including the 1983 Eleventh International Congress of Anthropological and Ethnological Sciences held in Vancouver, British Columbia. In a session entitled "Play and Ritual as Communication," chaired by Dr. Alyce T. Cheska, I read a paper on the ritual clown and chiasm—"Łibayé: Chiasm and Continuity." It is fully presented in a chapter, "Clowning and Chiasm," in *Living Life's Circle*.

5. See pp. 99–102 of my *Thunder Rides a Black Horse*, 2nd edition, for a brief discussion of dreams as wishes.

REFERENCES

FARRER, CLAIRE R.
1980   Singing for Life: The Mescalero Girls' Puberty Ceremony. *In* Southwestern Indian Ritual Drama. Charlotte J. Frisbie, ed. Pp. 125–159. Albuquerque and Santa Fe: University of New Mexico Press and the School of American Research, Advanced Seminar Series.
1987   On Parables, Questions, and Predictions. *In* special section, Parables of the Space Age, M. Jane Young, ed., of Western Folklore 46:281–293.
1988   Generating Balance. Friends Bulletin 57:89–91.
1990   Play and Inter-ethnic Communication: A Practical Ethnography of the Mescalero Apache, unrevised Ph.D. dissertation published by Garland

Publishing, Inc., New York, in the series "The Evolution of North American Indians: A 31-volume series of outstanding dissertations," under the general editorship of David Hurst Thomas. The original dissertation was accepted in 1977.

1991 Living Life's Circle: Mescalero Apache Cosmovision. Albuquerque: University of New Mexico Press.

1996 Thunder Rides a Black Horse: Mescalero Apaches and the Mythic Present, 2nd edition. Prospect Heights, IL: Waveland Press, Inc.

OPLER, MORRIS E.

1965 An Apache Life-Way: The Economics, Social, and Religious Institutions of the Chiricahua Indians. New York: Cooper Square Publishers.

SEVENTEEN

Don't Mess with Eagle Power!

JAMES CLIFTON

Afterwards I asked myself, "Why the devil did I let myself fall into the clutches of that old bird?" My defense was always the same. Anthropologists must double-check data and interpretations, diligently searching for evidence that might require changing strong first impressions, even the firmest conclusions. We have to track down fresh leads, more so to open-mindedly cross-check the contrary findings of other scholars. Nothing other than scientific responsibility pushed me into old *Menisi's* grasp.[1] That and some simple curiosity: what did an apparently much feared, allegedly self-confessed, reputedly all-too-successful Potawatomi Indian wizard really look like?

Two compelling questions nudged me toward an interview—and a confrontation—with the aged, illusive *Menisi* (Swoops Down). For more than a year I had studied the Kansas Potawatomi "Dream Dance" rites. These I knew centered on six large, richly decorated, much venerated sacred drums, each in its liturgical turn addressed as *Mishomonon* (Our Grandfather). Then I heard allusions to a seventh important drum, one never seen in public. This was the "oldest great drum," I was told, "maybe the original Potawatomi drum." "What is its name?" I asked. "The old flat drum," was a standard reply. "What does it look like?" I persisted. "You'll have to see for yourself," came the response.

The Young Dawn Man tried to advise me fully and to warn me off, I realized too late. "you could call that old flat drum the 'Vanilla' drum, maybe the 'Joker,'" Young Dawn Man told me, saying everything in a few words that were, to my later misfortune, utterly beyond my understanding. I never did pay close enough attention to Young Dawn Man's austere metaphors or his cautions. "Who is the Old Flat Drum's 'owner'?" I asked. "There's no 'owner.' That drum belongs to the *Neshnabek* [The People].[2] Swoops Down's got it at his place but won't give it up." These were the replies.

There was a seventh important drum, I concluded, tentatively. It might be the Potawatomi's first Dream Dance drum, perhaps. Or it could have some other significance. So, to solve the "Mystery of the Old Flat Drum," I went hunting for the secretive *Menisi*. I would do my Columbo routine. That ancient recluse, suitably coaxed, would play show and tell,

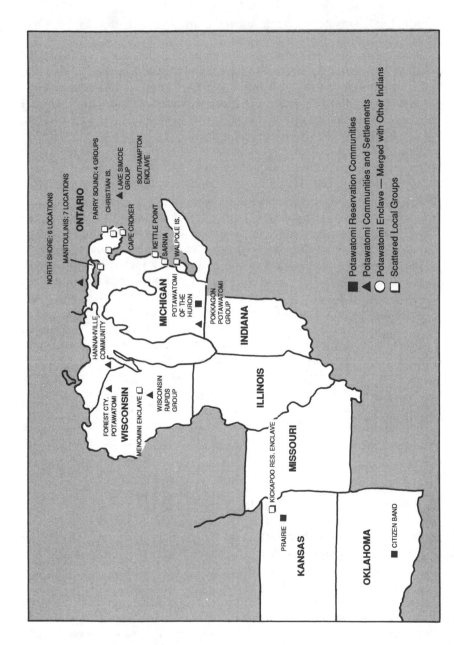

Potawatomi Indian Communities

unlocking his mysteries. Such was my plan. As events developed, I had more confidence than good sense.

Solving the mystery of the old flat drum was the lesser of two sound reasons for seeking out *Menisi*. The second was far more important. After a year's productive research, I thought I had the fundamentals of Prairie Potawatomi culture and society pretty well pegged. Then I learned an esteemed predecessor, the renowned Ruth Landes, had studied these *Neshnabek* during the mid-1930s. Because her work was still unpublished, I did not locate it in my library search. Nonetheless, a brief exchange of correspondence brought back in the mail two twenty-year-old manuscripts, one for her monograph *Potawatomi Medicine*, the second for her *Prairie Potawatomi*.[3]

The first of these instantly threw me off balance. *Potawatomi Medicine* opened with the line "Not often can even a simple culture be understood from the clue of one powerful bent." Landes followed this lead with a full description of a community menaced, oppressed, and abused by a class of sorcerers. The sorcerers she met and described were private practitioners who regularly bullied, intimidated, and magically assaulted their victims, then boasted publicly of their evil exploits. Magical "hooliganism," "terrorism," Landes called this openly avowed diabolic wizardry, and her key informants (themselves self-proclaimed perpetrators) gleefully applauded her assessment.[4]

More than a year of close observation and in-depth interviewing by myself, my wife, and several keen-eyed apprentice anthropologists had detected no hint of any such occult oppressors. We had closely studied the Dream Dance religion's seasonal rites, funeral and naming rituals, peyote religion sessions, and assorted other religious ceremonies and beliefs, even interviewing the only three remaining adherents (an elderly Ojibwa married to a Prairie Potawatomi woman and his two adult sons) of the classic *Midewiwin* (the Grand Medicine Lodge). I knew the Prairie Band community was perennially embroiled in a noxious internal conflict; however, this was a secular affair fought out in the political arena, covertly as well as publicly. But not the slightest glimmer of anything like the terror tactics of a gang of arrogant sorcerers had come to me, not between 1962 and the summer of 1963.

I was faced with the classic ethnographer's dilemma: Anthropologist Masterful studies Community Hermetic and discovers cultural patterns X; then Anthropologist Proficient studies the same Community Hermetic but describes a dramatically different ethos Y. I was not personally disposed to prosecuting a *Derek Freeman* v. *Margaret Mead* style indictment before the court of Anthropological Loyalties.[5] At any rate, had I been so inclined, Ruth Landes was alive, vigorous, and would have clobbered me had I been so presumptuous. Plus, in my own training I was taught to expect just such contradictions. Hadn't my teacher, Robert Redfield, responded civilly and intelligently to the contrary findings of Oscar Lewis in their separate studies of Tepoztlán with the suggestion that he had asked, "What made these people happy?" whereas Lewis was asking, "What made them miserable?" Even more sensibly and recently, when Jack Fischer and Ward Goodenough discovered they had produced opposite conclusions about Trukese social structure, they put their heads together cooperatively to find out why so, pushing anthropological methods and theory forward a notch in the process, not dishonoring themselves by academic foul play.[6]

How could I explain the differences between what Ruth Landes found among the Kansas Potawatomi in 1935–36 and what I had learned about this same society in 1962–63? In part, I surmised, we started from different conceptual premises and asked unmatched questions in our separate ways. Her opening line in the *Potawatomi Medicine* monograph was a theoretical giveaway, I recognized. The comment about a "single powerful bent" characterizing Potawatomi culture, I knew, reflected classic Benedictine configurationalism in its heyday. Landes was viewing Potawatomi culture through the evil eyes of this community's sorcerers, much as Ruth Benedict had greatly simplified the Zuni "Apollonian" ethos by overemphasis on the ideals of that Pueblo's priests.[7]

By itself this assessment was not enough. It left me still at square one. For with much detail Landes had described the attitudes, behaviors, styles, and tactics of a good many *named* Potawatomi sorcerers, and I had encountered and heard of none. How had I missed them? Or, where had they gone? Knowing that in 1935–36 Landes's mystic hooligans were mainly elderly men, most long dead by my time, was no help. They should have had successors. So, substantial social and cultural change in the intervening decades was another possible explanation. Nonetheless, if Landes witnessed these mighty terrorists, however much she might have exaggerated their significance, there were some nasty sorcerers—in her time. Where stood Potawatomi sorcery in the 1960s?

And so that summer, on the stifling prairie lands making up the Potawatomi reservation, I went on a witch hunt. Now, finding a sorcerer when an anthropologist wants one is easier said than done. Flat out questions directed to respected informants—"Show me a sorcerer," or "Identify a witch for me, please," or "Tell me all you know of witchcraft"— bring only flat denials, disclaimers, or declarations of ignorance. A standard evasion was, "Well, there may have been somebody with power like that in the old, old, days, but not in my time." Part of my problem was that I had been concentrating on the sunny side of the Potawatomi ethos, I came to understand. So the people I knew best were letting me see only the good stuff. My new task was to penetrate into what anthropologists sometimes call the "back regions" of this culture. To do this I had to shift my research gears. The subject of sorcery, especially when dealing with reluctant (maybe intimidated?) true believers, had to be approached like an annoyed wolverine: obliquely, cautiously.

Since sorcery involves cultural commitment to a theory of intolerable, otherwise inexplicable calamity, that was the indirect trail I had to take with my prodding.[8] Among these *Neshnabek* were people with chronic illnesses cured or alleviated by neither American nor Potawatomi therapists. And there were many curious accidents, mysterious sudden deaths, and other baffling afflictions. Persistently asking about the "real causes" of such hardships eventually paid off. Soon I had collected many hesitant, fragmentary admissions (possibly . . . maybe . . . I'm not sure, but . . . people say . . . some still think, not me) that there was still around "somebody owning" the old malevolent powers like those bad actors Landes had known and described.[9]

But specific accusations there were none. No Potawatomi would point a blaming finger. Named wrongdoers? Not one. When I insisted on asking for an identification, people looked the other way or changed the subject, nervously so. I realized I was treading on a source of high anxiety, for no one scoffed or played the skeptic. The consternation, even fear, provoked by my inquiries itself was clear evidence of at least some continuing belief in the power of sorcery as described by Landes, no matter how few or submerged the actual practitioners might now be. Uncertainty and unpredictability were what plagued these *Neshnabek* most. And insecurity was precisely that mood which Potawatomi sorcerers played on for their own malicious purposes. No one was willing to risk their own welfare by being first to speak an accusatory name. Retaliation, I understood from Landes's pages, was what vengeance-minded Potawatomi conjurers most relished. In the end, Whirlpool Woman and Downward Lightning set me straight. "You'll have to figure it out for yourself," I was admonished—flatly, with finality.

Figuring it out for myself required some disciplined thinking, the sorting of information, and contextualizing. The power and reputation of sorcerers accumulates with age. So, because the Potawatomi cherish great age, almost putting their well-scrubbed old folks on outright display, which elder males still living on the reservation were rarely seen in public? Of those, *Menisi* was one of a scant few. Of these, which had no kin willing to show him off or to speak proudly and lovingly of him? Here, *Menisi* was nearly alone. Who closely held and would not share some object of general ritual significance much valued by the Potawatomi? Once more Swoops Down—he had the Old Flat Drum and kept it to and for himself. There were no other suspects I could identify. All circumstantial evidence pointed straight to *Menisi*. Asocial he surely was. Was he also supremely antisocial?

My deducting done, I sought confirmation: obliquely, cautiously. "I've found out where Swoops Down lives," I mentioned to Watching Over, hinting I might drop by for a pleasant chat. "I wouldn't if I were you," he retorted emphatically, adding, "He's got a *bad* reputation." "What kind of a reputation?" I probed. "Well, you know, the old people used to say he maybe could steal a man's tongue." (*Aha! A Potawatomi sorcerer's favorite trophy was his victim's tongue.*) "How about driving out with me and introducing me to Swoops Down?" I asked Half

Day Sky. "Not me!" he responded. "Next week I'm going out to talk to *Menisi* about the Old Flat Drum," I told North Wind Woman, committing myself firmly. "Don't go out there alone! Don't let him look you in the eye! Don't go there after dark! Don't go in that shack of his with him!" she worriedly counseled. Oh that I might have had sense enough to follow all of North Wind Woman's grandmotherly advice!

Now better equipped to identify and chase my prey, I turned to trusty Young Dawn Man. If anyone around had supernatural power equal to some time-worn witch, it was he. "I hear Swoops Down is a shape-changer, that he claims he can hurt people," I suggested.[10] "Yup. Maybe so. Some people say that," he responded noncommittally. "I'm going out to his place tomorrow to see the Old Flat Drum, talk to him about things," I said, suggestively. Abruptly, Young Dawn Man sat up straight and leaned forward, sighed with resignation and cautioned me. "Clifton," he said, "he's got the power. He's killed thirteen people we know of, two just last year, and sickened plenty more. And he *brags* on it." The implication was *Menisi* had power enough to flaunt his triumphs, but Young Dawn Man, proper Potawatomi, was not about to tell me flatly not to go. A man will do what he's gotta do, was his philosophy. I was on my own. He concluded his admonitions: "Clifton, *we* don't mess with Eagle power!"

Forewarned, if not forearmed, the next afternoon I set out to corner *Menisi*. No flicker of vigilant doubt troubled my mind as I drove west along the gravel section line road. "Technique was everything," I advised myself. I drew near the turnoff. "Approach him gently," I rehearsed, "politely, indirectly, respectfully, firmly." I cut right, down a disused dirt road, doing my inventory while watching the ruts and humps: "Got everything I need—questions, note cards, ball-points, some Prince Albert and roll-your-own papers if that's his smoke, two packs of Luckies if he prefers tailor-mades." In the back of the dusty Chevy wagon was my ace in the hole: a cooler with a six-pack of Miller's High Life on ice, complete with church key. "I'm prepared for anything"—optimistic, poised, experienced. "Shoot, one sharp rational Ph.D. can handle one shabby braggart of a 'witch' any day. This old buzzard will soon be wagging his tongue for me."

The "road" soon narrowed into an overgrown footpath. Parking, I knelt to put my tracker's eye on the trail, searching for spoor. "Hmm. No sign. Not used for a couple of weeks, anyway. Not since the last rain. Is this turkey home?" Starting down the path afoot, every so often I called out: "*Menisi. Menisi!*" No answer came in the midafternoon heat. After a hundred or so paces I walked into a clearing, centered on a long unpainted, ramshackle cottage—Bureau of Indian Affairs modern, vintage 1905, never repaired since, sagging porch, holed roof, cracked windows, and all. I called out again, hearkening to a welcoming human voice or the unfriendly baying of hounds. Not a whimper.[11]

On my second circuit around *Menisi's* spread at last I noticed something promising. There a dozen yards west of the house lay a rusty iron bedspring. On the bedspring, face skyward, arms outstretched, was a form dressed in much bleached singlet and jeans, bare of foot and head covering. *"Menisi?"* I called. Not a murmur in return. "Has this old fart died on me?" I reflected. Stepping near, looking down at him, I could see the answer was no: wide open unblinking eyes staring upward but not seeing me, parched lips slightly parted though wordless—there *was* the faintest hint of respiration, but no response to my (unexpected?) coming.

Was he in a coma? In trance state? Meditating? Communing with his guardian spirit? Sunbathing? I was at the right place. He was old—*old* old. I had never seen him before. This had to be my quarry. None other. There lay Swoops Down himself in the sun-bronzed flesh like a Hindu fakir on his bed of nails, pondering some Potawatomi nothingness.

Polite, imperturbable, unswervable anthropologist, I presented myself. *"Bozhu, Bozhu,"* I said in greeting. "I'm Jim Clifton." Not a wink. "I'm Professor James Clifton from the university." Not a blink. "I'm the anthropologist who's been studying the *Neshnabek* the last couple of years." Not a twitch in response. "I hear you've got the Old Flat Drum . . . the one some folks call the 'Joker' or 'Vanilla.' . . . I'd sure like to learn more about that drum." Not the least breath of a comeback. None of my overtures produced a perceptible response. "Remember," I reflected with self-discipline, "there's nothing that unhinges an American more than a guy who won't chatter back in a two-person set. You're talking too much. You'll have to sit this sun-dried cow chip out." I cast around for something to perch on, spied a weathered milk bottle box, up-ended it a few feet from my uninformative informant, squatted, settled down, prepared to wait him out. The sun was now well past its meridian, falling toward the western horizon and into my eyes. I *had* forgotten something, my sunglasses.

Minutes passed. I grew restless. Another half-hour then three-quarters was gone. I was uncomfortable in the Kansas heat and humidity, half-blinded by the sun. Hauling out pipe and pouch I fired up, blowing a seductive cloud of smoke toward *Menisi*. Not a sniff in response. I waited a time, then displayed my presents: "Smoke? I've got some Prince Albert and papers." Not a whisker of movement from Swoops Down. I bided my time, puffing away, then tried again: "I've got some Luckies if you prefer them." Utter, total silence in return. An unsociable fellow, this one.

After another half-hour or so I grew restive. "Time's wasting," I reflected, "Now play your hole-card." "Pretty hot day," I observed coyly, adding, considerately, "You must be sweltering there. Happens I've got a six-pack of iced Miller's in the car. I think I'll have one. Care to join me?" There! Did I detect the least inclination of chin toward breastbone? A nonverbal affirmative? Surely it had to be. The old bugger was thirsty. I'd won the round. Gotcha!

Standing and stretching, I ambled around the house back to the car and broke out a pair of cold ones. When I returned, Swoops Down was still laid out, sizzling on his grill. I walked over, popped a cap, set the bottle down within *Menisi*'s reach, turned, sat down again, opened my own Miller's, downed half the bottle, then resumed my vigil, refreshed and expectant. There lay Swoops Down, eyes still skyward, moist lips slightly parted—but where was his bottle? Nowhere in sight. Had he eaten it?

I swallowed the last of my beer, then glanced up. Swoops Down was standing outlined against the red flare of the setting sun. I stood and faced him. He stepped forward. I stood my ground. "Over six feet," I observed, "maybe one seventy-five pounds, not an ounce of flab on him . . . striking, aquiline features. A handsome devil.'" He stared straight at me, flat-faced, expressionless, eyeball-to-eyeball. Not to be put down, I held his gaze. *Menisi* now was up on tiptoes stretching sideways with both arms, flexing and rippling his muscles like some overage Charles Atlas. "Jesus H. Christ!" I thought, "Look at those pecs and lats. He must have been one powerful bastard when he was younger." Swoops Down then rotated his wrists, spreading then curling his fingers into hooked . . .

Suddenly this huge snarling Eagle dove out of the sun at me, sharp open beak thrusting at my face, talons slashing at my eyes! I was hit by a massive adrenalin rush. Heart pounding I leaped back, fell ass-over-teakettle on top of the milk box, hit the dirt, hard.

Flee! My old combat training asserted itself reflexively. I did a clumsy double combat roll sideways, out of the line of fire, searching for a hole, a hump, any cover to protect me from this shocking attack.

Fight! Quickly I scanned around, looking for a weapon—a club, a rock—anything to defend myself against that damned eagle.

What eagle? Heart still thumping I looked up half fearfully, protecting my face with one arm. There was no eagle. That miserable sorcerer was standing there perfectly relaxed, arms at his side, the hint of a sneer on pursed lips, glancing at me contemptuously with a glint of a satisfied malice in his eyes.

I stood, stepped to one side to get the sun out of my eyes, peered sideways at *Menisi*, and started dusting off my dignity. We both stood there for minutes more. Then Swoops Down stepped around me toward the door to his coop. After a few seconds hesitation, I followed—a respectful distance behind.

Once on his ramshackle porch *Menisi* turned and spoke for the first time. Like some suave maître d'hôtel he gestured gracefully—one-handed, palm upward—toward the murky interior of his lair. "You wanna see my drum? Come along, it's inside." Then, gesturing, "You first." Momentarily, as dusk gathered around us, I pondered this proposition. I had already ignored Young Dawn Man's sound advice, much to my embarrassment. And to my chagrin I had violated three of North Wind Woman's four commandments for dealing with *Menisi*. Should I hazard ignoring the fourth?

　　Clifton. Be sensible! Walk through that door and see the Old Flat Drum! What's to be afraid of?

　　Clifton. You're tired. It's been a long day. It's time for home and a hot meal.

　　"No thank you," I replied, "not just now. I'll take a rain check on that. *Mgwetch*—Thanks. Nice meeting ya." I turned and left, keeping an eye out behind me as I retreated toward the sanctuary of my car.

　　On the drive homeward I sorted out the day's experience. What had I learned? Although easily the best performance I had seen so far, old *Menisi*'s attacking eagle stunt was part of a larger pattern of Potawatomi expressive culture. These people were once masters of the fine art of animal mimicry, in public gatherings usually delivered as ritual dancing.[12] Twice, for example, at the end of an all night funeral ritual, near dawn, I had "seen" four Thunderbirds swoop in from the east, gather up the corpse, and carry it off to the west. That is, much fatigued and half-mesmerized by hours of thudding drum beats and monotonous chanting in a confined space, I had seen four highly skilled dancers impersonate the Thunders. Old Swoops Down was a master of this art form, obviously.

　　Oh! He had plenty more witch's tricks in his kit bag. For weeks I had been muddling around asking about and looking for a sorcerer. The moccasin telegraph surely delivered this news to him. He was waiting for me, waiting and ready. When Clifton the Gullible arrived, he'd outsilenced me, stalled until I was nervous, dehydrated, suggestible, half-broiled, and more than half-blinded by the sun. Then Swoops Down pounced on his prey. A man of impressive deeds but few words, he delivered up a vivid, terrifying sampling of his repertoire. I had come looking for a witch. *Menisi* had shown me one in action.

　　Rationally, I could understand—now the front end of my brain was working again—that his tricks included a bit of prestidigitation, more than a little skilled playing with my own autosuggestability, maybe even some ventriloquism with that screaming eagle bit, and above all that marvelous—ghastly—plunging-eagle body language. Later, using my forebrain, I could reason this out. But face-to-face Swoops Down bypassed his victims' logical faculties and struck directly at their deepest, irrational emotions. Landes had been entirely right. There be Potawatomi wizards here—at least one of them.

　　But there was a then and now historical difference between Landes's observations and my own. Then, in 1935–36, these Potawatomi were generations closer to the time when many shamans—good or evil as the mood suited them—walked the earth. Swoops Down was born at a time when they were numerous, presenting him with many mentors. 1935–36 was also the height of the Great Depression, when Kansas was the heart of the Plains Dust Bowl, its topsoil and riches blown away. Then the Potawatomi were experiencing stress and poverty almost unparalleled in their history. In that historical context there was an outburst of great frustration and hostility turned inward, encouraged and facilitated by Potawatomi men-of-power working against their own. Such circumstances were fertile ground for the remaining Potawatomi wizards, all older men acting out their anger and their ambitions for power amidst a community containing many much deprived ardent believers.

Now, in 1962–64, was different. In the meantime there had been major efforts at political and social reform from within this reservation community. The Potawatomi had never exactly rejoiced in the terrors the old-time sorcerers dumped on them. Over the years they had worked at suppressing such fearsome disorder, striving for a greater sense of well-being, more supernatural and secular peace and quiet. By my time, except for the solitary *Menisi*, the sorcerers were pretty much gone, although the beliefs that supported such roles were still present, at least latently. Without much commotion, the Potawatomi had effectively stifled the evil influence of those flamboyant men and their grandiose claims to supernatural power. Anger, hostility, frustration, competitiveness, and rivalries there were still aplenty, but these were acted out in secular contexts, more often than not directed at outsiders, not themselves.[13]

A year or so later my nemesis Swoops Down died (under suspicious circumstances, others hinted). He had no apprentices and left no trained successors. After his death, the drum he had hidden surfaced again, but it was not thereafter given much ritual significance.

As for this "Mystery of the Old Flat Drum," I might better have stayed home. There was no great enigma to it. Its chief significance was that *Menisi* had it and would not share. When it passed into other hands and onto the public scene, it no longer possessed much import. It *was* an old drum I learned later, though not a Dream Dance drum, nothing like it. What it was was a simple, undecorated, one-sided tambourine drum, of the sort that Potawatomi shamans has used in earlier decades during curing rites or divining rituals. It was an heirloom. At last, when the moment was opportune, I asked Young Dawn Man the questions I should have asked in the beginning.

"When you told me you might call that flat drum the 'Joker' or the 'Vanilla' drum, what did you mean?" "Just what I said," he replied. "You could call it the 'Vanilla' drum cause it ain't got no rules on it, nothing special about it. And you can call it the 'Joker' like in a deck of cards, 'cause you can use it instead of any of the regular dream drums."

Young Dawn Man's interest in the Old Flat Drum, like that of other Potawatomi ritualists, reflected their efforts to cope with some serious problems. Mainly these had to do with the staffing and performance of their Dream Dance rituals. Each of the six sacred drums was supported by a set of "offices" (ritual roles), which totaled 282. There were far too few suitably disposed adult Potawatomi in 1964 for each of these offices to be taken and played by a separate individual, hence there was much doubling and tripling up. Young Dawn Man himself sometimes acted as Staffman for one drum, then North Pole Drummer for a second, Speaker for a third, and Waiter for another, as each drum took its turn in the ritual rounds.

Even with some ritualists doubling in brass, assembling enough skilled, knowledgeable performers to act out the required roles for a major seasonal rite was difficult. Bringing together the needed ceremonial crew on short notice, such as for a fast funeral in midsummer, was often near impossible. This was so because each "officer" had to be fully versed in the entire myriad of complex prescriptions and taboos, the hundreds of songs, the many courtesies and special ritual acts "belonging" to each of the drums. The Potawatomi's problem with the Dream Dance religion in 1964, simply put, was too few ritualists, too many ritual roles and rules.

In the Old Flat Drum, some like Young Dawn Man saw a possible solution. It was a drum with no rules whatever and no established offices "belonging" to it. If they could bring it into the public domain, the leading ritualists might be able to convert that venerable shaman's drum into a suitable liturgical instrument, one that could be used for a quickie funeral or an ad hoc naming ceremony, perhaps even a poorly atttended midwinter seasonal rite, whereupon there would be no worry about "not getting it done right." All of the talk about the Old Flat Drum I had noted represented an ongoing process of creative innovation. The Potawatomi were busy trying to invent a new religious tradition, one better fitting their circumstances in the mid-1960s.

The demise of active sorcerers and the rise of the Dream Dance rites as the Kansas Potawatomi's central religious institution were connected, I realized at last. The former represented successful efforts to suppress the influence of those who threaten with disruptive evil doing, the latter efforts to promote consensus and community well-being. Whether this good versus evil dialectic represented a durable ritual substitution, a recurrent, cyclic ebb and flow, or neither, I cannot say. A quarter century later, this is for someone else, double-checking Landes 1935 and Clifton 1964, to discover. But I do have some prudent, personally tested advice for any such venturesome, maybe overconfident young anthropologist: Why take unnecessary chances? *Don't mess with Eagle power!*

NOTES

1. The traditionalist Potawatomi I knew in Kansas resented (or feared) having their names used in publications, and I promised never to do so. All personal names used in this essay are pseudonyms. They are authentic clan names borrowed from pretwentieth-century historic figures. However, the Potawatomi for centuries have regularly bestowed the names of the dead on newborn children, so there may be living individuals with these same names. If so, they are not the people I write about here.

2. The ethnonym, or self name, of the people commonly called Potawatomi is *Neshnabek* (pl.).

3. Landes's studies were later published as "Potawatomi Medicine," *Transactions of the Kansas Academy of Science* 66 (1963): 553–599, and *The Prairie Potawatomi: Tradition and Ritual in the Twentieth Century* (Madison: University of Wisconsin Press, 1970). For more on Potawatomi sorcery, also see Alanson Skinner's *The Mascoutens or Prairie Potawatomi Indians,* Bulletin of the Public Museum of the City of Milwaukee, vol. 6, no. 1, p. 1 (1924): 204–209.

4. The public boasting about their exploits of self-proclaimed sorcerers characteristic of the traditional Potawatomi and related Algonquian peoples is rare elsewhere in the world. Witchcraft (or sorcery) is ordinarily a theory of misfortune. Those accused of being witches are thus scapegoats, ill-fated innocents for some reason suspected or accused by people who feel themselves mysteriously aggrieved for suffering a calamity. Potawatomi witches were different: They were the self-confessed *enemies* of society.

5. For a discussion of this travesty of academic justice, see Lowell D. Holmes's *Quest for the Real Samoa: The Mead-Freeman Controversy and Beyond* (Westport, CT: Bergin & Garvey, 1988).

6. See Jack L. Fischer, "The Classification of Residence in Censuses," *American Anthropologist* 60 (1958): 508–517.

7. Ruth Benedict, *Patterns of Culture* (Boston: Houghton-Mifflin) and John J. Honigman, *The Development of Anthropological Ideas* (Homewood, IL: Dorsey), pp. 169–179, 203–208.

8. For an excellent overview of the subject, see Lucy Mair, *Witchcraft* (New York: McGraw-Hill, World University Library, 1975).

9. Traditional Potawatomi believed that the power of sorcerers derived from ownership of a special, evil "medicine bundle," a decorated animal skin containing powerful charms and fetishes.

10. Traditional *Neshnabek* were convinced sorcerers would assume the shapes of various animals, mostly at night, to work their evil deeds.

11. Potawatomi witches/sorcerers were thought to own particularly ferocious dogs. So far as the author is concerned, all dogs are vicious and never to be trusted however harmless their owners. In any event, in *Menisi*'s case, one should beware of the master, not the dog.

12. The film *Neshnabek* contains some brief black-and-white scenes of Potawatomi animal mimicry in brief clips of clan feasts. If viewers watch closely, they can see Potawatomi men shambling like bears and stalking like wolves. This film is an edited montage of footage shot about 1936–37, and is available from the Department of Anthropology, University of Kansas.

13. A full scale ethnohistorical treatment of the background of these events and developments is in the author's *The Prairie People: Continuity and Change in Potawatomi Indian Culture, 1665–1965* (Lawrence, KS: Regents Press of Kansas, 1977).

EIGHTEEN

A Very Bad Disease of the Arms

MICHAEL KEARNEY

As a graduate student in the Anthropology Department at Berkeley in the mid-1960s I decided to go to southern Mexico to do my doctoral research. I had spent a previous summer in the Sierra Juarez of Oaxaca, and it was to this general area that I decided to return. After reconnoitering for several weeks, I chose the town of Santa Catarina Ixtepeji and took up residence there. Ixtepeji is splashed on the northern side of a rugged ridge high in the mountains east of the valley of Oaxaca. Winter days and nights are crisp and clear, but weeks can pass in the summer months without a ray of sun penetrating the dense fog and mists that shroud these high retreats.

At that time I was interested in relationships between the world view of the people of Ixtepeji and their social structure and environment. My primary ethnographic task was to discover the basic structure and content of the Ixtepejanos' world view. My theoretical perspective then, as now, was that the contents of a world view are largely a reflection of the lived in social and material environment (Kearney 1972, 1984). I also assumed that a dialectic relationship exists between world view and the social and geographic environment in that, insofar as human behavior is shaped by world view, it alters, it creates to a great extent, that very environment which is reflected in the world view. I thought of my own world view as scientific and materialist and quite consciously accepted that my perspective was the lens through which I was refracting the very different world view of the people of Ixtepeji.

What most fascinated me was that I and the Ixtepejanos could walk the same streets, abide in the same houses, eat the same foods, and yet live in such different cognitive universes. With my comfortable background and my financial and cultural capital resources, I faced each day with a sense of security and control over most conditions affecting me. I attributed my fortunes in life compared with the poverty of my hosts to the fact that our respective ancestors had been born into and swept along by very different currents of history which had been further textured by accidents of biography. They for their part attributed their lot in life to "fate," "the will of God," the intrusion into human affairs of spirits, and to the malevolence of witches and other "bad people."

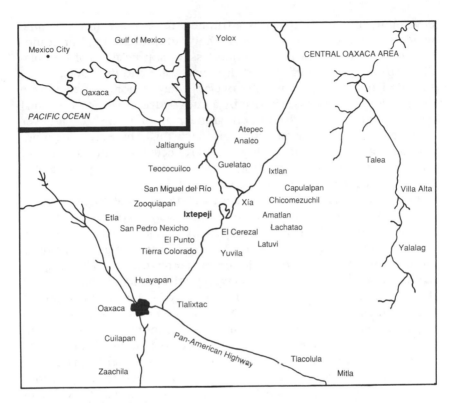

Ixtepeji, Oaxaca, Mexico

I came to realize that they perceived their world as virtually saturated with harmful, even lethal immaterial forces. The most potent of these were "bad airs" that could be sent into one's body by witches. Witches themselves personify evil and malevolence. They rely on deception and stealth to penetrate their victims' defenses. Some are thought to transform themselves into seemingly harmless animals and in this form do their evil. The most insidious of all may even take on the form of a person trusted by the victim and, so deceiving him or her, do that person great harm. Others can use black magic to send airs across town to harm or kill.

This then was the exotic and very different mental world in which my Ixtepejano friends and informants lived and which I was fascinated to document and to explain. Never for a moment did I doubt that these fantastic concepts and experiences of theirs were anything but the contents of a "nonscientific" world view. Ixtepejanos live in a world where death, suffering, and economic misfortune are common. Crops often fail, and dysentery and other diseases are endemic, and mortality rates of children and adults are high. These are conditions that demand explanations. To my mind they were all concomitants of "underdevelopment": the Ixtepejanos attributed these misfortunes to airs, witches, or the will of God because they did not have in their ethno-science any notions of germs, much less an appreciation of the relationships between contaminated drinking water and dysentery. Nor, I surmised, did they have any sense of class analysis, nor any perspective on their lot in life that is afforded by a knowledge of Mexico's colonial past and its position in the modern global economy. In short, it never occurred to me that their fantastic world view might have anything more than a certain metaphoric validity. It well reflected their precarious and dangerous existence, but did not, I was certain, accurately explain it. My complacence was soon to be shattered.

One morning after I had been living in Ixtepeji for about six months I was walking across town to resume talking with an old man who had been telling me his life history. I was lost in thought about the direction I wanted our dialog to take when I looked up to see a very anxious woman standing in front of me in the rock-strewn street. Wringing her hands she spoke to me in whispers with furtive glances to one side and then the other. I recognized her immediately as Doña Delfina, one of the two most notorious witches in town. Because I was interested in witchcraft and folk medicine I had tried some months before to get to know her, but she had rebuffed me in no uncertain terms. But now here she was seeking me out. "Señor Miguel, you're a stranger from far away and you certainly have much knowledge. You can perhaps help us with a terrible problem that we have in our house." I immediately forgot about my planned chore for the morning as my mind raced with expectations of getting to know this formidable woman and having her reveal to me the most esoteric and profound beliefs and practices associated with witchcraft.

"Well," I said, "I don't know, perhaps I can do something, but first please tell me what this bad problem is."

"Oh Señor Miguel, it's my sister-in-law, my brother's wife. She has a very bad disease in her arms, and she is going to die soon unless someone does something for her right away." Although it was a cool morning, she wiped perspiration from her face with her apron and implored me to come and look at her sister-in-law. With a naiveté born of inexperience and exuberance I agreed and followed her into her house where with little ceremony she presented the sick woman to me. Both of her forearms were ulcerated with deep ugly lesions that looked like infected third-degree burns. They were raw and oozing with pus and serum. The woman was in great pain and did not speak to me. Delfina explained that the condition was getting worse day by day and that her sister-in-law was now unable to grind corn or do any other household chores. I asked what they thought the cause could be, and she replied with the platitudinous "Only God knows."

I was at a loss to explain to them or to myself what this condition was and said that they should go and see the young doctor who was doing his tour of social service in Ixtepeji after having just graduated from medical school, but they said that he had left town for a few days. I then told them that the best thing I could do for her was to drive her down to Oaxaca City to see some other doctor. All they would have to do is get her several kilometers up the trail to the highway where my truck was parked.

"No, no. That's no good," said Doña Delfina. "Something has to be done right now. And anyway we're not going to take her to the doctor because they're no good for these kinds of things." Delfina was adamant about not going to a doctor, and when I asked her sister-in-law if she wanted to go to a doctor she morosely shook her head back and forth.

Since a doctor was out of the question, I remembered that I had up in my house an old can of army surplus sunburn ointment that I carried in my backpack. It had benzocaine in it, which takes the pain out of superficial burns and other skin traumas. I told them about it and suggested that we might put some on her arms for temporary relief. They both acted as if I had offered a miracle drug to a terminally ill patient and beseeched me to go and get this medicine. I did and gingerly daubed it onto the poor woman's sores. The anesthetic took effect almost immediately, and first the sick woman and then Doña Delfina were astounded. This was clearly, to their mind, very powerful medicine. They thanked me profusely and beseeched me to continue "the treatments." I came back that afternoon to see my patient and found that not only her general disposition but her arms were greatly improved. The wounds had stopped running and were only slightly uncomfortable. I gave her another treatment then and another that evening. By the next morning healthy scabs had formed over even the worst sores, and the woman was able to do light work. The following day she was completely recovered, and I was given credit for a "miraculous cure."

At that time I had an arrangement to eat lunch and dinner in the home of a friend of mine, Celedonio, who later become my compadre. As we were huddled around the fire after dinner a day or so after the "miraculous cure," he asked me to tell him exactly what had happened with Delfina. Word of what I had done had spread all through town. Feeling some not small sense of pride, I explained to him how I had responded to Delfina's request to cure her sister-in-law and how grateful they were that I had "saved her life." He looked at me incredulously and to my surprise asked me, "Why did you do that?"

"And why not?" I replied somewhat taken back.

"Because it was not a good thing to do," he said.

"It was not a good thing to help this poor woman who was suffering so?"

"You just shouldn't have done it," he said with a seriousness that irritated me because he seemed so unappreciative of my notable results.

"And so what was I supposed to have done, let this miserably sick woman die without trying to do anything for her?"

"You just shouldn't have gotten mixed up with those people," he said.

"And why not? I know that a lot of people don't like Delfina, but her sister-in-law is a good person and anyway she was suffering a lot. I had to help her." It all seemed very clear to me.

Then he leaned forward and said quietly, "You really don't know what was going on there, do you?"

Still somewhat indignant I said that all I knew was that a poor woman was in terrible pain and was maybe going to die and that perhaps I had saved her life.

Then he said, "I'm going to tell you what really happened so that you will know. The reason that she was so sick was because of your neighbor Gregoria." Gregoria, who lived in a house just across a small cornfield and above my house, also had a reputation of being a bad witch. What had happened, according to Celedonio, was that Gregoria had used black magic to take Delfina's brother away from his wife. Part of her strategy was to make his wife very sick and possibly to kill her. Just about everyone knew this except the contested man who was probably made dumb by poisons in his food and by other effects of Gregoria's powers. The proof was that he had been hanging around Gregoria's house and giving her money that should have gone to his wife and sister and also that his wife was dying. Delfina had been doing everything in her bag of evil tricks to get him back to their household, but to no avail. As Celedonio described it, these two titans of black magic were laying down artillery barrages of evil forces across the town and Gregoria, my neighbor, had been winning. Winning that is, he said, until I stumbled onto the scene and tipped the balance of power back to the other woman. Celedonio was thus not discrediting my cure but only taking me to task for my folly in having effected it.

"Until you came along Gregoria was winning. Now things have all changed. The husband is back with his wife and sister, and his wife is well again. Everyone knows what you did, and because of it Gregoria is very mad at you and you better be careful. Because she is so mean and hateful she will try and get you. You better be very careful."

"Oh come on. You don't believe in those superstitions, do you?" I said, appealing to his masculinity and budding sense of modernity.

"No, I don't—not very much," he said without conviction. "But just the same it's a good idea to defend yourself. Maybe you should leave town for a while until Gregoria calms down."

"Ah come on, Celedonio," I said, "you know that none of that stuff works, that it's all just a bunch of superstitions. That old woman can stick pins in dolls and burn them all year long for all I care. As long as she doesn't come after me with a gun I don't care what she does."

"You may be right," he said, "But just to be safe, you better be careful, because who knows what she is doing to you."

I went home that night and didn't think again about what Celedonio had told me. The idea that Gregoria could actually harm me did not even occur to me as something worthy of much further thought. As it was I had plenty of other things to keep me occupied.

About this time something else happened in Ixtepeji that I later realized was to be part of my encounter with these malevolent women. A cargo truck went off the road above the town, and as it crashed down through the forest on the side of the mountain a man riding on the back was killed. Since Ixtepeji was the seat of the municipality in which the accident occurred, the dead man's body was brought to the town. To be removed from the accident site, the body was lashed onto two branches and carried in this fashion. One night and part of the next day passed before the body was removed from the site, and in the cold air it had frozen into its final posture—eyes open, knees bent, and one arm raised in front of its chest as if gesturing. Since the doctor had returned, the authorities directed him to do an autopsy. Because I was a friend of the doctor and had expressed considerable interest in his work in the town, he invited me to assist him with the autopsy. On a dismal and cold afternoon the cadaver was placed for the procedure on a rough-hewn table in a low adobe building behind the courthouse.

When the time came to begin the autopsy, the doctor cleared the room of all but myself, the municipal secretary who was to take the doctor's dictation in a corner of the room as far from the cadaver as he could get, and two women in their late teens whom the doctor had been training as his assistants. These two young women were to do the main work of the autopsy. As the doctor instructed them, they began by cutting the dead man's clothes off and then sawing off the top of his cranium. The doctor had no bone surgery instruments and had to improvise with old rusty carpenter's tools. It was only after considerable exhortation and cajoling by the doctor and finally his help that the young women were able to finish the task of removing the cranium. One of their lesser difficulties was watching the action of the saw and yet avoiding the cold anguished stare of the cadaver's lifeless eyes. But the worst part was the opening of the chest and abdominal cavities with the crude shears and saw. The cold, rigid arm of the cadaver was constantly in the way, and the girls were not put at ease by the doctor's jokes about how they were going to wake up in the night and feel that same cold arm around them in their beds.

I had dissected animals and human cadavers and seen any number of surgical procedures but found myself feeling progressively more uneasy as the autopsy continued into the night, which was only lighted by a couple of smoky lamps. This unembalmed, unshaven body with its foul odors in this lugubrious setting was altogether too disagreeable for my tastes. When at last the final stitch was sewn in the cadaver's leathery skin with a large needle and twine, I was more than ready to escape out into the night air and see the reassuring glow of fireflies. But for the next few nights my sleep was disturbed by the dead man's swarthy face with its dark purple contusions and crown of Frankenstein-like sutures.

After about a week or so I stopped thinking about both Gregoria and the dead man, as I became absorbed in my work. In Ixtepeji most of the town goes to bed with the chickens, and I was accustomed to sit up late in my one-room adobe house on the edge of town and write and read at a small table that I had the local carpenter make for me. One particular night was not unlike most others in the late summer. Dense clouds blanketed the town blotting out the moon and stars. Cornstalks rasped against the wall of my house in the cold breeze that blew down the mountainside. Inside drafts made my oil lamps flicker and throw bizarre shadows on the walls. Mice scurried about in the rafters, and dogs barked and howled both near and far. But aside from these noises all other sounds in the town were dampened by the fog. I was writing some notes or possibly a letter when I became aware of an itch on my left forearm that eventually demanded scratching. My first thought was that I was being bitten by fleas again—a recurrent problem that required dusting my bedding with flea powder. The two cotton shirts, a sweater, and a jacket that I wore against the damp cold prevented me from scratching well and eventually I had to remove the jacket and roll up my sleeves to get at this persistent "fleabite." What I saw when my arm was exposed caused me to fall into a state of stark terror.

There on the side of my arm were several large angry welts. And not only that, they seemed to rise up and grow as I looked at them. Immediately the image of the chancrous arms of Delfina's sister-in-law exploded into my mind and right after that the realization that Gregoria's house was only some fifty yards away through the fog. The immediate assessment of the situation that, against my will, spontaneously rose into my consciousness was that "she's got me!" While I had been sitting complacently in my little house she must have been, as she was probably at that very moment, doing something to kill me. A weak voice that I recognized as my rapidly fading rationality said, "Bullshit." And then there came into my mind's eye the horrendous, contorted, and bruised face of the cadaver and the overwhelming fear that tomorrow I would be lying on that rough table as the ribald doctor directed my autopsy with those crude carpenter's tools. One part of me castigated another by saying, "Why didn't you leave town while you had a chance like Celedonio told you to, while you were still alive?" My mind began to race like a motor with its throttle stuck while I witnessed the disintegration of my own rational, scientific, materialist world view. The unsuppressable assertion rose into my mind that it was all false, that the people among whom I had been living with what I had assumed were quaint backward customs and superstitions were aware of and in touch with knowledge and forces with which I was in no way prepared to deal. I feared for my life as I never had before. It was going to take more than some sunburn ointment to save me.

This state of absolute terror lasted for I don't know how long, perhaps thirty or forty seconds, perhaps several minutes. Then slowly I began to struggle against it. I thought about fleeing to Celedonio's or to one of my neighbors. But I didn't want to go out into the pitch black darkness and have to stumble through the steep, dripping cornfields around my house. There was no way of telling what was out there—perhaps even Gregoria. But at the same time I desperately wanted to do this, to go to people who understood what was happening to me and who could possibly do something to save me. But another much weaker voice in me said, "What kind of nonsense is this; are you really going to capitulate to these superstitions?" And then too I thought that if I went for help, what would I say—"Help me, help me. I'm dying of witchcraft?" This seemed rather ridiculous—me the scientific anthropologist banging on someone's door and raving about being witched. But then as I looked at the welts on my arm I said to myself, "These are not superstitions." They were indeed very real facts, the kind that science is based on. And the inescapable hypothesis was that they were evidence of witchcraft. I was too preoccupied to think of it at the time, but much later I realized that I was then in a state of extreme cognitive dissonance. Reality was all askew. I had the most intense sense of being suspended between two different worlds. One was that of the rural Mexican Indians that I lived among, the other was my own world view, which until now I had never seriously questioned. But now it seemed different, not in me but back very far away in Berkeley with its abstract intellectual life and security. But now I wasn't in my comfortable little cottage in the Berkeley hills. I was deep in these dark foreboding mountains of dangerous and mysterious forces.

After I don't know how long I began to calm down as my own basic world view feebly started to come back into ascendancy. I heard a voice in the back of my mind asking in what other way could this bizarre phenomenon be explained and then I heard myself saying, "Maybe I've been hypnotized." My father had used hypnosis in his medical practice and had taught me how to attain anesthesia and deep relaxation. And, on my own, I had attained complete anesthesia for extensive dental work. I knew that by using hypnosis it was possible to moderate heart rate and even the temperature of the extremities. I was also generally aware of the hysterical conversion reactions that sometimes underlie cases of presumed witchcraft. I started to think that perhaps, just perhaps, I was suffering from such a conversion reaction and wasn't going to die a miserable death in these lonely mountains after all.

As I regained more composure I began to review my encounter with Delfina and her sister-in-law and what Celedonio had told me. I also started to think about all the cases of witchcraft that I knew of and the people who were said to have been made sick and died from it. I started to realize that while I had presumably been cataloging these events as interesting ethnographic data and then letting them fall from my conscious mind they must have been registering somewhere else in my memory to emerge on this night and to manifest themselves as this strange body language on my arm. I found this explanation to be extremely comforting since it continued to sweep away more of the fear and anxiety. Little by little the reality that I was experiencing became more structured by my own world view. And within a half-hour or so I had effected another "miraculous" cure.

But gone now was the cavalier insouciance and pride that I had after curing Delfina's sister-in-law. More than this, though, I now had a much deeper appreciation of world view and of cultural differences in general. Whereas before these were intellectually interesting and analytically powerful concepts, now that I had seen my own world view temporarily shattered and in some way overwhelmed by another, the concept of world view and especially a concern with differences among world views took on a new significance for me. The next day, as I was thinking about my experience, I recalled a passage I had read a year or so earlier in Lévi-Strauss's *Tristes Tropiques*, which chronicles his fieldwork in Brazil. Somewhere in this very personal book he says that a person who had done ethnographic fieldwork is forever afterward a "marginal man." The ethnographer will never completely become a native because he will always acquire his new cultural perceptions as an overlay on his own natal culture. But then too, when he returns home to his own milieu, he will be seeing his world through eyes that have lost their innocence and now refract reality differently.

After my experience I was left with an appreciation of witchcraft that lent a new dimension to what previously had been a strictly intellectual grasp of it. Now the anxiety of Delfina, the terror of her sister-in-law, and Celedonio's concern for me were emotions and ideas that I had briefly experienced much as they must experience them. And furthermore, this appreciation of their realities gave me a new and much deeper appreciation of the intellectual task in which I was engaged. I became more enthusiastic about my fieldwork. It now was more real and exciting. I felt that my own disease of the arms was an important milestone in my work, that it was an indication that in some important ways I was starting to understand the reality of the people with whom I was living.

This experience has also colored fieldwork that I have since done in other settings. For example, in the 1970s I worked with a cult of spiritualists in Baja California, the main figures of which are mostly older women who in all essential ways are shamans (Kearney 1977, 1978). One of these remarkable women, Micaela, who was also one of my key informants, lived in a lonely shack in the hills outside of Ensenada. She was engaged in a constant struggle with a "bad woman" down the road. I first became aware of this conflict one morning when I walked from my campsite to have my morning coffee with Micaela. She was haggard and disheveled from not having slept that night. When I asked her what was the matter she said, "Didn't you hear that owl in the tree outside my house? It was Josefa who was doing that to worry me and make me sick."

For country people in Mexico owls are harbingers of death, and for Micaela the presence of this one was a serious assault. On another occasion I arrived at Micaela's to find that she had spread a ring of ashes from her stove all around her shack and the little chicken house along side it. When I asked her what the ashes were for, she said they were to see tracks and confirm that Josefa was coming in the night in the form of a coyote to steal chickens.

These perilous ordeals of Micaela and the fear and hatred she had of her neighbor made me think back to the battle between Delfina and Gregoria. Had I not gotten caught up in it I don't think I would have been able to appreciate as well as I did the intense, florid shamanistic experiences of Micaela and her spiritualist sisters.

In the first years that I knew Micaela, she lived with a man who was a hopeless alcoholic for whom she would buy pure grain alcohol in a drug store when we went into town. Eventually his health disintegrated, and for some weeks before he died he was incontinent and had severe dysentery. As he was unable to leave his bed, Micaela kept him in improvised diapers.

By chance I arrived in Ensenada the day after he died. Neighbors down the road had sent for an undertaker, and the graduate student with whom I was working and I found Micaela in the mortuary with several of her spiritualist sisters. The hearse was just leaving for the public graveyard as we arrived. At the cemetery we found a grave that was almost completely dug and got gravediggers to come and finish it. Since there had been no money for a coffin, his body was in a battered cardboard box tied together with strips of an old sheet. The sun had already set when I finally found two boys to help me and the elderly undertaker carry the box to the gravesite. The box kept coming apart such that our friend's head dangled out. The first time I saw his head come out of the box the face of the dead man in Ixtepeji came into my mind and with it a shivering remembrance of the intense awe and fear that gripped me the night I had the problem with my arm.

It was almost dark when we finally got him into the ground and found the gravediggers again and had them come and fill the grave. As we were zigzagging around the mounds of freshly filled graves on our way to the car, I was almost certain that I saw an owl silently float through the black silhouetted trees and out of the graveyard in the direction of Micaela's house.

REFERENCES

KEARNEY, MICHAEL
1972   The Winds of Ixtepeji: World View and Society in a Zapotec Town. New
        York: Holt, Rinehart & Winston. Reissued Prospect Heights, IL: Wave-
        land Press, 1986.
1977   Oral Performance by Mexican Spiritualists in Possession Trance. Journal
        of Latin American Lore 3:309–328.
1978   Spiritualist Healing in Mexico. *In* Culture and Curing. Peter Morely and
        Roy Wallis, eds. Pp. 19–39. Pittsburgh: University of Pittsburgh Press.
1984   World View. Corte Madera, CA: Chandler & Sharp.

NINETEEN

Too Many Bananas, Not Enough Pineapples, and No Watermelon at All: Three Object Lessons in Living with Reciprocity

DAVID COUNTS

NO WATERMELON AT ALL

The woman came all the way through the village, walking between the two rows of houses facing each other between the beach and the bush, to the very last house standing on a little spit of land at the mouth of the Kaini River. She was carrying a watermelon on her head, and the house she came to was the government "rest house," maintained by the villagers for the occasional use of visiting officials. Though my wife and I were graduate students, not officials, and had asked for permission to stay in the village for the coming year, we were living in the rest house while the debate went on about where a house would be built for us. When the woman offered to sell us the watermelon for two shillings, we happily agreed, and the kids were delighted at the prospect of watermelon after yet another meal of rice and bully beef. The money changed hands and the seller left to return to her village, a couple of miles along the coast to the east.

It seemed only seconds later that the woman was back, reluctantly accompanying Kolia, the man who had already made it clear to us that he was the leader of the village. Kolia had no English, and at that time, three or four days into our first stay in Kandoka Village on the island of New Britain in Papua New Guinea, we had very little Tok Pisin. Language difficulties notwithstanding, Kolia managed to make his message clear: The woman had been outrageously wrong to sell us the watermelon for two shillings and we were to return it to her and reclaim our money immediately. When we tried to explain that we thought the price to be fair and were happy with the bargain, Kolia explained again and finally made it clear that we had missed the point. The problem wasn't that we had paid too much; it was that we had paid at all. Here he was, a leader, responsible for us while we were living in his village, and we had shamed him. How would it look if he let guests in his village *buy* food? If we wanted watermelons, or bananas, or anything else, all that was necessary was to let him know. He told us that it would be all right for us to give little gifts to people who brought food to us (and they surely would), but *no one* was to sell food to us. If anyone were to try—like this woman from Lauvore—then we should refuse. There would be plenty of watermelons without us buying them.

The woman left with her watermelon, disgruntled, and we were left with our two shillings. But we had learned the first lesson of many about living in Kandoka. We didn't pay money for food again that whole year, and we did get lots of food brought to us . . . but we never got another watermelon. That one was the last of the season.

LESSON 1: *In a society where food is shared or gifted as part of social life, you may not buy it with money.*

TOO   MANY   BANANAS

In the couple of months that followed the watermelon incident, we managed to become at least marginally competent in Tok Pisin, to negotiate the construction of a house on what we hoped was neutral ground, and to settle into the routine of our fieldwork. As our village leader had predicted, plenty of food was brought to us. Indeed, seldom did a day pass without something coming in—some sweet potatoes, a few taro, a papaya, the occasional pineapple, or some bananas—lots of bananas.

We had learned our lesson about the money, though, so we never even offered to buy the things that were brought, but instead made gifts, usually of tobacco to the adults or chewing gum to the children. Nor were we so gauche as to haggle with a giver over how much of a return gift was appropriate, though the two of us sometimes conferred as to whether what had been brought was a "two-stick" or a "three-stick" stalk, bundle, or whatever. A "stick" of tobacco was a single large leaf, soaked in rum and then twisted into a ropelike form. This, wrapped in half a sheet of newsprint (torn for use as cigarette paper), sold in the local trade stores for a shilling. Nearly all of the adults in the village smoked a great deal, and they seldom had much cash, so our stocks of twist tobacco and stacks of the Sydney *Morning Herald* (all, unfortunately, the same day's issue) were seen as a real boon to those who preferred "stick" to the locally grown product.

We had established a pattern with respect to the gifts of food. When a donor appeared at our veranda we would offer our thanks and talk with them for a few minutes (usually about our children, who seemed to hold a real fascination for the villagers and for whom most of the gifts were intended) and then we would inquire whether they could use some tobacco. It was almost never refused, though occasionally a small bottle of kerosene, a box of matches, some laundry soap, a cup of rice, or a tin of meat would be requested instead of (or even in addition to) the tobacco. Everyone, even Kolia, seemed to think this arrangement had worked out well.

Now, what must be kept in mind is that while we were following their rules—or seemed to be—we were *really still buying food.* In fact we kept a running account of what came in and what we "paid" for it. Tobacco as currency got a little complicated, but since the exchange rate was one stick to one shilling, it was not too much trouble as long as everyone was happy, and meanwhile we could account for the expenditure of "informant fees" and "household expenses." Another thing to keep in mind is that not only did we continue to think in terms of our buying the food that was brought, we thought of them as *selling it.* While it was true they never quoted us a price, they also never asked us if we needed or wanted whatever they had brought. It seemed clear to us that when an adult needed a stick of tobacco, or a child wanted some chewing gum (we had enormous quantities of small packets of Wrigley's for just such eventualities) they would find something surplus to their own needs and bring it along to our "store" and get what they wanted.

By late November 1966, just before the rainy season set in, the bananas were coming into flush, and whereas earlier we had received banana gifts by the "hand" (six or eight bananas in a cluster cut from the stalk), donors now began to bring bananas, "for the children," by the *stalk!* The Kaliai among whom we were living are not exactly specialists in banana cultivation—they only recognize about thirty varieties, while some of their neighbors have more than twice that many—but the kinds they produce differ considerably from each other in size, shape, and taste, so we were not dismayed when we had more than one stalk hanging on our veranda. The stalks ripen a bit at the time, and having some variety was nice. Still, by the time our accumulation had reached *four* complete stalks, the delights of variety had begun to pale a bit. The fruits were ripening progressively and it was clear that even if we and the kids ate nothing but bananas for the next week, some would still fall from the stalk onto the floor in a state of gross overripeness. This was the situation as, late one afternoon, a woman came bringing yet another stalk of bananas up the steps of the house.

Several factors determined our reaction to her approach: one was that there was literally no way we could possibly use the bananas. We hadn't quite reached the point of being crowded off our veranda by the stalks of fruit, but it was close. Another factor was that we were tired of playing the gift game. We had acquiesced in playing it—no one was permitted to sell us anything, and in turn we only gave things away, refusing under any circumstances to sell tobacco (or anything else) for money. But there had to be a limit. From our perspective what was at issue was that the woman wanted something and she had come to trade for it. Further, what she had brought to trade was something we neither wanted nor could use, and it should have been obvious to her. So we decided to bite the bullet.

The woman, Rogi, climbed the stairs to the veranda, took the stalk from where it was balanced on top of her head, and laid it on the floor with the word, "Here are some bananas for the children." Dorothy and I sat near her on the floor and thanked her for her thought but explained, "You know, we really have too many bananas—we can't use these; maybe you ought to give them to someone else. . . ." The woman looked mystified, then brightened and explained that she didn't want anything for them, she wasn't short of tobacco or anything. They were just a gift for the kids. Then she just sat there, and we sat there, and the bananas sat there, and we tried again. "Look," I said, pointing up to them and counting, "we've got four stalks already hanging here on the veranda—there are too many for us to eat now. Some are rotting already. Even if we eat only bananas, we can't keep up with what's here!"

Rogi's only response was to insist that these were a gift, and that she didn't want anything for them, so we tried yet another tack: "Don't *your* children like bananas?" When she admitted that they did, and that she had none at her house, we suggested that she should take them there. Finally, still puzzled, but convinced we weren't going to keep the bananas, she replaced them on her head, went down the stairs, and made her way back through the village toward her house.

As before, it seemed only moments before Kolia was making his way up the stairs, but this time he hadn't brought the woman in tow. "What was wrong with those bananas? Were they no good?" he demanded. We explained that there was nothing wrong with the bananas at all, but that we simply couldn't use them and it seemed foolish to take them when we had so many and Rogi's own children had none. We obviously didn't make ourselves clear, because Kolia then took up the same refrain that Rogi had—he insisted that we shouldn't be worried about taking the bananas, because they were a gift for the children and Rogi hadn't wanted anything for them. There was no reason, he added, to send her away with them—she would be ashamed. I'm afraid we must have seemed as if we were hard of hearing or thought he was, for our only response was to repeat our reasons. We went through it again—there they hung, one, two, three, *four* stalks of bananas, rapidly ripening and already far beyond our capacity to eat—we just weren't ready to accept any more and let them rot (and, we added to ourselves, pay for them with tobacco, to boot).

Kolia finally realized that we were neither hard of hearing nor intentionally offensive, but merely ignorant. He stared at us for a few minutes, thinking, and then asked: "Don't you frequently have visitors during the day and evening?" We nodded. Then he asked, "Don't you usually offer them cigarettes and coffee or milo?" Again, we nodded. "Did it ever occur to you to suppose," he said, "that your visitors might be hungry?" It was at this point in the conversation, as we recall, that we began to see the depth of the pit we had dug for ourselves. We nodded, hesitantly. His last words to us before he went down the stairs and stalked away were just what we were by that time afraid they might be. "When your guests are hungry, *feed them bananas!*"

LESSON 2: *Never refuse a gift, and never fail to return a gift. If you cannot use it, you can always give it away to someone else—there is no such thing as too much—there are never too many bananas.*

NOT ENOUGH PINEAPPLES

During the fifteen years between that first visit in 1966 and our residence there in 1981 we had returned to live in Kandoka village twice during the 1970s, and though there were a great many changes in the village, and indeed for all of Papua New Guinea during that time, we continued to live according to the lessons of reciprocity learned during those first months in the field. We bought no food for money and refused no gifts, but shared our surplus. As our family grew, we continued to be accompanied by our younger children. Our place in the village came to be something like that of educated Kaliai who worked far away in New Guinea. Our friends expected us to come "home" when we had leave, but knew that our work kept us away for long periods of time. They also credited us with knowing much more about the rules of their way of life than was our due. And we sometimes shared the delusion that we understood life in the village, but even fifteen years was not long enough to relieve the need for lessons in learning to live within the rules of gift exchange.

In the last paragraph I used the word *friends* to describe the villagers intentionally, but of course they were not all our friends. Over the years some really had become friends, others were acquaintances, others remained consultants or informants to whom we turned when we needed information. Still others, unfortunately, we did not like at all. We tried never to make an issue of these distinctions, of course, and to be evenhanded and generous to all, as they were to us. Although we almost never actually refused requests that were made of us, over the long term our reciprocity in the village was balanced. More was given to those who helped us the most, while we gave assistance or donations of small items even to those who were not close or helpful.

One elderly woman in particular was a trial for us. Sara was the eldest of a group of siblings and her younger brother and sister were both generous, informative, and delightful persons. Her younger sister, Makila, was a particularly close friend and consultant, and in deference to that friendship we felt awkward in dealing with the elder sister.

Sara was neither a friend nor an informant, but she had been, since she returned to live in the village at the time of our second trip in 1971, a constant (if minor) drain on our resources. She never asked for much at a time. A bar of soap, a box of matches, a bottle of kerosene, a cup of rice, some onions, a stick or two of tobacco, or some other small item was usually all that was at issue, but whenever she came around it was always to ask for something—or to let us know that when we left, we should give her some of the furnishings from the house. Too, unlike almost everyone else in the village, when she came, she was always empty-handed. We ate no taro from her gardens, and the kids chewed none of her sugarcane. In short, she was, as far as we could tell, a really grasping, selfish old woman—and we were not the only victims of her greed.

Having long before learned the lesson of the bananas, one day we had a stalk that was ripening so fast we couldn't keep up with it, so I pulled a few for our own use (we only had one stalk at the time) and walked down through the village to Ben's house, where his five children were playing. I sat down on his steps to talk, telling him that I intended to give the fruit to his kids. They never got them. Sara saw us from across the open plaza of the village and came rushing over, shouting, "My bananas!" Then she grabbed the stalk and went off gorging herself with them. Ben and I just looked at each other.

Finally it got to the point where it seemed to us that we had to do something. Ten years of being used was long enough. So there came the afternoon when Sara showed up to get some tobacco—again. But this time, when we gave her the two sticks she had demanded, we confronted her.

First, we noted the many times she had come to get things. We didn't mind sharing things, we explained. After all, we had plenty of tobacco and soap and rice and such, and most of it was there so that we could help our friends as they helped us, with folktales, information, or even gifts of food. The problem was that she kept coming to get things, but never came to talk, or to tell stories, or to bring some little something that the kids might like. Sara didn't argue—she agreed. "Look," we suggested, "it doesn't have to be much, and we don't mind giving you things—but you can help us. The kids like pineapples, and we don't have any—the next time you need something, bring something—like maybe a pineapple." Obviously somewhat embarrassed, she took her tobacco and left, saying that she would bring something soon. We were really pleased with ourselves. It had been a very difficult thing to do, but it was done, and we were convinced that either she would start bringing things or not come. It was as if a burden had lifted from our shoulders.

It worked. Only a couple of days passed before Sara was back, bringing her bottle to get it filled with kerosene. But this time, she came carrying the biggest, most beautiful pineapple we had seen the entire time we had been there. We had a friendly talk, filled her kerosene container, and hung the pineapple up on the veranda to ripen just a little further. A few days later we cut and ate it, and whether the satisfaction it gave came from the fruit or from its source would be hard to say, but it was delicious. That, we assumed, was the end of that irritant.

We were wrong, of course. The next afternoon, Mary, one of our best friends for years (and no relation to Sara), dropped by for a visit. As we talked, her eyes scanned the veranda. Finally she asked whether we hadn't had a pineapple there yesterday. We said we had, but that we had already eaten it. She commented that it had been a really nice-looking one, and we told her that it had been the best we had eaten in months. Then, after a pause, she asked, "Who brought it to you?" We smiled as we said, "Sara!" because Mary would appreciate our coup—she had commented many times in the past on the fact that Sara only *got* from us and never gave. She was silent for a moment, and then she said, "Well, I'm glad you enjoyed it—my father was waiting until it was fully ripe to harvest it for you, but when it went missing I thought maybe it was the one you had here. I'm glad to see you got it. I thought maybe a thief had eaten it in the bush."

LESSON 3: *Where reciprocity is the rule and gifts are the idiom, you cannot demand a gift, just as you cannot refuse a request.*

It says a great deal about the kindness and patience of the Kaliai people that they have been willing to be our hosts for all these years despite our blunders and lack of good manners. They have taught us a lot, and these three lessons are certainly not the least important things we learned.

TWENTY

Lessons in Introductory Anthropology from the Bakairi Indians

DEBRA S. PICCHI

The Bakairi Indians interacted with many types of non-Indians. Yet they had never worked with an anthropologist before I came to study in their village. I spent fourteen months with them, and at times, I am certain that my inexplicable customs frustrated them to the point of anger. I know I had plenty of opportunities to consider both the superficial and profound cultural differences that separated us. I, like so many who preceded me, found myself learning more than I ever thought possible about a people's traditions as well as relearning in more meaningful ways basic tenets taught in introductory anthropology courses.

I planned to study how the Bakairi used their natural resources and to compare their methods with those employed by other, similar groups in central Brazil. As an ecological anthropologist, I was less interested in such aspects of culture as child rearing than in modes of production and labor organization.

Yet participant-observation, still one of the hallmarks of anthropological fieldwork, disallows selective learning about a people. Adjusting to a new culture provides on a daily basis many different types of experiences that prevent anthropologists from concentrating too assiduously on any one aspect of a people's traditions.

I had done my homework before I entered the field to begin research. I knew that the Bakairi Indians inhabited a small reservation in Mato Grosso, a central Brazilian state. About 280 of them lived in a single village on the banks of the Paranatinga River. The village was made up of some sixty wattle-and-daub houses in which small extended families resided. A ceremonial men's house, where the men congregated to discuss politics and to perform rituals, was situated in the center of the village. The Bakairi were fishermen and horticulturalists, raising manioc and rice in gardens carved out of the gallery forests that lined the river. They also hunted to a certain extent. Their religion was animistic, and shamans, who were responsible for curing diseases and performing witchcraft, were the only religious specialists.

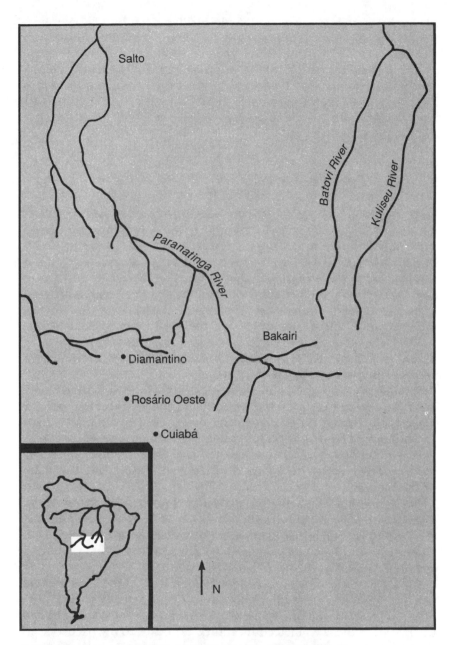

Bakairi Indian settlements in Mato Grosso, Central Brazil

I entered the reservation in March, the beginning of the dry season. I flew in a two-seater plane, carrying with me four hundred kilograms of supplies. Although I wanted to live with an Indian family, a technique I had successfully used in another Indian group with which I worked,

I brought enough food so that I could survive if left on my own. I anticipated staying two to four months before leaving the reservation to restock.

As the plane touched down on the grassy airstrip beside the village, I felt extremely nervous. I wondered if I brought enough trade goods and medicines. I speculated about whether my coffee and cigarette supplies would hold out. Yet, most important, I worried about whether the Bakairi would like me.

HUMANS AND LANGUAGE

Rays from the setting sun colored the water purple as I turned away from the river bank and clambered awkwardly up the steep path to the village. After only a month in the Bakairi village, I was still unsure of which stones were safe to walk on, so I moved slowly, not wanting to risk a sprained ankle. Indian women, agile and strong, passed me as if I were standing still even though many of them carried huge aluminum pots of water balanced on their heads. Snippets of a conversation spoken in Portuguese drifted back to me as I followed them to the village.

"She doesn't speak well," Cici, a young mother of two, complained loudly to her friends. "I think she must be as stupid as those giant anteaters that wander around the jungle."

Domingas, a frail old woman, answered Cici softly, "You ask too much. She has been with us only a few weeks. You cannot expect her to speak Bakairi as well as we do. Be patient and she too will be a human being."

They turned onto the main path leading up to the center of the village with me trailing behind. The warmth of the sun was gone, and dusky shadows crept toward the village from the Urubu Mountain, the home of the vulture.

Maisa, another young mother, spoke up. "I don't know. I'm worried. The *Alemao* really is not learning very fast at all. Geraldina told me that she tried to explain to her the story of how the jaguar copulated with a human to produce our people. Geraldina said she didn't think that girl understood two words of what she told her."

I made a mental note to record in my field journal the term *Alemao* as it was applied to me in this discussion. *Alemao* actually means "German" and refers to the nationality of the first Europeans who contacted the Bakairi in the late nineteenth century. I quickened my pace to keep up with the Indian women.

Domingas's placid voice rose again. "Brazilians visited here before. They stayed for as long if not longer than the *Alemao*, and they didn't even attempt to learn to speak our language. Why say hurtful things about this girl who at least tries?"

A flap of wings made me look up in time to see a black cloud of bats shoot out from a huge tree to the right of the path. They veered sharply upward, on their way to forage fruits and berries in the forest before returning to the tree before dawn. My mind automatically registered that they were too large to be vampire bats that suck the blood of animals and humans, sometimes communicating dangerous diseases such as rabies.

Then Inês spoke sharply, perhaps too sharply for a woman of her age when addressing an elder, "*Alemaes* and Brazilians are different, Domingas, and you know it. They are from different parts of the world. Your mother herself met one of the first *Alemaes* who entered our lands so many years ago."

Cici chimed in, "Yes, the *Alemaes* have always asked us questions about our ways and written things about us on paper that they take away with them. Brazilians are not like that. They bring us medicine and take care of the sick. How can you expect Brazilians to learn our language and become like us? That is the job of the *Alemao*, and I tell you, this girl will fail."

Domingas sniffed while the other women gave a collective sigh of discouragement. I had heard them give similar sighs in other contexts, such as when Maria's husband had come back drunk from a nearby town. He bought *pinga* with all the money he had made working for two weeks on a nearby ranch. The sigh meant something like, "The situation is impossible, but what can you do?"

We approached the first houses of the village. Children played outside while women and men conversed in small groups. Shouts of laughter rose from further down the lane as some of the girls flirted with eligible young men. The discussion terminated as the women separated to go to their own homes.

I slowly made my way back to my hut, calling out to those I knew and stopping to chat with those I especially liked. Inside my house, I lighted a candle and closed the shutters so that insects would not come in. Then I hung up my towel to dry and made some coffee on the alcohol stove. As I sipped the steaming beverage, I puzzled through what I had just heard.

I did not doubt that the women carefully planned what had just transpired. They spoke in Portuguese so that I could understand them, rather than in Bakairi, which they normally would have used among themselves. In addition, they had made certain that I would overhear them. This allowed for effective criticism to take place without a direct confrontation, which is avoided at all costs in an Indian village. In other words, their behavior was beyond reproach. They were disturbed about my performance and communicated their displeasure in a way consistent with Bakairi etiquette.

Yet I felt angry, believing they were being unjustly critical without giving me the opportunity to defend myself. It was true I was not intensely studying Bakairi. Most of my energy went toward gathering data on demographics and garden harvests, which were the focus of my research. What time I had left went toward language acquisition, but my progress was slow.

I blew out the candle and climbed into my hammock. I continued to feel perplexed about why my ability to speak Bakairi was so important to the women. Many people in the village spoke Portuguese, which allowed me to communicate in that language about most subjects. Why was Bakairi so important?

Then I remembered Domingas's comment about becoming a human. Perhaps to them, the ability to speak Bakairi was the essence of being a human. Without it, one would be relegated to the status of a Brazilian, who brought medicine, or an *Alemao*, who wrote things on paper. Although there was nothing intrinsically wrong with either of these identities, assuming a role closer to that of the Bakairi was preferable from the anthropological point of view.

The equation looked more interesting as I closely considered it. I knew from the anthropological literature that one of the key aspects of the definition of *Homo sapiens* was the ability to use language. The sophisticated capability to handle symbols and to move back and forth conceptually in time marked the beginning of a unique period in history. Cultural evolutionary rates exploded when our species began to use language.

The Bakairi were merely reaffirming a basic principle and extrapolating from it as they applied it to their culture. They believe that humans speak Bakairi. Without this ability, one could not understand Bakairi culture in all of its intricacies. The women were trying to tell me that a grasp of the language was a necessary precondition for an effective study of their traditions.

As I dozed off, I realized that I had just relearned a basic anthropological lesson—one that is discussed in the first month of every introductory course I have ever taken or taught. Yet somehow its significance had recently been obscured by other specialized considerations more germane to my research.

A pair of tarantulas caught my eye as they scurried across the earthen floor of the hut. I decided that I was too tired to care.

HUMANS AND SEXUAL MORES

The rains came. Torrential sheets of water fell on the village every day, transforming paths into muddy streams. My hut leaked but no more than any other. The palm thatch that served as a roof was relatively new so that it shed water easily. Other people with older huts complained of rivulets of water falling on them.

Everything inside was soggy or moldy. My cotton hammock, my clothes, my notebooks became limp in the humidity. A coating of mold covered the inside of the lens of my camera, and my leather shoes sprouted something that looked distinctly alive.

The humidity and heat were incredible. My shirt stuck to my back, and beads of sweat dripped regularly off my nose. Armies of mosquitoes swarmed audibly around me whether I was down at the river, in the forest, or sitting near the men's house in the center of the village.

I felt dejected and was not surprised when I came down with a cold. My symptoms were normal: a runny nose, aches and pains, and digestive tract disorders. I took decongestants and aspirin and waited for it to pass.

One rainy afternoon I was resting in my hammock reading a novel, a luxury I allowed myself on special occasions, such as when I was sick. Space was so limited on the small plane I used that I brought only a few books into the reservation. I treasured them and read them as slowly as I could.

When Maiare entered the hut, I had been absorbed in the dry and clean southern town described in *To Kill a Mockingbird.* I sat up with a start as he flicked the water from his hair all over me.

"Maiare, you're getting me all wet," I said severely.

"Sorry," he responded in a despondent manner. "I just got back from fishing and caught nothing as usual."

"I thought you said fishing was impossible when it rains because the fish don't bite. They are full from eating what washes into the water from the forest," I said. "Why did you even bother to go out on the river? Surely you must have just sat in a wet canoe and got rained on."

Maiare sat on the small plank of wood that I had pushed up against the clay wall of the hut. It served as a chair when visitors came to see me. He made an impatient gesture with his hand.

"Why?" he snapped. "You ask why? I'll tell you why," he continued with the frustration in his voice becoming increasingly apparent. "My wife is making me crazy. I had to get out of the house."

I made a humming noise that the Indians used to signal agreement or openness to hearing more. I started to heat some water on the alcohol stove. Clearly Maiare could use some strong sweet tea. As I moved around the hut, dodging leaks, his voice became bitter.

"And I'll tell you something. If she thinks I don't know what's going on, then she's dumber than a parrot in a cage. I know she's having sex with Jeremi."

I poured the hot water into a mug and stirred in lots of sugar, which I knew the Indians liked. Then I handed the cup to Maiare and went back to swing in my hammock. I tried to act in a casual manner, but I was excited. None of the Bakairi had ever confided in me about their personal problems. If I could get Maiare to tell me more about his situation, then I might understand better how sexual behavior was organized and how conflicts were resolved in the village.

"So," I said in a vague way, trying to disguise my interest, "Jeremi is sleeping with Balbina. Does Vita know about this?"

"Of course she knows. She's Jeremi's wife, isn't she? She'd be the first to realize it," Maiare said with surprise.

"Well," I replied, "it isn't always like that with my people. They say the spouse is always the last to know." I paused and then asked, "Is Vita upset?"

Maiare gave me a look of disbelief. "You ask the strangest questions, *Alemao.* Vita is very upset. A few days ago, she kicked Jeremi so hard he fell out of his hammock."

Maiare handed me back the empty mug, and I jumped up quickly to make more. I had additional questions to ask so I intended to ply him with tea for as long as possible. I again pumped up the alcohol stove and began heating more water. Maiare moped with his head in his hands.

I chose my words carefully as I asked my next question. "If you know and Vita knows, and you are both upset, then what can you do?"

Maiare's face brightened. "Vita could threaten to visit her parents, and Jeremi would get very upset because, without her, who would cook? Who would take care of the children? Who would wash his clothes?"

He chuckled gleefully as he pictured his enemy in such dire straits. The rains had stopped, and the cackle of chickens could be heard. One hen regally entered my hut, pausing on the doorstep as if to decide whether it was worthwhile to enter.

"Couldn't you go home to your parents?" I asked as I shooed it away. I didn't want it going to the bathroom on my floor.

Maiare shook his head sadly. "A man would lose face if he did that. No, we men must stay in the houses we build, pretending that nothing is wrong, even if it means we go hungry because there is no one to cook our food." He sighed as he stood up, "I guess I could beat her with my belt. Then she might stay home more often."

I was alarmed and asked quickly, "You would do that?"

Maiare turned to me and said grimly, "If I did, she would probably go to stay with her parents for a few months, and then I'd be stuck with no one to take care of the house. Plus she might leave the children, and then I'd really have problems." He turned and strode off down the path.

Later I sat in my hut, paper and pen before me, and tried to organize what I had learned. "Fact one," I said to myself, "the Bakairi have extra-marital affairs." Both men and women were allowed to have multiple sex partners, unlike some societies where only men are allowed to have affairs.

"Fact two," I went on, "the Bakairi experience jealous feelings when they discover their spouses are sleeping with other people." Maiare was obviously very troubled, and hadn't he said that Vita had become so angry one night that she had kicked Jeremi? The reactions of the spouses suggested to me that the Bakairi did not casually accept affairs as many people believed they did.

Some anthropologists contend that jealousy is a function of capitalist society. That is, as people begin to control labor, the means of production, and capital, they view their own personal relationships in the same way and react possessively when threatened with loss. If a society lacks capitalist structures, as did Bakairi culture, then jealousy would be absent. "So much for that theory," I thought.

"Fact three," I continued, "the Bakairi appear to have few options when faced with infidelity on the part of their spouses." Men had fewer choices than women did, it seemed. They were able to beat their wives, but this was not considered an effective way to terminate an affair because the wife might leave. Or they could stoically wait for the affair to end, as Maiare seemed to be doing. I noted that he had not brought up attacking or killing Balbina's lover. Also, the option of divorce had not come up. Although the Bakairi recognized the practice, adultery apparently was not a legitimate reason for it.

A woman could leave the house of her husband and return to her parent's home for extended visits. Or she could wait for the affair to end, as I supposed Vita was doing. Violence and divorce did not appear to be appropriate responses for a woman either.

What puzzled me was what kept Bakairi couples together. Why was divorce not an option? It is in many cultures, especially in those cases where it is essential to know the father of a woman's child. For example, if the transfer of great wealth or title is contingent upon the identity of the child's father, then a wife's infidelity is a much more serious matter.

Then I recalled Maiare's parting words. He said that if Balbina left him, he would be responsible for housework and child care, as well as for his own duties. That suggested that the division of labor in Bakairi society was complementary: Men depended on women, and women on men, to perform specific key tasks. Divorce would rip the social tapestry apart. As Maiare said, he could not wash clothes at the river with the women. It was ludicrous to even imagine it. Furthermore, Balbina could not fish and cut down trees in the forest to make a garden. That was "men's work."

The rain began again, and I crawled back into my hammock. Another basic anthropology lesson had been endorsed by Maiare. He had reminded me that interlocking role definitions between the sexes are critical for the smooth functioning of a society. Much would be forgiven between men and women if they needed each other in profoundly basic ways.

Lightning cracked the sky. I wondered where Balbina was.

HUMANS AND THE SUPERNATURAL

"You know what I think?" young Marcedes asked darkly. "I think Bolo has bewitched me and that's why I'm sick and confused. I believe he got Vincente to cast a spell on me so that I'd be destroyed. I'm going to Paulino's tonight to be cured. Then he'll see."

I did not think this was the time to remind Marcedes that he had recently visited a nearby Brazilian town where he had gotten drunk, according to some of the other men who had gone on the trip. In addition he probably picked up a flu or a cold. The Indians always came back tired and sick when they left the reservation.

I kept quiet as Marcedes sat and brooded. We were perched on a plank of wood outside his hut. I heard his wife, Lita, pounding rice with a pestle in back of the house. The rhythmic thumping was relaxing.

"So Marcedes is going to be cured tonight," I thought. I was interested in seeing a Bakairi curing ritual. I had not witnessed one since I had been in the village. Curing took place regularly and openly in another Indian culture I had studied. However, the Bakairi viewed it as a secret practice that took place at night in private.

I did not know how to ask Marcedes to take me to Paulino's that night. I took a risk and asked, "I have some lovely red cloth Lita might like to have. Do you think I should give it to her?"

Marcedes cheered up immediately. I knew that Lita had been angry with him since he returned from town because he had spent so much money on food and liquor that he had little left over to make household purchases. He could give her the red material as a peace offering.

"However," I said slowly and then paused. "However, perhaps you could do something for me in return. I would very much like to go with you to Paulino's tonight to see you cured."

"I can manage that," he smiled as he helped me get up from the bench. "Let's go get that cloth."

That night was blacker than any I could remember. Usually a moon or stars provided some illumination. However, it seemed that a blanket had been thrown over the village preventing even my flashlight from helping us pick our way along the path to Paulino's hut. I was a little nervous because recently a snake had bitten a man as he was walking home on a dark night such as this. I walked slowly, hoping anything ahead of us would have time to get out of our way.

Paulino's wife, Judite, met us at the door and efficiently shepherded us inside. Paulino was waiting by the fire, already partially drugged from sucking on the huge green tobacco cigar he held in his hand. He started to say something to Marcedes but vomited instead.

Paulino's eyes were clearer after he had finished retching, and for the first time he seemed to notice me.

"Oh yes," he said with slurred speech, "I heard you were coming. Why don't you sit down with my wife over there."

He pointed vaguely in the direction of Judite, and we women retired to sit on a skin placed on the floor. Marcedes lay down on a hammock, while Paulino started to chant in a low voice. Soon he began to stamp one of his feet, circling Marcedes's hammock several times. Then there was quiet, and I saw in the glow of fire that Paulino was lighting his cigar again. He blew smoke onto Marcedes, muttering in a muffled voice. Then he discarded the cigar and began to massage Marcedes's arms and legs. The smoke-blowing and massaging continued for nearly half an hour.

My legs cramped, and my attention wandered as the curing ceremony wore on. I looked around the hut and saw that, although it was small and simple like mine, expensive machetes and rifles were hanging from the walls. They suggested that Paulino was wealthy by Bakairi standards. I knew that shamanism, or religious curing and sorcery, paid well, so I was not surprised.

Paulino sucked deeply on the cigar again and apparently became so dizzy that he fell on the floor. I saw his hands fumbling in a dark corner. He turned away from us and began to vomit again. After he had exhausted himself, Judite got up and put more wood on the fire. She helped him over to a skin that lay spread out. An eager Marcedes joined him there.

"What did you find?" he asked anxiously. "What did you discover?"

Paulino shook his head sadly. "It is good that you came because it is certain you were bewitched."

He opened his hand and showed Marcedes a small, smooth amber-colored stone, a piece of red material, and some fecal matter that looked like it came from an animal.

"The stone was lodged near your heart where it weakened you, and the droppings are from the spirit who chased away all your good luck," Paulino explained.

"And the red thing?" asked Marcedes, who was obviously strongly affected by what Paulino had just related.

"The red is from your blood, which has been poisoned by the sorcery of the enemy who tries to rob you of your life."

Judite began to bustle around, a cue for us to leave. Marcedes profusely thanked Paulino for saving him and gave him a small bag of fishhooks and line in payment for his work.

We started to walk home just as a light rain began. It was the end of the rainy season, and occasional showers still unexpectedly occurred. I wrapped myself in the plastic slicker I had gotten into the habit of carrying with me and asked Marcedes what would happen now.

"Happen? What should happen?" he answered. "Everything is going to be all right. I'll be better tommorrow. You'll see."

I groped my way back to my hut after waving good night to Marcedes. I lighted a candle and then found a cigarette, which I slowly smoked. The shamanistic curing ritual I had just observed was so obviously chicanery that I had trouble understanding how Marcedes, whom I considered to be an intelligent and perceptive man, could have been so easily duped. I realized that Paulino had really been drugged by tobacco and that the substance in such strong doses induced vomiting. However, I also knew that the stone and droppings were not placed in Marcedes's body through witchcraft and that Paulino had not removed them with magic. I believed Paulino hid them on the floor until he needed them. He picked them up when he fell down.

I was clearly not thinking like an anthropologist. Maybe the rainy season had sapped me of the energy I needed to emotionally grasp the cultural realities around me. I needed a break. Could I afford the time to take a few weeks off and go to Brasilia? I'd stay in a hotel, take baths every night, eat tons of chocolate, and go to the movies. I promised myself to consider the possibility of leaving the reservation for a while just as soon as I woke up in the morning.

I am not sure what woke me that night. It had cleared, and the moon was up. Some beams made their way through the cracks in the shutters and shimmered on my blanket. I thought some more about Marcedes and Paulino.

Maybe the practical reality of curing or sorcery really made no difference. "Did that really happen?" was not a legitimate question to ask because the scientific validity of Bakairi witchcraft was not the issue. Rather, what was crucial was how people like Marcedes related the supernatural to their daily lives. The vitality and significance of witchcraft were obvious when one observed Paulino's commitment to his art and Marcedes's concern about his personal problems. Theirs was a living ideological system that helped the men conceptualize and act within their cultural world.

The question of whether a spirit literally did leave those droppings was of no value. The central issue was whether or not the shamanistic ritual rendered Marcedes's experience comprehensible to him.

As the moonbeams climbed up the walls of my hut, I realized I had rediscovered another fundamental anthropological tenet as a result of my evening with Paulino and Marcedes. The supernatural plays a very real and critical role in the lives of humans. And we do not find anything comparable to it among other animals. We are unique in this way.

A shaft of moonlight illuminated the rafters of my hut. I went back to sleep.

BASIC LESSONS RELEARNED

I had given away everything that would not fit in the plane. The usual arguing about "who should have what" took place, but in the end everyone seemed satisfied. I was not too concerned about a completely equitable distribution of goods since I knew that kinship networks and ritual festivities would ensure a far more just allocation of my possessions than I could hope to achieve.

The past fourteen months had gone by rapidly. At first each hour crawled by, and I carefully marked off the days on my calendar. However, by the end of my field trip, I lost track of time. I would have liked to have stayed a few more months because it was the dry season again, and those were my favorite months. Yet I knew it was time to leave.

I had secured a great deal of ecological data, and I believed I would be able to complete my report as planned. I checked points off in my head. Yes, I had information on fishing and hunting catches. And I had weighed garden harvests. Plus I was lucky enough to secure some demographic records that went back some fifty years. I had verified them with the Bakairi for accuracy and knew I had some great material.

Nevertheless, other experiences I had undergone with the Indians somehow overshadowed my project. Weighing manioc in Geraldina's garden seemed far less significant than overhearing the women who had passed me on the river path complaining that I was learning Bakairi too slowly. Maiare's pain and frustration over his wife's affair had a greater impact on me than did my discovery that the Bakairi consume less high-quality protein than they probably should. Marcedes's attempt to understand his sick and confused feelings upon returning from a trip to a Brazilian town was more interesting than the natural and actual population increase rates I calculated.

These were the people who retaught me the basic lessons of anthropology. They took me to the heart of the discipline where it is affirmed that we are all human and that the differences between us are merely variations of the same theme.

I heard the engine of a plane and walked over to the landing strip. We said goodbye with little ceremony because it is believed that one must leave sorrow behind quickly. The plane took off, and I watched the huts that lined the big green river fade into the distance.

SUGGESTED READING

PICCHI, DEBRA S.
2000   The Bakairí Indians of Brazil: Politics, Ecology, and Change. Prospect Heights, IL: Waveland Press.

TWENTY-ONE

Arranging a Marriage in India

SERENA NANDA

Sister and doctor brother-in-law invite correspondence from North Indian professionals only, for a beautiful, talented, sophisticated, intelligent sister, 5′ 3″, slim, M.A. in textile design, father a senior civil officer. Would prefer immigrant doctors, between 26–29 years. Reply with full details and returnable photo.

A well-settled uncle invites matrimonial correspondence from slim, fair, educated South Indian girl, for his nephew, 25 years, smart, M.B.A., green card holder, 5′ 6″. Full particulars with returnable photo appreciated.

Matrimonial Advertisements, India Abroad

In India, almost all marriages are arranged. Even among the educated middle classes in modern, urban India, marriage is as much a concern of the families as it is of the individuals. So customary is the practice of arranged marriage that there is a special name for a marriage which is not arranged: It is called a "love match."

On my first field trip to India, I met many young men and women whose parents were in the process of "getting them married." In many cases, the bride and groom would not meet each other before the marriage. At most they might meet for a brief conversation, and this meeting would take place only after their parents had decided that the match was suitable. Parents do not compel their children to marry a person who either marriage partner finds objectionable. But only after one match is refused will another be sought.

As a young American woman in India for the first time, I found this custom of arranged marriage oppressive. How could any intelligent young person agree to such a marriage without great reluctance? It was contrary to everything I believed about the importance of romantic love as the only basis of a happy marriage. It also clashed with my strongly held notions that the choice of such an intimate and permanent relationship could be made only by the individuals involved. Had anyone tried to arrange my marriage, I would have been defiant and rebellious!

At the first opportunity, I began, with more curiosity than tact, to question the young people I met on how they felt about this practice.

Sita, one of my young informants, was a college graduate with a degree in political science. She had been waiting for over a year while her parents were arranging a match for her. I found it difficult to accept the docile manner in which this well-educated young woman awaited the outcome of a process that would result in her spending the rest of her life with a man she hardly knew, a virtual stranger, picked out by her parents.

"How can you go along with this?" I asked her, in frustration and distress. "Don't you care who you marry?"

"Of course I care," she answered. "This is why I must let my parents choose a boy for me. My marriage is too important to be arranged by such an inexperienced person as myself. In such matters, it is better to have my parents' guidance."

I had learned that young men and women in India do not date and have very little social life involving members of the opposite sex. Although I could not disagree with Sita's reasoning, I continued to pursue the subject.

"But how can you marry the first man you have ever met? Not only have you missed the fun of meeting a lot of different people, but you have not given yourself the chance to know who is the right man for you."

"Meeting with a lot of different people doesn't sound like any fun at all," Sita answered. "One hears that in America the girls are spending all their time worrying about whether they will meet a man and get married. Here we have the chance to enjoy our life and let our parents do this work and worrying for us."

She had me there. The high anxiety of the competition to "be popular" with the opposite sex certainly was the most prominent feature of life as an American teenager in the late fifties. The endless worrying about the rules that governed our behavior and about our popularity ratings sapped both our self-esteem and our enjoyment of adolescence. I reflected that absence of this competition in India most certainly may have contributed to the self-confidence and natural charm of so many of the young women I met.

And yet, the idea of marrying a perfect stranger, whom one did not know and did not "love," so offended my American ideas of individualism and romanticism, that I persisted with my objections.

"I still can't imagine it," I said. "How can you agree to marry a man you hardly know?"

"But of course he will be known. My parents would never arrange a marriage for me without knowing all about the boy's family background. Naturally we will not rely only on what the family tells us. We will check the particulars out ourselves. No one will want their daughter to marry into a family that is not good. All these things we will know beforehand."

Impatiently, I responded, "Sita, I don't mean know the family, I mean, know the man. How can you marry someone you don't know personally and don't love? How can you think of spending your life with someone you may not even like?"

"If he is a good man, why should I not like him?" she said. "With you people, you know the boy so well before you marry, where will be the fun to get married? There will be no mystery and no romance. Here we have the whole of our married life to get to know and love our husband. This way is better, is it not?"

Her response made further sense, and I began to have second thoughts on the matter. Indeed, during months of meeting many intelligent young Indian people, both male and female, who had the same ideas as Sita, I saw arranged marriages in a different light. I also saw the importance of the family in Indian life and realized that a couple who took their marriage into their own hands was taking a big risk, particularly if their families were irreconcilably opposed to the match. In a country where every important resource in life—a job, a house, a social circle—is gained through family connections, it seemed foolhardy to cut oneself off from a supportive social network and depend solely on one person for happiness and success.

Six years later I returned to India to again do fieldwork, this time among the middle class in Bombay, a modern, sophisticated city. From the experience of my earlier visit, I decided to include a study of arranged marriages in my project. By this time I had met many Indian couples whose marriages had been arranged and who seemed very happy. Particularly in contrast to the fate of many of my married friends in the United States who were already in the process of divorce, the positive aspects of arranged marriages appeared to me to outweigh the negatives. In fact, I thought I might even participate in arranging a marriage myself. I had been fairly successful in the United States in "fixing up" many of my friends, and I was confident that my matchmaking skills could be easily applied to this new situation, once I learned the basic rules. "After all," I thought, "how complicated can it be? People want pretty much the same things in a marriage whether it is in India or America."

An opportunity presented itself almost immediately. A friend from my previous Indian trip was in the process of arranging for the marriage of her eldest son. In India there is a perceived shortage of "good boys," and since my friend's family was eminently respectable and the boy himself personable, well educated, and nice looking, I was sure that by the end of my year's fieldwork, we would have found a match.

The basic rule seems to be that a family's reputation is most important. It is understood that matches would be arranged only within the same caste and general social class, although some crossing of subcastes is permissible if the class positions of the bride's and groom's families are similar. Although dowry is now prohibited by law in India, extensive gift exchanges took place with every marriage. Even when the boy's family do not "make demands," every girl's family nevertheless feels the obligation to give the traditional gifts, to the girl, to the boy, and to the boy's family. Particularly when the couple would be living in the joint family—that is, with the boy's parents and his married brothers and their families, as well as with unmarried siblings—which is still very common even among the urban, upper-middle class in India, the girl's parents are anxious to establish smooth relations between their family and that of the boy. Offering the proper gifts, even when not called "dowry," is often an important factor in influencing the relationship between the bride's and groom's families and perhaps, also, the treatment of the bride in her new home.

In a society where divorce is still a scandal and where, in fact, the divorce rate is exceedingly low, an arranged marriage is the beginning of a lifetime relationship not just between the bride and groom but between their families as well. Thus, while a girl's looks are important, her character is even more so, for she is being judged as a prospective daughter-in-law as much as a prospective bride. Where she would be living in a joint family, as was the case with my friend, the girl's ability to get along harmoniously in a family is perhaps the single most important quality in assessing her suitability.

My friend is a highly esteemed wife, mother, and daughter-in-law. She is religious, soft-spoken, modest, and deferential. She rarely gossips and never quarrels, two qualities highly desirable in a woman. A family that has the reputation for gossip and conflict among its womenfolk will not find it easy to get good wives for their sons. Parents will not want to send their daughter to a house in which there is conflict.

My friend's family were originally from North India. They had lived in Bombay, where her husband owned a business, for forty years. The family had delayed in seeking a match for their eldest son because he had been an Air Force pilot for several years, stationed in such remote places that it had seemed fruitless to try to find a girl who would be willing to accompany him. In their social class, a military career, despite its economic security, has little prestige and is considered a drawback in finding a suitable bride. Many families would not allow their daughters to marry a man in an occupation so potentially dangerous and which requires so much moving around.

The son had recently left the military and joined his father's business. Since he was a college graduate, modern, and well traveled, from such a good family, and, I thought, quite handsome, it seemed to me that he, or rather his family, was in a position to pick and choose. I said as much to my friend.

While she agreed that there were many advantages on their side, she also said, "We must keep in mind that my son is both short and dark; these are drawbacks in finding the right match." While the boy's height had not escaped my notice, "dark" seemed to me inaccurate; I would have called him "wheat" colored perhaps, and in any case, I did not realize that color would be a consideration. I discovered, however, that while a boy's skin color is a less important consideration than a girl's, it is still a factor.

An important source of contacts in trying to arrange her son's marriage was my friend's social club in Bombay. Many of the women had daughters of the right age, and some had already expressed an interest in my friend's son. I was most enthusiastic about the possibilities of one particular family who had five daughters, all of whom were pretty, demure, and well educated. Their mother had told my friend, "You can have your pick for your son, whichever one of my daughters appeals to you most."

I saw a match in sight. "Surely," I said to my friend, "we will find one there. Let's go visit and make our choice." But my friend held back; she did not seem to share my enthusiasm, for reasons I could not then fathom.

When I kept pressing for an explanation of her reluctance, she admitted, "See, Serena, here is the problem. The family has so many daughters, how will they be able to provide nicely for any of them? We are not making any demands, but still, with so many daughters to marry off, one wonders whether she will even be able to make a proper wedding. Since this is our eldest son, it's best if we marry him to a girl who is the only daughter, then the wedding will truly be a gala affair." I argued that surely the quality of the girls themselves made up for any deficiency in the elaborateness of the wedding. My friend admitted this point but still seemed reluctant to proceed.

"Is there something else," I asked her, "some factor I have missed?" "Well," she finally said, "there is one other thing. They have one daughter already married and living in Bombay. The mother is always complaining to me that the girl's in-laws don't let her visit her own family often enough. So it makes me wonder, will she be that kind of mother who always wants her daughter at her own home? This will prevent the girl from adjusting to our house. It is not a good thing." And so, this family of five daughters was dropped as a possibility.

Somewhat disappointed, I nevertheless respected my friend's reasoning and geared up for the next prospect. This was also the daughter of a woman in my friend's social club. There was clear interest in this family and I could see why. The family's reputation was excellent; in fact, they came from a subcaste slightly higher than my friend's own. The girl, who was an only daughter, was pretty and well educated and had a brother studying in the United States. Yet, after expressing an interest to me in this family, all talk of them suddenly died down and the search began elsewhere.

"What happened to that girl as a prospect?" I asked one day. "You never mention her any more. She is so pretty and so educated, what did you find wrong?"

"She is too educated. We've decided against it. My husband's father saw the girl on the bus the other day and thought her forward. A girl who 'roams about' the city by herself is not the girl for our family." My disappointment this time was even greater, as I thought the son would have liked the girl very much. But then I thought, my friend is right, a girl who is going to live in a joint family cannot be too independent or she will make life miserable for everyone. I also learned that if the family of the girl has even a slightly higher social status than the family of the boy, the bride may think herself too good for them, and this too will cause problems. Later my friend admitted to me that this had been an important factor in her decision not to pursue the match.

The next candidate was the daughter of a client of my friend's husband. When the client learned that the family was looking for a match for their son, he said, "Look no further, we have a daughter." This man then invited my friends to dinner to see the girl. He had already seen their son at the office and decided that "he liked the boy." We all went together for tea, rather than dinner—it was less of a commitment—and while we were there, the girl's mother showed us around the house. The girl was studying for her exams and was briefly introduced to us.

After we left, I was anxious to hear my friend's opinion. While her husband liked the family very much and was impressed with his client's business accomplishments and reputation, the wife didn't like the girl's looks. "She is short, no doubt, which is an important plus point, but she is also fat and wears glasses." My friend obviously thought she could do better for her son and asked her husband to make his excuses to his client by saying that they had decided to postpone the boy's marriage indefinitely.

By this time almost six months had passed and I was becoming impatient. What I had thought would be an easy matter to arrange was turning out to be quite complicated. I began to believe that between my friend's desire for a girl who was modest enough to fit into her joint family, yet attractive and educated enough to be an acceptable partner for her son, she would not find anyone suitable. My friend laughed at my impatience: "Don't be so much in a hurry," she said. "You Americans want everything done so quickly. You get married quickly and then just as quickly get divorced. Here we take marriage more seriously. We must take all the factors into account. It is not enough for us to learn by our mistakes. This is too serious a business. If a mistake is made we have not only ruined the life of our son or daughter, but we have spoiled the reputation of our family as well. And that will make it much harder for their brothers and sisters to get married. So we must be very careful."

What she said was true and I promised myself to be more patient, though it was not easy. I had really hoped and expected that the match would be made before my year in India was up. But it was not to be. When I left India my friend seemed no further along in finding a suitable match for her son than when I had arrived.

Two years later, I returned to India and still my friend had not found a girl for her son. By this time, he was close to thirty, and I think she was a little worried. Since she knew I had friends all over India, and I was going to be there for a year, she asked me to "help her in this work" and keep an eye out for someone suitable. I was flattered that my judgment was respected, but knowing now how complicated the process was, I had lost my earlier confidence as a matchmaker. Nevertheless, I promised that I would try.

It was almost at the end of my year's stay in India that I met a family with a marriageable daughter whom I felt might be a good possibility for my friend's son. The girl's father was related to a good friend of mine and by coincidence came from the same village as my friend's husband. This new family had a successful business in a medium-sized city in central India and were from the same subcaste as my friend. The daughter was pretty and chic; in fact, she had studied fashion design in college. Her parents would not allow her to go off by herself to any of the major cities in India where she could make a career, but they had compromised with her wish to work by allowing her to run a small dressmaking boutique from their home. In spite of her desire to have a career, the daughter was both modest and home-loving and had had a traditional, sheltered upbringing. She had only one other sister, already married, and a brother who was in his father's business.

I mentioned the possibility of a match with my friend's son. The girl's parents were most interested. Although their daughter was not eager to marry just yet, the idea of living in Bombay—a sophisticated, extremely fashion-conscious city where she could continue her education in clothing design—was a great inducement. I gave the girl's father my friend's address and suggested that when they went to Bombay on some business or whatever, they look up the boy's family.

Returning to Bombay on my way to New York, I told my friend of this newly discovered possibility. She seemed to feel there was potential but, in spite of my urging, would not make any moves herself. She rather preferred to wait for the girl's family to call upon them. I hoped something would come of this introduction, though by now I had learned to rein in my optimism.

A year later I received a letter from my friend. The family had indeed come to visit Bombay, and their daughter and my friend's daughter, who were near in age, had become very good friends. During that year, the two girls had frequently visited each other. I thought things looked promising.

Last week I received an invitation to a wedding: My friend's son and the girl were getting married. Since I had found the match, my presence was particularly requested at the wedding. I was thrilled. Success at last! As I prepared to leave for India, I began thinking, "Now, my friend's younger son, who do I know who has a nice girl for him . . . ?"

FURTHER REFLECTIONS ON ARRANGED MARRIAGE

The previous essay was written from the point of view of a family seeking a daughter-in-law. Arranged marriage looks somewhat different from the point of view of the bride and her family. Arranged marriage continues to be preferred, even among the more educated, Westernized sections of the Indian population. Many young women from these families still go along, more or less willingly, with the practice, and also with the specific choices of their families. Young women do get excited about the prospects of their marriage, but there is also ambivalence and increasing uncertainty, as the bride contemplates leaving the comfort and familiarity of her own home, where as a "temporary guest" she has often been indulged, to live among strangers. Even in the best situation, she will now come under the close scrutiny of her husband's family. How she dresses, how she behaves, how she gets along with others, where she goes, how she spends her time, her domestic abilities—all of this and much more—will be observed and commented on by a whole new set of relations. Her interaction with her family of birth will be monitored and curtailed considerably. Not only will she leave their home, but with increasing geographic mobility, she may also live very far from them, perhaps even on another continent. Too much expression of her fondness for her own family, or her desire to visit them, may be interpreted as an inability to adjust to her new family, and may become a source of conflict. In an arranged marriage, the burden of adjustment is clearly heavier for a woman than for a man. And that is in the best of situations.

In less happy circumstances, the bride may be a target of resentment and hostility from her husband's family, particularly her mother-in-law or her husband's unmarried sisters, for whom she is now a source of competition for the affection, loyalty, and economic resources of a son or brother. If she is psychologically or even physically abused, her options are limited, as returning to her parents' home or getting a divorce is still very stigmatized. For most Indians, marriage and motherhood are still considered the only suitable roles for a woman, even for those who have careers, and few women can comfortably contemplate remaining unmarried. Most families still consider "marrying off" their daughters as a compelling religious duty and social necessity. This increases a bride's sense of obligation to make the marriage a success, at whatever cost to her own personal happiness.

The vulnerability of a new bride may also be intensified by the issue of dowry that, although illegal, has become a more pressing issue in the consumer conscious society of contemporary urban India. In many cases, where a groom's family is not satisfied with the amount of dowry a bride brings to her marriage, the young bride will be harassed constantly to get her parents to give more. In extreme cases, the bride may even be murdered, and the murder disguised as an accident or a suicide. This also offers the husband's family an opportunity to arrange another match for him, thus bringing in another dowry. This phenomenon, called dowry death, calls attention not just to the "evils of dowry" but also to larger issues of the powerlessness of women as well.

TWENTY-TWO

'Pigs of the Forest' and Other Unwritten Papers

TERENCE E. HAYS

The smoke stung my eyes, I was tired and hot in the midday sun, and boredom had reached its high point. Though the occasion differed, the earth oven feast was just like all of the others I had attended in Ndumba, a Highlands community in Papua New Guinea.[1] The pit had been opened in the morning, stones were heated on gigantic fires and then placed in the bottom, grass and leaf coverings were placed over the stones, vegetable food was dumped in unceremoniously, and the whole was covered with more banana leaves and finally a high mound of dirt. Now we waited—usually about three or four hours—until the steamed food could be removed and distributed for the eating.

A feast should be exciting, but obviously *feast* was a misleading way of labeling such an event. Small groups of women sat around talking or performing mundane tasks such as weaving string bags, while most men and youths had wandered off to while away the waiting period in some other—any other—way. As dutiful observer and note taker, I sat off to one side bored to distraction, which I hoped would come soon.

There were always children to play with, of course. My wife and I were the first "red people" these children (and adults as well) had ever come to know on a daily basis, and the novelty of just looking at us and delightedly responding to any attention we gave them was still compelling. Among the children hovering about on that day was Foringa, a young boy I had not seen around the hamlets for some time. One look at him suggested the reason, as he clearly was not feeling well.

In the past, children in the New Guinea Highlands were almost inevitable sufferers from yaws. Now that scourge is gone, but skin diseases and tropical ulcers continue to be common sources of discomfort and systemic infection. Foringa, his body virtually covered with festering, fly-blown sores, was the most pitiful-looking case that I had ever seen. He managed a small smile but continually grimaced and squinted at me through crusted, swollen eyelids. I tried to speak pleasantly to him, imagining his pain and wondering whether he might usefully go to the nearby mission medical aid post for treatment. They would certainly wash his lesions, probably daub them with the purple liquid used for nearly every skin condition, and then send him back home.

As I speculated and sympathized, I caught a glimpse of his father, Haangguma, who had just arrived at the feast ground. I approached him and, after the requisite greetings and small talk, asked about his son: What was Foringa's problem, and how was he having it treated? His response was both startling and intoxicating, smacking of impending revelation of ethnographic treasure. Haangguma told me that he was treating his son's condition by no longer hunting in Maatarera, a section of primary forest claimed by his patriclan.

Haangguma went on: His wife had, some months before, given birth to a new brother for Foringa. Ndumba birth customs required that a successful birth be followed by a "coming-out party" for the mother and child, at which scores of smoke-dried game animals (*kapul,* in New Guinea Tok Pisin) would be distributed to all of her patriclan members. This entailed considerable effort on the part of the father and his kinsmen and friends, as they scoured the forest during the months of birth confinement to hunt and trap the needed possums and other marsupials that abounded in the high forest.

It seemed, according to Haangguma, that he had overdone it this time. He had obtained the number of *kapul* he needed, but all from one part of the forest. Large though it was, as he appreciated upon having to go increasingly higher to find prey, the section was now depleted of game through his and his fellows' activities. This was why his son was now suffering.

At this point I expressed my confusion. Had Foringa been with his father on these trips to the forest? Had he caught the sickness there? Was that the problem?

Haangguma, like other Ndumba adults, had learned to accept the profound ignorance of "anthropologists" (whatever that might mean, that was what we said we were), and patiently filled in the necessary background, as he might with a small child.

I knew about *faana,* right? The spirit beings that inhabit the forest, especially in its upper reaches?

Well, the *faana* of the upper forest are like people in many respects, including a having a taste for meat. Since they are unable to raise pigs, as people do, the *kapul* are their "pigs." That is, *faana* look after the game animals and regard them as their property, just as people do with their pigs. Now, *faana* realize that men will hunt and trap these "pigs" of theirs, and up to a point they tolerate that situation, though when in the high forest Ndumba men try to avoid excessive noise or anything else that might draw the attention of *faana* to their presence.

But, he stressed, if one takes too many *kapul* from the *faana,* they become angry. (What he meant by "too many" was left vague, but clearly Haangguma's haul of over a hundred animals was judged, ex post factor, as qualifying.) This anger gets expressed in various ways. Disturbed *faana* might follow a hunter home and interfere with his sleep; they might only cause bad luck on future expeditions; or, in extreme cases, they might make the wife or children of a hunter sick as a message. Clearly, in Haangguma's mind, this last had been his fate. His first-born son was now suffering from the condition I had observed. Nothing could really be done except to avoid the section of forest where the transgression had occurred, hoping that with a long enough cooling-off period, the local *faana* would forgive him or forget about the incident. Then Foringa would recover and Haangguma could resume his exploitation of Maatarera.

I scribbled furiously in my notebook—this was wonderful stuff! Visions of Ballantine labels danced in my head! Venn diagrams! "Institutions," "customs," and "beliefs" all interlocked in a tight whole—hunting, medical beliefs, and religion inextricably intertwined, the way I had learned they must be for a society to function. What was more, these customs and beliefs were *adaptive!* Avoidance of a section of forest would give the game population a chance to recover; the area would become a buffer zone, allowing the environment to restore its intricate balance with the demands of its human inhabitants. I had discovered a link between seemingly nonrational Ndumba beliefs and the practical world!

As my head swam with the possibilities, Haangguma slipped away. The earth oven was being opened, and for him the appeal of freshly cooked food and intelligent conversation with his peers could not be compared with dealing any further with my silly questions.

No matter. Details could be followed up later. I was already drafting in my mind the articles that would make my career and render the doctoral dissertation I was supposed to write almost irrelevant. Or perhaps that could be my dissertation topic as well! "Pigs of the Forest: Natural Conservationists in the New Guinea Highlands," "Spirit Beliefs and the Conservation of Resources in Ndumba," and other titles for the papers I would write buzzed around in my brain and gave rise to mental outlines until I could bear the tension no longer. Hot sweet potatoes could wait; further details could wait; I hurried back to our house to begin work on my ethnographic masterpiece.

After the initial excited discussion with my wife, of course, further details were needed. It happened that another man, Waanggusa, stopped by our house to visit that evening. Anytime we attended a feast there were sure to be visitors later—particularly those who hadn't attended it but who might benefit from a secondary food distribution from the generous portions we usually received. I seized the opportunity and pumped Waanggusa for more information about the "pigs of the forest."

As things developed, my linguistic clumsiness was not the only reason for the confused look on his face as my tale unfolded. Without identifying who specifically had told me about the *faana*–skin disease connection, as we generally tried to avoid the risk of confounding interpersonal conflicts with "ethnographic truth," I indicated that I had just learned of all this, but still had some questions. For example, how many *kapul* were "too many"?

First, Waanggusa asserted that it was possible to overhunt a given section of the forest. This led him to go on at some length about another area of bush where concern had arisen recently over birds of paradise. Some people were afraid, he reported, that the introduction of shotguns (a dreamed-of and often discussed prospect, but still not a reality in Ndumba at that time, or even as late as 1985) would mean the rapid extinction of these birds with their highly prized plumes, and . . .

I interrupted him to get back to the questions at hand. Digressions certainly have their place, and we all owe a great deal to the serendipity of chance remarks and conversational meanderings—indeed, that day's wondrous revelation was just such a case. But at the moment I had bigger fish to fry.

Unfortunately, my attempts to get Waanggusa back on the track continued to lead only to more digressions and confusion. What about skin diseases and lesions? Well, Waanggusa knew a story about the origin of skin diseases—did I want to hear it? Aha! Of course I did, and so he told me. As it turned out (when would I learn?), it wasn't a story about the origin of such conditions at all, but about how trading partnerships with the Baruya Anga to the south developed, in the "time of the ancestors," when a man from there miraculously cured a Ndumba man whose skin resembled the lichen-covered bark of a beech tree. Good stuff, this, but *not* what I was so singlemindedly, even obsessively, after at the time.

Tell me about the "pigs of the forest," I insisted. Did all *faana* have them? Did female *faana* feed them, the way human women tended real pigs?

Seemingly impatient now, Waanggusa wanted to know where I ever got the idea that *faana* kept pigs. He had never heard of such a thing! I explained that of course I wasn't referring to actual pigs, but to *kapul* that were analogous to pigs as far as *faana* were concerned.

Waanggusa chuckled at the thought of such an arrangement. It was preposterous, he said (or words to that effect). Yes, there were *faana* that lived in the forest, and yes, they sometimes punished men for various transgressions, but hunting, or overhunting, wasn't one of them. Like a member of the Ndumba Chamber of Commerce, he reminded me of the vast tracts of forest claimed by Ndumba, especially in contrast to the grassland peoples to the north, and the local abundance of game. In any case, *kapul* were not looked after by *faana*, who had rather loftier matters to occupy their attention.

What about skin diseases, then? What caused them? Why did some children seem to suffer so badly—Foringa, for instance (I sneaked in)?

Waanggusa couldn't say for sure about Foringa, but severe cases were, like most ailments and misfortunes, caused by sorcery. Knowledge of such magic was possessed by people downriver to the west. Living at a slightly lower elevation—in "hot country" by Ndumba standards, though still a mile above sea level—many of them were said to suffer from skin diseases and to be especially proficient at causing them. If someone from here angered someone from there, Waanggusa opined, he or his wife or children might experience such a form of revenge. "Look to strained interpersonal relationships," Professor Waanggusa might have phrased it, "rather than to *faana* for an explanation."

My ethnographer's heart was sinking. Had Haangguma made up this whole thing? Was he covering himself by blaming spirits instead of his own problems with neighbors? Had I been duped? Or was Waanggusa the culprit? Was he, for some reason, trying to snatch away my Nobel Prize? Or was he simply ignorant? Could a mature adult man *not know about* "Mystical Illness Causation and Ecological Balance"?

I was still foundering as Waanggusa left our house, shaking his head and snickering over my silly notions. I had met Two Crows.

I remember being rather shocked than pleased when in my student days I came across such statements in J. O. Dorsey's "Omaha Sociology" as "Two Crows denies this." This looked a little as though the writer had not squarely met the challenge of assaying his source material and giving us the kind of data that we, as respectable anthropologists, could live on.

Thus Edward Sapir (1938:7) voiced his dismay when faced with Dorsey's (1884) particular resolution of a major dilemma of ethnography—the one I had to wrestle with in Ndumba and one which cannot be avoided. We go to the field, equipped with the concepts of *society* and *culture,* in search of groups with beliefs, customs, and institutions. But what we confront, as did Dorsey before us, is "a finite, though indefinite, number of human beings, who [give] themselves the privilege of differing from each other" (Sapir 1938:7).

As A. L. Kroeber is reported to have said, "Cultures don't paint their toenails." The ethnographer in the field is set down in the midst of a Heraclitean world where some informants paint their toenails, while others do not; some did previously, but have given up the practice; others begin to do it, having been stimulated by the posing of the question; and Two Crows, perhaps thinking of particular persons, says that no one—or that everyone—does it. How, then, is this reality of variation and disagreement to be abstracted into the kind of data that anthropologists can live on? For the ethnographer seeking authoritative statements about Omaha culture, Two Crows must be absorbed into, or even become, the Omaha.

What was I to do with the conflicting statements of Haangguma and Waanggusa? How could they be accommodated in my descriptions of Ndumba culture?

Perhaps one of them was simply wrong. Maybe Haangguma was making it all up—to divert attention from his sorcery troubles, to play a trick on me, or just to entertain me (I clearly manifested excitement at what he was telling me at the time). After all, I had seen little evidence of a conservation ethic elsewhere in Ndumba behavior. Children happily robbed birds' nests of fledglings and eggs—for amusement, not food—carelessly destroying the nests in the process, and no one seemed distressed except me. The grassland that covered much of Ndumba territory was "created" by their burning activities. Burning secondary growth was an essential part of their gardening pattern, but I had also witnessed huge areas set alight out of casual mischief or curiosity as to how far a grass fire would burn before extinguishing itself. Amid such waste (from my point of view, at least) Haangguma's story had been all the more remarkable, suggesting concerns for the conservation of resources—however they might be rationalized—that were inconsistent with my experiences to that point.

But maybe it was just Waanggusa who was wrong, or simply uninformed about the *faana* of the forest and their "pigs." Yet this was not an immediately persuasive conclusion, except that reaching it would enable me to get on with my career more quickly. After all, the two men were of about the same age and comparable standing in the community. Moreover, as father of several children by two wives and veteran of many childbirth *kapul* feasts, Waanggusa had taken countless numbers of game animals from the high forest. How could this aspect of his fellows' belief system never have come to his attention?

Apart from questions about the distribution of the "*faana*'s revenge" belief in the community, what about its supposed effects on the environment? If, in the most extreme scenario, the belief was held only by Haangguma, then surely his abstention from hunting in Maatarera would have little effect as long as others hunted there. Similarly, if some others shared his belief but it was not universally held and followed, or if even a sizable minority was not influenced by such notions, again it would be difficult to presume that the ecological balance was maintained by this aspect of Ndumba cosmology.

As I pondered these complications and felt my Nobel Prize slipping from my grasp, I had to wonder where the culture I had come so far to study was. Having grown up in schools and libraries, I had come to view the world as consisting of things to be known and populated by people who knew them and people who didn't, with the latter needing only to turn to the ones who did to fill the void. Yet here were my authorities disagreeing with each other, obstructing my attempts to identify and describe the system.

The trap I had fallen into was one to which scholars may be especially prone, but one that awaits any who would reify belief systems that are continually being negotiated by their users. Living in a world of *Robert's Rules of Order,* instruction manuals, and encyclopedias, it is easy to lose sight of the fact that culture is neither static nor fully shared, even among those who enshrine "authorities" in seemingly timeless printed forms. In a nonliterate society the situation is no different, even though it would be easier for the analyst if there were analogues to reference works and card catalogues, waiting to be tapped by identifying and questioning the "right informant" who retains "the culture" in his or her head. Like consensus, culture has to be built up, though never seamlessly, from the individual and various versions of it. As Sapir (1938:11) advised, the starting point is "to operate as though we knew nothing about culture but were interested in analyzing as well as we could what a given number of human beings accustomed to live with each other actually think and do in their day to day relationships."

Two Crows, in one of his many guises, will always be there to frustrate attempts to abstract simple and clear cultural rules from the actions and statements of people who live in worlds of contingencies. Yet contingencies need not result in chaos, but in life as it is lived. Some beliefs, one will find, are held by virtually all members of a community; others are only shared by some; and still others—the ones that give us delight more often than not, when you think about it—may be unique to specific individuals, such as Haangguma (or was it Waanggusa?). The process of discovering that *patterned diversity* is the real system—and that some differences need to be resolved, others are just tolerated, and still others may only surface with an outsider's probings—is what keeps us all alive. That realization, and the new *kinds* of questions it raises, have brought me more understanding than ever could have come from the papers Waanggusa and others kept me from writing.

NOTE

1. A degree of literary license has been taken with this account, though possibly no more than is common in the classroom. The conflicting statements and explanations reported are faithfully rendered, but reattributed (pseudonymously) for narrative purposes, and are representative of quandaries that plagued me during fieldwork in the Eastern Highlands Province of Papua New Guinea in 1971–72, 1981, and 1985. Despite all of that I am grateful to my mentors in Ndumba and to those who have supported my research there: the National Institutes of Health, the Institute of Papua New Guinea Studies, the National Endowment for the Humanities, Rhode Island College, the Australian-American Eduational Foundation, and the Australian National University, Research School of Pacific Studies.

REFERENCES CITED

DORSEY, J. OWEN
1884 Omaha Sociology. Smithsonian Institution 3rd Annual Report (1881–1882), pp. 205–370. Washington, DC: Government Printing Office.

SAPIR, EDWARD
1938   Why Cultural Anthropology Needs the Psychiatrist. Psychiatry 1:7–
       12.

SUGGESTED   READINGS

HAYS, TERRENCE E.
1987   Initiation as Experience: The Management of Emotional Responses
       to Ndumba Novices. *In* Anthropology in the High Valleys: Essays on
       the New Guinea Highlands in Honor of Kenneth E. Read. L. L.
       Langness and Terrence E. Hays, eds. Pp. 185–235. Novato, CA:
       Chandler & Sharp.
1979   Plant Classification and Nomenclature in Ndumba, Papua New
       Guinea Highlands. Ethnology 18:253–270.

HAYS, TERRENCE E., AND PATRICIA H. HAYS
1982   Opposition and Complementarity of the Sexes in Ndumba Initia-
       tion Ceremonies. *In* Rituals of Manhood: Male Initiation in New
       Guinea. Gilbert H. Herdt, ed. Pp. 201–238. Berkeley: University of
       California Press.

TWENTY-THREE

Lessons from the Field: Gullibility and the Hazards of Money Lending

CINDY HULL

In the months prior to my grand departure into "the field," I listened with awe and admiration to my mentors, those of the faculty, whose tales of trials and tribulations had inspired me to proceed with my academic endeavors. I also listened to my peers who had just returned, their faces still tanned, their memories fresh. Among the stories told at department colloquia and informal gatherings were scattered subtle warnings: "Don't drink the water, always soak the beans so you can scrape the bugs off the top before cooking, never step on a female tarantula, to kill a scorpion, separate its tail from the body, and never, ever loan money."

My husband and I took these warnings to heart. We promised to never fall into the traps that our predecessors had been foolish enough to experience. We would not be gullible. Our fieldwork experience would be flawless, our memories all pleasant, and my research extraordinary in its insights and conclusions.

Such, I suspect in retrospect, are the expectations of most graduate students, thrown, as it were, to the wolves, with no protection except those words of wisdom spoken in blissful reminiscence. However, like all anthropologists before me, I found the graduate student's concept of ethnographic reality, more often than not, falling short of that of their subjects.

We arrived in the small village of Yaxbé, causing a small stir as the 1,800 souls learned of the arrival of the gringos. Yet, in their usual generosity, they accepted us, or at least their children did. After a time the adults, too, began to come to visit to discover if all the stories of the strange gringo customs were indeed true. Did they really boil their water and soak their beans? Did they really sleep on cots and cook over a dangerous kerosine stove?

During those first weeks, the roles of anthropologist and subject were reversed. The villagers were understandably curious about our presence.

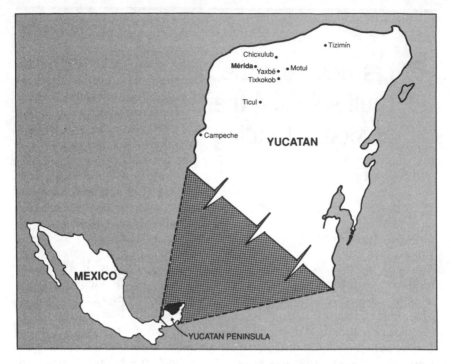

Yucatan Peninsula, Mexico

The braver of the villagers were persistent in their questioning. They wanted to know about our families and why they would allow us to journey so far from home. They wanted to know if we knew their cousin José who lives in Texas. They wanted to know why we didn't have any children. Nevertheless, by the end of the first month, they no longer thought we were complete idiots because we could not speak their Mayanized Spanish with any degree of fluency. They now believed we were only mildly retarded.

It did not take long for us to make friends, for the villagers were friendly and patient. Among our first visitors were a sister and her two younger brothers. Maria, the oldest and spokesperson for the trio, was a lanky ten-year-old with shoulder-cropped thick black hair. She wore skirts shorter than the norm for the village, and her shirts were too short for her tall frame. Marcos, who appeared to be around seven years old, was a subdued, middle child and Carlos, four, was the tagalong.

Since it was summer when we arrived, our presence was a special treat—a new diversion—for the children. Yet, for the duration of our stay, the Chan children and several others represented the core of our fan club, and they spent many hours in our nine-by-twelve-foot cement room. When they invited us to their home to meet their parents and grandparents, we were especially thrilled.

The Chan *solar,* or enclosed homestead, was one of the first that I had formally visited. It was located several streets off the two main intersecting roads, which I used to coordinate the four sectors of the village. As I stood outside the limestone wall, awaiting acknowledgment, I was moved by the austerity of the homestead. The wall, which surrounds all Maya homesteads and lines up with those of all the families along the road, was nearly nonexistent. The limestone boulders had fallen along the roadway, and no one had bothered to move or replace them in their proper spot. A gate, carelessly constructed of small sticks and rope, fell into the yard as I unhooked the latch.

Maria and her mother, Doña Carmen, met me at the opening where the gate had fallen in and, with an apologetic smile, picked up the meager door and replaced it behind me as I entered. Doña Carmen was dressed in a plain white *huipil,* which lacked the embroidered neck and hem characteristic of traditional garments. That she had been making tortillas was obvious by the raw cornmeal carelessly smeared on her dress. She wore her hair in the characteristic fashion of Maya women, pulled tightly and knotted at the back of the skull with a small comb. Her face had sharp, non-Mayan features. The nose was long and thin, the face quite narrow. Her smile was friendly and I estimated her age at fifty. I was later to learn that she was thirty-five and pregnant. Maria was dressed in one of three dresses that she wore continuously, and she was smiling widely as she introduced me to her mother.

Doña Carmen motioned me into the yard with a downward cupping of her hand, and as she led me to the main house she persistently apologized for their poverty. Indeed, the house was much poorer than those along the main road of the village. The mud and cement daub had fallen from the wattle sticks, exposing the interior of the house to view. The thatch on the roof was old and thinly spread, with gaping holes. Inside, the house had a packed dirt floor. Four hammocks were strung from a center pole and extended to the sturdier posts that supported the traditional oval structure.

At the rear of the main house was the cooking shelter, like most of those in the village but with a much smaller cooking area. Two pans hung from hooks on one of the supporting beams. On the ground, the cooking fire was smoldering under a large metal cooking sheet. Two low three-legged stools were placed on either side of the fire pit. A hollowed-out coconut shell covered with a small cloth indicated that she indeed had just finished making tortillas.

The yard itself was characteristic of the Mayan *solar.* Another house, as meager as the first, stood to the rear, slightly tilted and sagging. Further back a small shower building, made of wooden planks, was barely visible. The ground was packed from constant pressure of feet upon the hard limestone surface. Limestone rock jutted out from the ground at intervals, a danger to unaccustomed toes and very slippery after the rain. Between the two living houses, the children's maiden aunt, Fidelia, was extracting water from a well that was also in dire need of repair. Large chunks of limestone, once the body of the well, were now dislodged and laying haphazardly in the yard.

As we finished the tour, Maria's father entered the *solar.* Doña Carmen's husband, Gustavo, was a striking man, with mutant blue eyes that contrasted handsomely with his dark, Mayan features. He wore a panama hat and immediately struck up a friendly conversation. He introduced me to his parents, who had entered with him and stood timidly behind.

Gustavo's father and mother lived in the small house behind theirs, and the children ran to bring them to meet their honored guests. The old man, Estebán, was stooped and moved with the help of a homemade cane. He spoke to us in Maya, interspersed with Spanish. He smiled a toothless grin and even though I did not understand his words, I knew that his mind had known more coherent days.

We met many people in those first months, some poorer, many more affluent than the Chan family. Because of the obvious poverty of the Chan's, we both felt sympathy and compassion for them. When cold December winds blew, chilling our cement house, we took blankets to the Chan house and hung our army tarps over the most blatant gaps in their walls. When Don Gustavo asked for a small loan, thirty pesos, for some thatch, we gladly loaned it to him. With that first loan we fell headfirst into the trap.

After the second small loan, we began to feel uncomfortable. I recalled the warnings about loaning money, though I had forgotten who had made them, revered faculty with many years in the field or embittered returning graduate students who had one negative experience. Yet, something began to eat at me. Something had gone awry. We had crossed an invisible line between friendship and patronism.

Don Gustavo talked often about the many hours he worked in the *ejido* (village-owned fields) cutting and weeding the henequen plant, which is the backbone of the Yucatecan economy. He complained about the poor pay and the corruption by the team leaders, who often cheated the workers. We sympathized with him for we knew how hard he worked—he had told us so. We also knew that he sold vegetables in the village and was involved in both the legitimate and the illegitimate lottery. The children sold enchiladas and other prepared foods within the village, and we were told how his father, old Estebán, had to sell limes and other fruits in the surrounding towns and in Merida, the capital.

One day Doña Carmen came to our door with a letter she wanted to send to an *ejido* official in a nearby *municipio.* She asked that I type it so that it looked better. My better judgment told me that I should decline, but my curiosity about the contents of the letter overcame my reticence. In the letter, Doña Carmen was denouncing certain actions by village *ejido* leaders, several of whom we knew. Because I did not want to be implicated, even indirectly because of the use of my typewriter, in the denunciations, I refused to allow the Chan family further use of my machine, even though they were fairly prolific in their complaints about the local henequen leaders.

Meanwhile, some of our newly found friends began to speak to us about a certain man, whose *apodo* (nickname) was Flojo (not his real *apodo*). It seems Flojo was a deceitful man who took advantage of people who helped him. He was poor, but the money that he borrowed did not go to the care of his family, but to his own uses. He did not work in the fields, but spent his time in neighboring villages, selling lottery tickets. We thought this interesting but did not think it concerned us, since we did not know who Flojo was.

It was when Doña Carmen had her baby that we began to put together the pieces of our ethnographic puzzle. Don Gustavo came to us one day to say that Doña Carmen had to be transferred from the local medical clinic to the hospital in Merida since the baby was *otra forma* (of another form). This sounded ominous, and of course, we sympathized. My husband drove Don Gustavo to the hospital to visit his wife several times until we realized that he had the habit of arriving at our house just after the Merida bus passed through the village.

Don Gustavo began to ask for money. He claimed that because he had to take care of the other children, he had not been able to work; his compadre was in Mexico and could not help with the family expenses. Could we please loan him three hundred pesos. This was an outrageous amount for us, for we were on a limited budget, and we had to refuse.

When Doña Carmen returned home with her new baby, we were asked for one hundred pesos for clothing and food. Again we declined, saying that we would be glad to buy some food and blankets but that we could not afford to loan them that much money. He refused the offer of goods and reiterated that he needed the money so he could buy the food.

After Don Gustavo left, my husband and I discussed these events. We wanted to help our neighbors yet, somehow, we felt trapped in an uncomfortable relationship. Generosity became obligation, and when I began to remember what other people had told us about Flojo, obligation transformed itself into humiliation.

During this time of rumination and depression, Don Gustavo's daughter, Maria, arrived at our house with a note that she had written. In the letter, she pleaded with us to help the family until their compadre returned from Mexico. She had included a list of goods that they needed and the cost per item. It totaled nearly one hundred fifty pesos. I asked Maria what her father's *apodo* was, and she turned red and said, "People call him Flojo."

Handwritten notes on scraps of paper glued to the pages of my notebook illustrate the steady stream of requests from various members of the Chan family. "When will you buy the *panuelos* [diapers]?" "Please take us to. . . ." Terse comments made in my field notebook reflect our growing frustration and eventual bitterness toward the family that we had nurtured and encouraged. We began to avoid them, yet almost daily one of the children or adults would come with yet another request or an inquiry about when we would comply with the last request. We were miserable and confused.

Once people learned about our problems with the family, they began to tell us stories, the usual village gossip concerning deceit in selling chickens, unpaid loans, and the fact that the children had to sell food in the streets to feed themselves. It was eventually disclosed that old Don Esteban, Gustavo's minstrel father, earned centavos as a beggar in various neighboring villages.

We learned later that Don Gustavo had been the *solidario* (work group) representative several times but had been fired for corruption and for stealing money. We were surprised to learn that he actually worked very little in the *ejido*, that he spent most of his time selling lottery tickets and vegetables. This information allowed us to fit together the pieces of our puzzle, for although we had been curious why Don Gustavo had spent so much time in the village and on the intervillage buses, we had never doubted his stories about the many hours he spent in the fields. We had always assumed him to be an industrious man.

As the days passed, I slowly regained my anthropological temperament. That is, I was able to laugh at myself, to accept my mistakes, and in doing so, I gained a new perspective on these events. We visited Doña Carmen regularly and brought small gifts of food and clothing for the baby, but we refused to loan them any more money. The older children continued to visit us, though Don Gustavo came less and less often, and after several months the letters pleading for money ceased.

We had hundreds of experiences in Yaxbé, some joyous, others, like this one, extremely disturbing. But none of the events taught us as much as this one did. It may have been because it happened so early in our visit. It could have been because we learned about gullibility. But mostly we learned about the villagers and about ourselves as visitors in their world.

Our stereotypes about the homogeneity and social perfection of rural villages were put expeditiously to rest. Although we never attempted to force the villagers into a Redfieldian utopia, we did have idealistic expectations about their behavior. And, with the exception of the Don Gustavos and the occasional drunk or malcreant, we were not disappointed. Eventually we knew the town drunks by name and we could recognize the village turkey thieves (one of whom stole our camera). These characters became part of the complex matrix of village life, not aberrations to a flawless equilibrium or evidence of conflict and tension.

We also learned about the impact of the researcher on the society. The suggestions that the researcher should not change the social or economic environment of his or her village are valid, but impossible to comply with totally. For what kind of human being is one who would not give a blanket to a cold family or give clothing, as we did, to a woman whose house burned to the ground?

To us, Yaxbé was our home, like Grand Rapids and Detroit and Ann Arbor had been homes to us over the past few years. We did not see ourselves as deus ex machina, dropping favors to the common creatures below us, yet we considered ourselves obligated in a strong sense to the villagers. They had, indeed, accepted us graciously and generously. We shared their water, imposed on their precious time, accepted their meals and food gifts, and most of all, lavished in their sometimes overwhelming attention. Above all, we learned from them more than they could tell us in words alone.

We wanted to be a part of the everyday flow of life in the village. As unrealistic as it seems in retrospect, we wanted to be Yaxbeños. We were excited, for example, when we had to stand in line like everyone else at the *tienda* (village store) and when the young girls or Don Juan took our order without giggling. We felt accepted when we could visit a home without having everyone scurrying around to wait on us, sending children out the back door to buy us a Coke. And we became very comfortable having children piled in our hammocks, listening to our radio and pounding on the infamous typewriter. We loved having the adults visit, women on their way to the store in the mornings and men in the lazy hot afternoons.

Yet we were not Yaxbeños, nor would we ever be, no matter how long we lived in the village. To the villagers we would always be gringos, "our gringos" as they would jokingly say. We were not like them, and our presence was always clouded in a sense of mystery and awe. To the villagers we were rich. We had no refrigerator or oven. No washing machine. But we were there. We had a 1974 Volkswagen Beetle, a short-wave radio, a portable typewriter, and no jobs. We had to be rich. And that perception had an impact on the villagers, especially those, like Don Gustavo, who already existed on the margins of their own society.

Had these events occurred in the latter days of our stay, their impact would have been negligible. The situation would not have reached the same climax had our initial expectations been more realistic and had our Spanish language skills been sharpened. As the days passed, we learned the subtleties of the verbal and nonverbal language. We learned to recognize innuendo and sarcasm, aspects of language we had never learned in the university classroom.

Yet, had this series of events not occurred, these valuable lessons would have been postponed and our misconceptions perpetuated. We would have lost a meaningful thread—one which, interwoven with many others, completed a brightly colored tapestry of the Maya.

TWENTY-FOUR

🪷 To Die on Ambae: On the Possibility of Doing Fieldwork Forever

WILLIAM L. RODMAN

MARGARET C. RODMAN

December 7, 1985:
LATE SATURDAY NIGHT, OUR HOUSE,
AMBAE—BEDSIDE

Bill

And then I said:

An anthropologist gets sick and dies while conducting fieldwork on the small South Pacific island of Ambae. Suddenly, there she is, standing in front of these big gates beside a man with a long beard and a scroll. "Hello," says the man, "I'm St. Peter and these are the Pearly Gates. I have some good news and some bad news for you. Which do you want first?"

"The good news," says the anthropologist.

"Okay," says St. Peter, "the good news is that you have been admitted to Heaven."

"That's just great," she says, "if I've been admitted to Heaven, then what could possibly be the bad news?"

"Well," says St. Peter, "Heaven consists of little worlds. People spend eternity in the same place where they drop. You planned a few months fieldwork on Ambae, but now it looks like you'll be doing fieldwork there forever."

It was a bad joke and I knew it. Still Margy managed a weak smile: "That's not very funny," she said. She thought for a moment and her expression became more serious: "You don't suppose . . ."

"No," I told her, "of course not. Dumb joke. Sorry."

Since last night she had run a fever and endured severe chills and worse sweats. She hadn't been able to keep down a thing—not medicine, not food, not even water. We kept thinking the fever would break, but it didn't, and she was getting weaker. She had been a trooper, but now I could see in her eyes she was getting scared.

"Bill," she said, "you've got to get me out of here."

I wanted to, God knows, but there was just no way, at least not for another few days.

Friday, December 6, 1985:

THE WAR MUSEUM IN THE RAIN FOREST

Margy

On our first field trip to Ambae in 1969 we discovered that the island was, for us, a place where the days last longer and time slows down. Back in Canada, we yearned to reset our mental clocks to Ambae time, and indeed we've returned to the island for three more field trips over the years. Our most recent trip, in 1985, provided both a respite from a demanding period of fieldwork elsewhere in Vanuatu and a chance to fill in some gaps in our material.

By early December, we were ready to leave the field. My last scheduled interview was with an old man named Charlie Siu, a collector and connoisseur of World War II memorabilia. Charlie lives in an isolated hamlet near the coast with his wife, Betty, a healer who likes to seem mysterious. For years I paid more attention to her than to him. I recorded her songs, photographed her medicinal plants, learned from her the sexual facts of life that she thought every Ambae woman should know. Charlie had wanted to tell me of his wartime experiences working for the Americans on Espiritu Santo, a huge medical and supply base for the Battle of the Coral Sea. It was a topic that interested our son Sean, then thirteen, so he decided to come along with me and help by taking pictures.

We set off early on Friday morning, exactly a week before we were due to bring the field trip to an end. I had a headache and hiking to Charlie's hamlet seemed an immense effort, but perhaps the weather was to blame. It had rained in the night and then again at dawn, a windless rain that left the air so damp I could see my breath. The rain forest steamed as we followed the path down the hill, our flipflops slipping and slapping a gritty spray of dark volcanic mud up the backs of our legs. We crossed a pile of mossy stones, once a garden wall, into Charlie and Betty's plantation, a raggedy stand of old coconut palms from which they earned a little money making copra—smoke-dried coconut meat, the "palm" part of Palmolive soap, and an ingredient in coffee whitener. Copra is the main cash crop in Vanuatu and it provides the only source of income for most people on Ambae.

Their hamlet occupies a clearing in the plantation. Sean and I stood on the plaza at the center of the settlement, looking down at the bare earth,

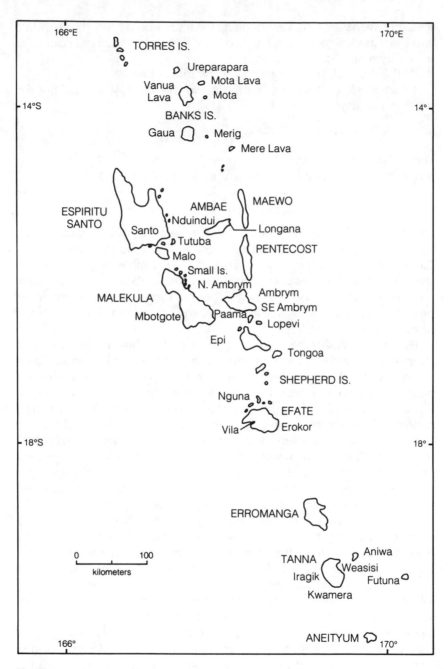

Vanuatu

shuffling our feet and clearing our throats, politely signaling our hosts that we had arrived. Sean picked up a piece of paper in the mud. "Mom, it's a pay slip from the U.S. Navy!" It was a blank, undated, unsigned, but the Navy hasn't been in the area since 1944. We knew we were in for a treat.

Charlie led us into a bamboo house where we sat on new copra sacks that smelled like freshly mown hay. He sang, his soft, whining old man's voice recalling the war as the islanders experienced it. The traditional melodic forms of Ambae warriors' songs contrasted with the sounds of a white man's war—*boom, ratatat, whirr*—and with songs he learned from soldiers: "God Save America Wan Gudfala Ples." Betty joined us and took charge of presenting Charlie's World War II collection for our inspection: forty-seven American dimes with dates ranging from 1928 to 1944, shell casings, bullets, blankets, dinner plates from Los Angeles, and forks marked USN.

"And see that big cooking pot in the corner? That's from the watime, too," Betty said. I nodded, and suddenly I felt my enthusiasm run out of me like water. I wasn't feeling well; my head still hurt and my bones ached, perhaps from the damp, hard earth beneath the copra sack.

Before we left, Charlie posed in front of a red hibiscus bush. Sean snapped a picture of him wearing a U.S. Navy cap, long-sleeved shirt, and fatigues with cuffs rolled several times to keep them above his bare feet and the muddy ground.

Sean and I climbed slowly through a soft rain to the hill village of Waileni, our field site during our three visits to the island since 1978. We walked past a fallen banyan that lay on the edge of the village like a great wooden whale beached in the last hurricane. We continued on to our compound, which consisted of a bamboo house, a separate kitchen, and a privy concealed in the bush. Our compound was part of a satellite hamlet just out of sight of the village plaza. It was the chief's hamlet: Chief Mathias Tariundu, a leader of the highest rank in the *hungwe,* an association in which men kill tusked boars in order to gain prestige. I was Chief Mathias's "daughter-in-law" because, in 1978, he adopted Bill as his "son." Since then, we have spent about twenty months living in his village.

Channing, our five-year-old daughter, hurtled down the path to greet us, village playmates in her wake. Sean ducked into the cool, dark kitchen in search of something for lunch and Channing followed, chattering, her eyes on the small ripe bananas hanging from the rafters. I wasn't hungry. I thought I'd lie down for a while.

It was a week before I got up again.

Bill

I, too, conducted my last scheduled interview that Friday morning. When I returned to our compound, I asked Sean where his mother was. "Mom isn't feeling well," he said. "She went inside to lie down." No big deal, I thought, and I left her alone to take what I thought was a nap.

I had mixed feelings about leaving the island. I was pleased that our field trip was almost over and sad for the same reason. Pleased that it had gone so well—Margy and I had gathered good data, and we'd renewed old friendships, some of sixteen years' duration. The kids had readjusted to village life and the family had remained in good health. I was sad mostly because I was leaving Mathias, my second father, almost certainly for the last time.

Once, Mathias told me he was as old as the century: I think he believed the birth date he assigned himself and thought of himself as not doing badly for an "olfala" of eighty five. He'd slowed down a bit, but not much: He mediated fewer disputes in the village but he still attended just about every rank-taking in the area, the art of killing tusked boars being his particular passion. He'd raised me to my first rank in 1978; on this field trip, I'd taken a second rank. Most days, we spent hours together in the shade of the canarium almond tree near his clubhouse. I'd heard most of his stories before but just being with him gave me pleasure. Most nights we drank kava together, he and I, and felt the sweet communion of the slightly stoned.

Toward nightfall Mathias came by our house. He leaned through an open window and I stopped typing the morning's interview. We talked for a moment in Bislama about the man I had visited, then he asked, "Where's Margaret?"

"Lying down. She's not feeling well," I said.

"Fever?" What he meant was, does she have malaria.

"I think so."

"Too bad." He paused, and then, with a smile, "Some men are coming over. Do you want to drink kava with us?"

"No, not tonight. I have to make dinner for the kids."

"Too bad," he said, and wandered off.

Saturday, Decemer 7:
AT HOME AT THE END OF THE LINE

Bill

Margy and I have always thought of malaria as a kind of dues. Everybody who works in northern Vanuatu gets it: It's part of the price you pay to conduct fieldwork there. We take antimalaria pills whenever we are in the field, chloroquine in the 1970s, newer and more sophisticated drugs in the 1980s, but still we've both contracted the disease twice. On one occasion, my fever went high enough—and stayed high long enough—that I heard two little village dogs talking to each other across the plaza from where I sat propped against a tree. That they were holding a conversation didn't surprise me at the time; however, I remember being impressed that dogs on the island speak English.

Most often, in my experience, the course of a bad case of malaria runs like this: You get a splitting headache, followed by a high fever, and then you become very cold, even though the weather is warm. Your teeth begin to chatter uncontrollably and you cover yourself with blankets. You have a miserable time out there on the ice floe, and then your personal thermostat swings into turnaround and you throw the blankets off because the room you are in has become a sauna and your sheets are soaked with sweat. By this point, you should have taken a "curative" dose of antimalaria pills, roughly three times the weekly suppressive dose, and after a while your temperature begins to fall as rapidly as it rose only hours earlier. You feel enormous relief, then you sleep, then you feel wrecked for about four days.

That's malaria as we knew it, awful but not lethal. In the late 1970s, new strains of the disease appeared in northern Vanuatu. The most recent types of malaria don't respond to chloroquin or any other medication an anthropologist might have in his pack. Left untreated, the disease can be deadly.

We worried about our children contracting malaria, so we took all the precautions we could. We chose a field site high in the hills of the island. There are no mosquitoes at night in Waileni: it's too cold for them. Sunday was pill day. Every Sunday, without fail, our whole family took the bitter-tasting pills that suppress the most common strains of malaria. One of the smells I associate most vividly with fieldwork is the smoky scent of mosquito coils made from pyrethrum, the dried flower heads of chrysanthemums; we burned a coil anytime we were in the house during the day. Deep-Woods Off was as much a part of our interviewing kit as a tape recorder and spare batteries. For all our precautions, Margy had every symptom of malaria with which we were familiar from experience, plus a few more. Her illness didn't respond to the initial dose of chloroquine; her fever remained constant. Starting late Friday night, she began to vomit and could hold nothing down. Medicine came up immediately; so did as much as a mouthful of water. My main concern was that she might have contracted cerebral malaria, an especially dangerous form of the disease, but I was almost equally concerned about the possibility that she might become severely dehydrated. How long can a person with a fever last without water? Three days? Less? A bit more, perhaps? I wasn't sure, but I knew that it wasn't very long.

On Saturday, the seriousness of our situation struck me with full force. Not only was Margy a very sick woman, but we were isolated, temporarily unable to leave our field site. Margy was in no shape to walk anywhere and the single motor vehicle in the village, an old, battered Toyota truck, belonged to a leader of the area's small population of Seventh Day Adventists. Saturday is the Adventist day of worship: They maintain a strict prohibition against work of any sort on Saturday, their Sabbath, and they count driving a truck as work. Even if we had transport, our options were limited. A truck could drive us to the cow pasture that served as a landing strip on that part of the island, but no plane was due until Monday or possibly Tuesday. A truck also could take us an hour over rough road to a small hospital located on the southeastern tip of the island. The hospital was staffed by two "doctors" whose titles were honorific: one held a degree in hospital administration while the other, "Dr." David, had received training roughly equivalent to a North American paramedic. Regardless of their qualifications, we perceived the hospital as our best hope for obtaining medical aid. But we had no way to get there.

All day Saturday I stayed in our compound. I transcribed interviews and every so often checked on Margy, remaining with her for as long as she wanted company, which was never very long. She was pale and her eyes had become dull and sunken. Her skin was hot, as if she had a furnace casting off heat inside her body. She couldn't read (a side effect of the malarial headache) and she couldn't sleep either. So she spent most of her time staring at four photographs of horses I'd torn from a Minolta calendar and taped to the bamboo wall of our room.

The village was quiet: all the kids, including our own, were off in the bush, hunting for crayfish or pigeons, gathering nuts, playing games. Around noon, Mathias came to check on Margy's condition. He leaned through the big open window in the bamboo wall of the house and rested his forearms on the sill. He looked very old and his eyes were troubled.

"How is she?" he asked.

"Not so good. About the same. She still has the fever."

He exhaled slowly, audibly, his eyes fixed on the floor. Then he looked up, directly at me.

"What do you think she has?"

I told him I still thought she had malaria.

"Did you give her the medicine?"

"Yes. But it won't stay down."

He thought about this for a moment and then shook his head. "You say it's malaria but if it is, then your medicine should help her." His statement didn't surprise me. I'd heard many times his view that Western medicine was made for white people; hospital medicine (as opposed to bush medicine) always helped restore white people to good health. Modern medicine sometimes worked with islanders; other times, bush medicine worked better.

"Well," I said, "I think it's a *different* kind of malaria."

He raised and lowered his eyebrows. It was an ambiguous gesture that could signify agreement or a withholding of judgment or even disagreement, but with a desire to avoid confrontation. He left abruptly, without saying another word, and retreated to the cool semidarkness of his men's house. I didn't see him again for the rest of the day.

Sunday, December 8:

THE FAREWELL FEAST

Bill

In the January before our August arrival in Vanuatu, Hurricane Nigel devastated most of the northern islands of the archipelago. On Ambae, only one person lost his life in the hurricane but damage to property was immense: According to the government newspaper, over 90 percent of the houses on the island were flattened. When we heard the news in Canada, we wanted to do something to help the relief effort on Ambae, especially that part of the island with which we had long-standing ties. We conduct our fieldwork in the Anglican sector of Ambae and at that time Margy attended the Anglican church in our neighborhood in Canada. She received permission from the minister of the church to give a Sunday sermon concerning the plight of the people in Vanuatu. Part of the collection was set aside for hurricane relief. A few weeks later, she showed slides and gave a talk to a church woman's group. They too made a generous contribution to the small relief fund we were accumulating.

Margy had planned to present part of the money she had collected to Waileni in church on our final Sunday in the village. She was too sick to attend the service, so I acted in her stead. I explained the origin of the donation and gave the treasurer of the village council the funds she had collected. Mathias stood up and made a short, graceful speech thanking us on behalf of the community. After church, I went immediately to find the man with the truck to take my wife to the hospital.

Margy

The very complexity of a passage that I had always performed simply and without thought brought home to me, and to our neighbors, how quickly I had become as weak as the oldest, feeblest widow in the village. To walk from our house to a waiting Toyota Landcruiser, pull open its heavy, squeaky door, clamber into the passenger seat, and close the door behind me was much more than I could accomplish on my own. I leaned heavily on Bill's arm as he led me across the few yards that separated our house from the truck. I tried to smile but the eyes that gazed back solemnly reflected my own discovery that, try as I might, I could not even create an illusion of being less sick than everyone feared. This scared me. And I could see that it scared Sean and Channing. Bill helped me into the passenger seat, closed the door, boosted himself into the truckbed, and signaled the driver that we were ready. The children waved as we drove off, Channing almost, but not quite, in tears and our teenage son beside her, dry-eyed and tall. Two brave kids, I thought.

I rode with my eyes closed as the Landcruiser lurched through potholes and ruts. The driver was proud that he had maintained this truck for nine years; he eased it carefully through washouts and down hills. Time slowed to walking speed, and I remember the journey mostly as a sequence of scents—the smell of gardens, the damp earth of the forest, woodsmoke from cooking fires, the rancid bacon odor of drying copra. When at last the driver shifted into third gear, I could smell cattle manure mixed with sea salt and I knew we had reached the flat coastal plantations. The hospital was nearby, just over the lip of an extinct volcanic crater that had blown open to the sea.

A local nurse in a crisp blue uniform and bare feet greeted us, seated me on the veranda which served as the waiting room of the colonial-style hospital, and took my temperature. She was young and shy; long thick lashes protected her downcast eyes from the intrusive gaze of outsiders. Her sympathetic bedside manner depended entirely on softly sibilant intakes of breath combined with clicks of the tongue. Nurses in Vanuatu all seem to be experts at producing this consoling sound, somewhere between that of a purring cat and a sitting hen.

Lulled by the nurse's care, I began to think everything would be all right. Then "Dr." David appeared, dressed in Sunday shorts and a Foster's Lager T-shirt. He was proprietary about my illness. I remembered his Australian predecessor haranguing us in 1970 when we complained of loose teeth: "No one on *my* island gets scurvy," he bellowed as he treated our vitamin deficiency. I don't know if the old doctor was really David's role model, but it was quite clear that no sick person would be evacuated from *his* island if he could help it. Go back to the village, take more antimalarial drugs and rest, he prescribed. He had seen more serious cases. Why, one man from a remote settlement came down with resistant malaria and had been unconscious for two days by the time his friends carted him to the hospital. He survived and so will you, David assured me. Turning to Bill, he signaled the end of our consultation with a cheerful "No worries, mate!"

Bill

In fieldwork, as in show business, there are times when the show must go on. Our farewell feast was one such occasion. The village had planned the feast for weeks. By Sunday, the event had a momentum of its own, an inevitability quite independent of the moods and wishes of its guests or even its planners. Some invited guests lived in the deep bush of a neighboring district. There was no way to contact them quickly in their own communities; in any case, by Sunday morning, they were on their way to our village. During the past few days, our neighbors and friends in Waileni had brought taro and yams from their gardens. They had grated and processed the tubers into the principal feast food in Vanuatu, lap-lap, a starchy pudding. In small compounds all around Waileni, lap-lap had been cooking in earth ovens since early Sunday morning.

Upon our return from the hospital, I was told to remain in our compound until preparations for the feast were complete in the main village. Sean posted himself at the window of our house overlooking the dirt track connecting our compound with the village. Around four P.M., he saw a small group of men leave the main village and walk down the road toward our house. He turned to me. "Better lighten up, Dad," he said. "It's party time!"

My mother's brother gave me a head of kava to take with me to the feast. He gave Sean and Channing each a small bundle of *lap-lap*. Then he led us to the meeting house, located on a small rise overlooking the plaza and fallen banyan in the village. When we arrived, the meeting house was filled with people. It had been decorated for the occasion with flowers and ornamental shrubs, gardenias shaped like ivory pinwheels, hibiscus as red as heart's blood, crotons with corkscrew leaves that look like a thermal map, splashes of sea green on a base of vivid canary yellow. The three of us were seated on a wooden bench. Facing us were ten heads of kava and twenty-six bundles of *lap-lap* wrapped in banana leaves, each weighing from ten to fifteen pounds—a lifetime supply unless you know the rules for disposing of it. Channing's friend, Ndiu, ten years old, placed an artificial lei around her neck. This was an honor indeed: In Waileni, real flowers are commonplace but plastic flowers (which bridesmaids carry in all church weddings) cost money and last indefinitely. Sean and I received wreaths of real frangipani. In fact, Ndiu placed two leis around my neck, one for the absent Margy.

There were speeches of welcome and thanksgiving, of friendship and the sorrows of distance, and then ten half coconut shells of kava were set out in front of the bench where I was sitting, and I drank the gray-colored, bitter liquid with all the chiefs, a kind of "kastom" communion. According to one local myth, kava first grew from the decomposing genitalia of a murdered woman and everyone agrees it tastes terrible. It is acceptable, even polite, to make loud phlegm-summoning noises and then spit after drinking kava. So the chiefs and I all rushed outside the meeting house as soon as we had drained our shells. There we all stood, lined up on the grass in front of the meeting house, spitting over the edge of the small rise, and at that precise moment the sun broke through the clouds, bathing the fallen banyan across the plaza in golden light.

It was the last light of late afternoon. Night fell quickly and I distributed the bundles of taro and yam pudding with the help of my adoptive kinsmen. Women and children began to leave the area of the meeting house for their own compounds. Most of the men stayed behind to drink more kava. The wife of my mother's brother sent one of her children to tell me that I was to remain with the men, that she would look after Margy and would summon me if I was needed. I trusted her and gratefully I accepted her offer. As I waited for my second shell of kava, some of the men asked me about Margy's condition. I told them she had malaria and they said "ahhhh" or "sori" or else they drew in their breath sharply through their teeth in an expression of sympathy. I had no idea at the time how thoroughly the villagers rejected my diagnosis in favor of their own judgment.

I returned home after my second shell of kava. As soon as I stepped through the door of our house, I wondered if I was hallucinating. Margy was sitting up in bed. By the light of a single kerosene lantern at her bedside, I could see that she was grinning. That struck me as odd, but odder still was the way she smelled. She smelled smoky, funky, as if she had spent the last few hours putting out a brush fire in a coconut plantation. "You'll never guess what happened while you were away," she said.

Margy

As I lay in my bed, drifting with the fever, I became aware that not everyone was at the feast. The corrugated iron roof creaked as it expanded to absorb the heat of the day; but the bamboo floor also creaked, and for no apparent reason. From time to time, I saw worried brown faces peeking through the open window above my bed or watching me from the darkness of a doorway as I staggered to the privy. By evening, the worried faces had settled down at the foot of my bed to stay.

Woibani, the local kindergarten teacher who lived next door, acted as the spokesperson for the other women. I should realize, she explained, that while I might be ill with malaria, I was clearly suffering from something more serious.

"Like what?" I asked.

"Well, like spirits," she said, her dark eyes shining with excitement and concern.

"Oh," I said.

"The women—my mother and the others—want to do something to help you."

It soon became evident to me that I was being made an offer I couldn't refuse. "No" was not an acceptable response; what I didn't have was a choice. Looking back, I realize that the village women had no choice either. To fail to give me the appropriate customary treatment would have been like a doctor withholding a tetanus shot from someone who had rolled through a barnyard full of rusty barbed wire.

Woibani's mother inched forward from where she had been standing at the foot of the bed. She held a tiny green coconut in one hand and in the other a fistful of crustlike fibers of dry coconut husk. I felt the round smoothness of the coconut move down my right side from my cheeks to my thights, while the coarse, scratchy fibers followed the same course on my left side. Then she took the coconut and the husk away and faded into the outer dark. Woibani explained to me that she was taking the implements to Eva, a local healer. Eva would say a spell over the coconut and the husk and that would begin my cure.

Eva must have been nearby. In a few minutes I heard voices ouside the house: "Woibani, *pssst!*" Woibani slid off my bed and conversed softly with her mother through the slats in the thin wall. As she listened to her mother, Woibani looked down at the dry woven bamboo floor of the bedroom, shook her head, and said, "No, Mother, I think I'd better do it in the kitchen." I began to be apprehensive about what was going to happen next.

Soon I found myself, unsteady but upright, standing in our kitchen, surrounded by Woibani's younger sisters. They drew back as Woibani carefully put a match to the crusts of coconut husks. First she held the burning husks and solemnly wafted the smoke around my body like a priest with a censer. The sisters cringed from the smoke, which was meant for me alone. Then she placed the little fire right between my feet. I was relieved that Woibani had the good sense to suggest the coral floor of the kitchen for this event.

Someone handed me the small green coconut and said, "Here! Drink this in one swallow!" I did, and promptly threw up. That didn't seem to matter. Woibani helped me back to bed, and I lay there, reeking of smoke, feeling that—in a small way—I had given my body for science.

Monday, December 9, 1985:
DENYING THE RIVER SPIRITS

Bill

The night passed. Margy seemed to sleep well enough—sheer exhaustion will do that—but when we took her temperature first thing on Monday morning, I became alarmed. During the last few days she had a relatively low fever in the morning, and then her temperature had risen gradually during the day, reaching a peak at night. Today she was starting out close to 103 degrees Fahrenheit. I tried again to give her some food and medicine; none of it stayed down. I decided that I had to get her out—today.

Mathias came to our house at about six A.M., as soon as he saw we were awake. He looked grim. His eyes were serious and his mouth was set in a deep frown. I had assumed that he agreed with my diagnosis that Margy had malaria, even if he didn't understand the technicalities of chloroquine-resistant strains. I had further assumed that he would be relieved if I put her on the plane to Espiritu Santo, where Western doctors could treat her. He listened to me in silence as I tried to reassure him that proper medical care could cure her and told him my plan to get her to Santo. I expected agreement, sympathy, and relief. Instead he wore a curious expression on his face, one I had never seen before. There was something about the set of his eyes and a certain tightness around the edges of his mouth. Then I knew: I recognized with a shock that he disbelieved and discounted what I was saying. But there was something else, too, in his expression, something more than mere disbelief, an emotion closer to contempt. What was the matter? Why was he looking at me like that? Then he told me, his voice cold and harsh:

"You white men think you know everything," he said. "You may *think* this illness is malaria, but that's just not right. If you take Margaret to Santo right now, you will kill her. She must stay here in the village."

"What are you talking about?" I asked him angrily. I felt confused and defensive and not fully awake.

"I'm talking about *wande,* river spirits, the ones that killed Elsie a few years ago. When your medicine had no effect on Margaret's illness, we knew it couldn't be malaria. We began to consider other possibilities, other ways of explaining why she is so sick. I thought it might be *wande* because I know she went swimming at Waisala last week. That's their place, you know; that's where they live. Last night Eva took the young coconut that the women rubbed over Margaret's body and she dreamed on it. Early this morning—before dawn—she came to see me. She told me her dream. She said she saw rows of little houses on the banks of the Waisala, dwellings just like our own but much smaller. As Margaret swam with her friends, the *wande* watched her from the other side of the river. They liked her and they decided she must come live with them. They lined the riverbank and waved at her, but she couldn't see them. She couldn't hear them either, but they were calling to her: 'Come live with us. Come live with us.'

Mathias's voice became melodic, almost pleading as he imitated the *wande.* "Come live with us" was a bush-siren's call, entrancing, irresistible.

He continued: "Eva spoke to them in her dream. She told them that Margaret couldn't come to live with them, that they must release her. The *wande* agreed, but now Margaret must take the medicine that will cure her."

"What medicine?" I asked.

"It's *our* medicine," he said, "special leaves. Eva prepared some to give to Margaret. She must take it."

"No," I said sharply, and knew immediately that our relationship had been altered forever. With one word, I had shown him the limits of my trust in him and the boundary of my belief in his world. Damn it, life has its bottom lines: Mosquitoes, not bush spirits, made Margy sick; proper medical care would cure her, not concoctions made to guard against invisible enemies. I had known Mathias for sixteen years. I had spent almost two of the last eight years living with him, much more time than I spent with my own kinsmen during the same period. During all the time we had known each other, we played our roles well: He was my teacher and I was his eager student, he was a warm father and I tried to be his loving son; he was the chief and I was his follower, bound to respect his word. Suddenly it all seemed like play-acting. If the stakes were high enough, and I thought they were, then I was willing to take off my mask called "anthropologist" and kiss cultural relationships good-bye. What I didn't consider at the time was that he thought the stakes were high too, and he too was willing to take off his mask.

"She *must* take the medicine," he said.

Margy

Bill didn't know that Mathias's will had already been done. While the old leader confronted Bill in the front yard, Woibani slipped through the bushes and came silently in the side door. She stood by my bed, breathless for a moment, holding another little coconut and a green leaf folded as if something was wrapped inside of it.

"You have to drink this. Drink it all at once," she said handing me the coconut. "And here, you must eat this medicine. Eva made it for you."

She opened the leaf wrapper, revealing a paste made of chopped greens. Mixed with the greens were dark brown chunky bits, like dry cat food in pureed spinach.

"It's useless, Woibani. I'll just throw up."

"That doesn't matter," she said reassuringly. "Just eat it and see what happens!"

"See what happens, eh? What if I take a bite of that stuff and grow so big I fill this entire house? Or would I find myself tiny as a mouse, swimming in a pool of tears?" I really didn't say that, except in my mind. In fact, I said nothing at all as I reached out for the medicine. I heard Mathias's and Bill's voices outside, in front of the house, and I wondered what they were arguing about. I envied them their strength to argue and knew I was too tired to do likewise. The simplest thing was just to do as I was told. How could a few leaves make much difference to my poor body?

Later, Bill asked me what the leaves tasted like. They tasted green, that's all I remember. What did strike me as remarkable at the time was that they were the first thing I'd eaten since Friday that stayed down. Woibani smiled the smile of the vindicated. *She* knew the leaves would help me. Before she left, she told me with something like pride in her voice that she would bring me another round of medicine in only a few hours.

I didn't want to be around for that. Not that I felt the medicine was harmful. I simply had no faith that herbal cures could prove effective against a new strain of malaria. The women meant well—they really cared about me—but I'd had enough.

And so I left the village. It was a visit cut short and not properly ended. The women stood at the edge of the clearing in front of our house; they did not approach the truck that came to take me to the airport. I wanted to assure them that I would be all right, but for them to really believe me, I would have had to stay in Waileni. Anyway, I was having difficulty putting words together coherently. My head had begun to buzz. I felt as if I were underwater listening to people speak on the surface. As the truck pulled out of the village and headed for the airfield, what had been ordinary daylight began to pulse and flare.

Bill

Semiconscious and still smelling strongly of smoke, Margy must have been quite a sight to the young French pilot of the Britten-Norman "Islander" that landed on the airstrip on Ambae. He helped me carry her to the plane and settle her in the copilot's seat. I kissed her on the cheek and whispered to her that I loved her. Then, when the pilot got ready to close the door of the aircraft, I let go of her hand and walked back to the bush shelter at the end of the runway. A few minutes later the plane raced down the cow pasture that served as an airstrip, gathered speed, lifted, and then headed out over the coconut plantations, toward the sea. Santo was only thirty miles away but it might as well have been on another planet. My separation from Margy was complete, as complete as if she had been in the *Voyager* passing the dark side of the moon.

That afternoon I packed our bags. Getting ready to leave Waileni was lonely work. Except for Mathias, the compound was empty of people: No kids played under the almond tree, no women clustered around our kitchen, no men squatted on the bare packed earth in front of the clubhouse. It was an ordinary Monday in an average week. Children were in school and, for their parents, there was work to be done in the gardens, copra to be made, pigs to be tended. Mathias often remained behind when others set off to work; he was an old man, entitled to an old man's rest. Every so often he would come to my house and sit in the place where he always sat, just inside the door, on the bamboo floor. Neither of us felt like talking. Silently he watched me pack, and then, as silently, he would leave, only to return a little while later. His anger at me was gone but I could still feel his concern and his sadness. He *knew* I'd made a terrible mistake in sending Margy to Santo before her cure was complete. He'd done what he could, but in the end I had acted just like the white man I was. There was nothing else to say.

Tuesday, December 10, 1985:
FINAL ACTS

Bill

Getting out of the field is simple in concept (pack only two suitcases; everything else stays) but difficult in practice (you must dispose of the rest of the stuff). I arose at three A.M. and went into the kitchen, my storeroom and staging area. I lit a kerosene lamp and looked around me: There, on tables and on the coral floor, was the detritus of our stay in Waileni— plastic buckets, gray trade-store blankets, a machete, bright blue calico curtains, spare flipflops, a half-empty sack of rice, a can of shaving cream, a case of corned beef, an unopened bottle of French champagne Margy and I had planned to open on our last night in the village, and more, much more. My problem was how to distribute our belongings fairly—that is, how to give everybody in the village *something,* with special gifts for special friends. I made myself a cup of coffee and sat down at a table with two pads of Scotch Post-its.

By dawn, every item in the kitchen bore a little yellow sticker with someone's name on it. I woke up the children.

Outside the house, people were gathering—under the almond tree, in the clubhouse, on the road. I could hear men's quiet laughter and women shushing noisy children. I carried the first bundles outside. It was like Christmas morning, two weeks early. Mathias received the lion's share, as was his due. He sat apart from the rest of the men and received my gifts without comment. To Eva, I gave our very best lengths of calico; to my mother's brother's wife, a silver-plated necklace I had brought from Canada for just this occasion; to Woibani, many small gifts, including Margy's favorite brush and comb. And so it continued, the final act, with everybody on stage except Margy.

Then the stage emptied: I'd given my last gift, shaken everyone's hand, said my good-byes. For the people of Waileni, it was the beginning of another ordinary day and there was work to do. Only Mathias stayed behind, waiting for the truck that would take us to the airfield. When it arrived, I slung our suitcases up to Sean, who had clambered into the back of the truck. I lifted Channing into the Toyota's cabin beside the driver and shut the door. I stood beside the truck on the road with Mathias, not knowing how to end it, what to do or say.

"I don't know when I'll see you again," I said awkwardly, "maybe soon, though. You never know."

He just stood there.

"Good-bye," I said, and stuck out my hand.

He just looked at it. Slowly his gaze returned to my face, and he said loudly "Awwww, *buggerit!*" which is not a local word at all. He smiled and put his arms around me in a short, strong embrace and then let go of me forever.

The Australian doctor's wife in Santo is the only woman in town with freckles and long red hair. As we landed, before we disembarked, I saw her standing behind the wire fence bordering the airstrip. We had become close friends, and with dreadful certainty I knew she'd come to the airfield to meet me. My God, I thought as the plane rolled to a standstill, what's happened to Margy? I raced across the tarmac toward her, my mind a broth of nightmares: Margy flown out to a larger hospital, Margy in coma, Margy dead. "She's going to be all right," I heard the red-haired woman say. "I thought you'd want to know immediately."

RECOVERY TIME

Margy

"You *ate* those leaves!" The young, bearded Australian doctor at the Santo hospital looked appalled. He was my friend, and one reason we had become friends is that we seemed to share so much in common. He had visited us in the village, drunk kava with the men, and gone swimming (without ill effects) in the Waisala. I had assumed that his attitude toward customary medicine would be rather like my own: It can't do any harm and it might do some good . . . *they* take leaf potions themselves when they are sick . . . and anyway, who knows, maybe the cure for cancer grows wild in the rain forests of Ambae.

There's a certain expression that humans reserve for friends who have acted foolishly. The doctor wore that expression—incredulous, bemused, embarrassed *for* me—as he stood by my bedside. He didn't want to tell me he thought my views on customary medicine were naive and romantic, but that's what he let me know. As he took my temperature, he said he had seen many patients arrive at the hospital unconscious and half dead from the effects of "bush cures." Indigestible leaves sometimes caused intestinal blockages. In any case, he said gently when he finished taking my pulse, "the medicine probably *did* have an active agent. From your symptoms, I imagine they were trying to ward off the spirits with leaves that contain atropine."

My recollections of the first few days in Santo are vague. I lay in bed in the doctor's house, my jaws and every muscle in my body clenched tight, a side effect of the massive doses of quinine the doctor gave me. He also gave me medicine to inhibit the vomiting, which had resumed some hours after Eva's treatment.

We left Santo on Thursday, four days after I'd arrived, but before I was really well enough to travel. According to the hospital scales I had lost fifteen pounds: I weighed less than when I was fourteen years old. I still couldn't walk steadily. Both my vision and hearing were impaired from the malaria or the quinine or the leaf medicine, or all three.

In Port Vila, the capital, we stayed on the outskirts of the town in a house more suited to the plantations of Mississippi than those of Vanuatu. It was a mansion in a state of genteel decay, redolent of rotting flowers and the sea breezes and mildew. We were houseguests of a British public servant who spent early evenings and weekends whacking away at decorative shrubbery gone wild. Hibiscus flowers, purple bougainvillea vines, avocado trees, all fell to his machete and left a swath like a firebreak between the house and the jungle. I lay in bed looking out the window, listening to the hum of tropical fields and to the slap of the knife, growing stronger, and gaining distance from what had happened on Ambae.

"THAT WHICH DOES NOT KILL ME (GETS NO SECOND CHANCE)": CONCLUSIONS FROM EXPERIENCE

Margy

Would I go back to Ambae? Certainly. In part, I want to return so that I can make a proper leavetaking. I want Woibani and the others to see that I have regained good health. I've written letters but I'm sure some people in the village wonder if I'm telling the whole truth. Maybe I'm shaving the edges of the truth to save them worry or maybe I'm unaware of some lasting effects of my brush with the spirits: Maybe the *wande* are not so easily denied. Peoples' residual doubts will be stilled only when they see me. That's the way things are on Ambae. Seeing is believing.

When I return to Ambae, there's one thing I *won't* do: I won't swim in the Waisala. *Wande* may exist only in people's minds, but I am not brave enough to mock them or fool enough to risk another invitation to come live with them. Fieldwork is the most tempting of fates for an anthropologist, but in doing fieldwork you don't tempt fate, not unless you're willing to do fieldwork forever.

Bill

Nietzsche said, "That which does not kill me makes me stronger," and Hemingway believed him. Me, I'm not so sure. I think experience makes us wiser, wilier, sometimes sadder, but seldom stronger. If anything, a crisis such as the one we experienced is more apt to introduce new hesitancies to the human soul than build character. To do fieldwork in a remote area, an anthropologist needs self-confidence, a sense of being able to cope with the islandness of islands, the secret ways of jungles, or the emptiness of deserts. This can lead—easily—to a soldierly illusion of invulnerability, a fiction that the slithergadee (which comes out of the sea) "will get all the others, but won't get me." It is not the mere fact of isolation that makes us vulnerable. Nor is it a lack of caution or preparation that is most apt to get us into trouble. What renders us helpless most often is circumstance. Even where there are planes, there always is a last flight out. If you need to be on it and you are not, then—for you—there might as well be no flights at all.

Another thing I learned from the events surrounding Margy's illness concerns a hidden element in the economics of fieldwork. Anthropologists never view themselves as being a burden on their hosts; we all try to repay the many kindnesses of the people we study in whatever ways we can. It's true that there is a sense in which our exchange with our host communities always is imbalanced: Without fieldwork, we would have no careers as anthropologists. We never repay the people we study for the benefits we receive in our own societies from our fieldwork. But it's also true that reciprocity always underlies a good relationship between a fieldworker and a host community—we exchange goods for glimpses into lives, the rewards of learning for the pleasures of teaching, big gifts for oceans of story and a host of intangibles. Everyday exchange and mutual generosity come to feel natural, balanced, value given for value received, a relationship between equals who like each other. What I learned during our last fieldwork was that some people had been giving us gifts that we hadn't even recognized, let alone repaid. Margy's illness cast into bold relief the degree to which our presence in the village was a burden to Mathias. We chose to live with him because we respected his knowledge and liked his personality. It was easy for us to choose him; it was an added burden for him to accept us. He likes us, of that I'm sure, but he also felt very, very responsible for our well-being. We were babes in the woods and as such a source of worry for him. He knew about hazards to our well-being (river spirits, bush spirits, God knows what else) of which we were either unaware or else did not take seriously as threats. He loved us, I think, and I also think he must have counted the days until our departure. When we left him, we were sad; he may have been sad too, but he also was relieved. It couldn't have been otherwise. Looking back, I am a bit mystified that he managed to tolerate us for so long with such apparent ease and good humor.

The final lesson I learned was the hardest of all, and it has to do with the *real* politics of fieldwork. In most places, at most times, anthropologists conduct fieldwork in an atmosphere of political relativism: We observe but do not interfere; the people we study tolerate our observation and do not attempt to exercise authority over us. A crisis can change all that. During our final days in Waileni, Margy and I became key participants in a small-scale drama involving the politics of curing, and by so doing we became less innocent about the political realities of fieldwork. I had always thought that my relationship with Mathias was based on rough and ready equality and bonds of mutual goodwill. After all, he adopted me; I interpreted that as having to do with kinship and amity, not politics. But Mathias understood something I did not: Ordinary sentiments of friendship and affection are inappropriate to extraordinary times. He is the chief of a territory—we were in his territory at the point at which Margy became ill. I assumed (incorrectly) that he would never try to impose his will on us. He assumed (incorrectly) that I would not challenge his decision in a time of crisis. Being in conflict with each other was a learning experience for us both. We both learned something about ourselves, about each other, and about each other's culture.

There are other lessons I learned that are less cautionary and more personal; they are implicit in the story we have told and need no underlining. The lessons we learn breed lessons we continue learning. Even when anthropologists return from the field, they continue to do fieldwork as they remember and interpret their experiences and learn from them. In that sense, for as long as we care, we do fieldwork forever.

ACKNOWLEDGMENTS

Sharon Tiffany, Isabel Brymer, and Richard Brymer provided us with valuable comments on earlier drafts of this story. We are grateful for their editorial advice and for their insights into the experiences we describe.

SUGGESTED READINGS

ALLEN, MICHAEL

1981 Vanuatu: Politics, Economics, and Ritual in Island Melanesia. Sydney: Academic Press. The only major collection of articles on Vanuatu.

FITZGERALD, FRANCES

1986 Vanuatu: The Original Bali-h'ai. Islands 6:34–53. The author of this travel article (which has beautiful photographs) is a Pulitzer Prize winner. And Ambae, our fieldsite, is the island James Michener used as a model for *Bali-h'ai*.

HARRISON, TOM

1937 Savage Civilization. New York: Knopf. A lively and very readable early ethnography of the New Hebrides. He describes a cannibal feast on Malekula but his title is ironic: The British and French colonialists, not the native people, are the "savage" civilization.

RODMAN, MARGARET

1988 Deep Water: Development and Change in Pacific Village Fisheries. Boulder, CO: Westview Press. Looks at development from the point of view of the participants—both developers and islanders—and how and why it works (or doesn't work), focusing on the interaction of the island culture, the culture of North American volunteers, and the outside impetus for development.

RODMAN, WILLIAM

1985 'A Law Unto Themselves': Legal Innovation in Ambae, Vanuatu. American Ethnologist 12:603–624. This article describes what happened when colonial rule ended on Ambae. When the state withdrew from participation in local legal affairs, the people reorganized their villages, codified their laws, set up their own courts, and became—for more than eight years—"a law unto themselves."

TWENTY-FIVE

A Letter from the Field

MARTY ZELENIETZ

November 14, 1977
Ongaia, Kilenge
West New Britain
Papua, New Guinea

Dear Joel,

Can't remember when I last wrote you—months ago, as I recall. We're head over heels into our research, pushing ourselves about as hard as we can in this heat and humidity. I'm glad that my advisor, Dave Counts, steered us to this field site. We couldn't have conjured up a better group of people to work with. The people of Ongaia tolerate our strange ways and incessant questioning, look after our welfare, and support us and our work every way imaginable. They've even stopped calling us "Masta" and "Missus" (the usual appellations for white people) and have pulled us into the village system by giving us local names.

Jill and I make a good team. Asking her to come was the smartest move I've ever made. I'm sure I'd go stark raving bonkers without a sympathetic soul to speak my own language, to share my own cultural background. Bush living offers the ultimate challenge to our relationship—if we make it through the next few months without loathing each other, I guess we'll get married.

Early on we gave up trying to run our own separate research projects. It just didn't work. Now we cover the same topics from different angles. I handle the male perspective, and Jill discovers the female view. This saves us both agony and frustration, and fills in otherwise inevitable gaps. By myself, I'd never find out what women think and say. Married women and single girls generally avoid me. I could never sit down for personal or confidential interviews with them, for the Kilenge *know* what a man and a woman do alone together. Now if Jill came to the village alone, she would have to "unsex" herself, become some sort of nonwoman, in order to gain access to male gossip, rituals, and secrets. So I work with the men, and Jill with the women. Our gender identities secure, we sit down together to work with families and couples. I think we get the broadest perspective possible.

Jill picked up a bit of Male'u (the local language) in the last few months, while I basically work in Tok Pisin (the lingua franca spoken by nearly all Ongaians) Her knowledge allows us to cross-check what our informants tell us. Most men (but not the women) don't credit her with understanding Male'u, so they frequently use Male'u to discuss their answers to our questions before giving an answer in Tok Pisin. Usually we get the same answers in both languages, but not always. Differing responses give us clues to questions we should ask, issues we should pursue.

It's not all work and no play for us. We took a quick trip to Lae in September. Lae, ah, lovely Lae—my vision of the perfect tropical town. Lush flowers, tree-lined streets, relaxed pace of life, all that you could want. After five months in the bush, Jill and I flipped out: take-out food, white tile bathrooms, showers, flush toilets (quite a contrast with our current "facilities"), paperback novels galore, and booze that we didn't have to ration by the thimble full. We dropped a fortune on supplies and gifts for friends in the village. I think economists call this the "trickle-down" effect.

The only disconcerting note of the trip came at a party on our last night in town. A loudmouthed overseas volunteer claimed that five days in a village gave her *total understanding* of life in the bush. Worse yet, given the opportunity, she would convert that village to her worldview—cultural missionaries we don't need! What a contrast to Jill and me: After five months in Ongaia, we only began to learn of the depth of our ignorance about village life, organization, and customs.

As I wrote to you earlier, in our first months here I hadn't made much headway trying to study sorcery. I thought sorcery might tie in to my work on political and social change, but people just didn't want to discuss it. Villagers responded to my pointed questions with vague generalities and closed the topic by saying that they banished sorcery long ago. Either sorcery had disappeared or people didn't want to talk about it, so I dropped that line of investigation and moved on to other things. Rule number one in this business: Don't push anything people don't want pushed.

But surprise, surprise! We found a dramatically different situation when we returned from Lae. In our absence, somebody announced his suspicions: An unknown sorcerer had attacked him. With a sorcery accusation out in the open, with the threat of sorcery exposed in the village, people not only talk about sorcery now, they're preoccupied with it. The preoccupation transcends mere discussion—someone actually gave me the chance to learn some potent homicidal sorcery spells and techniques! I might use that kind of knowledge to work wonders on my supervisory committee when I get back, but meanwhile having that knowledge would blow my fieldwork by compromising my position in the village, so I declined. Let me tell you the story. . . .

We only left Ongaia for a week in September, but returned to find a prominent man in the village deathly ill with a mysterious ailment that no one (mission hospital or local healers) could seem to cure. The people at the mission hospital, just up the hill from the village, think that Herman has a form of TB, but the poor man believes someone sorcerized him. Herman's talk of sorcery opened a floodgate of fear, information, and debate. The Kilenge see sorcery as we do nuclear armaments: If you don't think or talk about it, fine, but once it hits your consciousness, the consequences horrify and overwhelm you. A hidden, latent fear of sorcery and its destructive potential lurks beneath the surface of village life. With sorcery now a public affair, with gossip buzzing about the validity of the sorcery diagnosis and the identity of the assailant (and people wondering who would next fall victim), our friends and informants have inundated us with detailed cases from the not-so-distant past. And my guess panned out. Much to my relief, a lot of the sorcery stuff ties in with my research on leadership and social control.

To pick up the narrative, in the beginning of October, we heard that a famous sorcerer, Tangis, would come from a Lolo (mountain people) village to attempt a cure of the afflicted Herman. I'd never met Tangis, but his reputation preceded him—a real man of "power," a suspected homicidal sorcerer. Just the way people whisper about Tangis echoes their fear and respect for the man. Mind you, the Kilenge regard all Lolo with suspicion, see all Lolo as potential sorcerers, but they hold Tangis in special awe.

On October 5, Tangis (who villagers describe as the Number One Doctor) showed up at the mission hospital. Assisted by another Lolo man of power, Akone, Tangis performed a curing ceremony on Herman. We got lucky: some friends alerted us, so we grabbed our notebooks and camera and charged up the hill. Receiving permission to attend, I witnessed the ceremony and documented the event. Jill commiserated with Herman's female kin gathered outside the room. No one minded our presence; in fact, they made us feel welcome. As he performed the cure, Tangis explained each stage to the onlookers. He rubbed leaves on the patient to locate and neutralize pain, spat ginger to "heat things up," and chanted spells and songs.

Later, my adopted father Steamship formally introduced me to Tangis and Akone. (You probably think that no one could *really* have the name "Steamship," but here people often take a "death name" when a close relative dies. My adopted father's son died while on board a ship—hence the name Steamship.) Steamship explained that since Tangis called him "big brother," I could cell Tangis "smol papa," or junior father. Such instant relationships derive from the Kilenge notion of cognatic descent and a kind of Hawaiian kinship terminology. Don't let the anthropological jargon get to you. Translated into plain English, it means that if you're related to anyone, you're probably related to everyone.

I felt a little awed meeting Tangis. He carries such a heavy reputation and commands such respect. Oddly enough, he's a quiet, unassuming man, short even by local standards, and not at all fierce—not my mental picture of a killer sorcerer. After we met Tangis, we headed back for the village and spent the rest of the day and night recording villagers' views of why someone attacked Herman and who they thought did it. No matter how I looked at the episode, no matter whose interpretation of events I examined, people generally agreed that some unknown sorcerer had targeted Herman. Somehow the sorcery attack on Herman tied into local power struggles for social standing and leadership status. Many villagers felt that Herman had moved too far, too fast, in his bid for leadership status.

A few days later, the evening of the eighth, Tangis and Akone came to our house for a chat, accompanied by a man from the village next to Ongaia. As a general rule I don't tape interviews; I usually take extensive notes and then write up the material the following morning. But I taped the session with Tangis and Akone, partly for accuracy, partly because they enjoyed listening to themselves talking on the tape, and partly, I guess, because I hoped for some bit of esoteric knowledge too precious to lose. So the five of us crowded around the tape recorder, with only one hurricane lamp for light, as Tangis talked about Herman's case. He described how he and Akone diagnosed the malady, how they located the "infection," and the steps they took to draw the sorcery out of Herman's body. Tangis then talked in general terms of his life as a man of power, of his father's instructing him in various spells, rituals, and techniques for the communal good. His teachers enjoined him never to use his powers to hurt others, unless others tried to hurt someone in his group.

In talking about defending family and kin, Tangis digressed to describe how to sorcerize a person, how to make them sicken and die. He discussed the procedures and actions for sorcerizing (with Akone adding a comment here and there). He carefully avoided telling us what spells to use, what powers to invoke. (Okay, Joel, I know this must sound strange as you read it in the relatively civilized surroundings of Chicago, but remember I came here to study these things, and in the still of the night, wedged in a creaking hut between the ocean and the jungle, this stuff is not only believable, it's reality! And no, I'm not suffering malarial hallucinations!) Tangis said he couldn't tell us the spells, not here in the village, and he could never say them in front of Jill (some things women may never know). In essence, Tangis gave us an empty gun which was useless without the ammunition.

What Tangis said next really caught me by surprise. He casually offered to take me into the bush, up the mountain, for a few days of instruction on the proper spells to cure people of various kinds of sorcery. On the surface an innocuous offer, but the way sorcery works here, if you can remove a spell or illness from someone, then you can (so common belief and knowledge goes) also put that spell or illness on somebody. One implies the other: Those who cure can kill, and vice versa. Tangis, so it seemed, invited me to join the ranks of homicidal sorcerers. After presenting his offer, my "smol papa" and his assistant gave us a couple of spells for making the new gardens grow better—our consolation prize of esoteric knowledge for the night. Shortly thereafter, they left.

Jill and I talked long into the night about Tangis's offer. Honestly, I felt ambivalent, a bit frightened, a bit intrigued. Days and nights in the mountain bush could drag me out physically. Then again, gaining that priceless knowledge might more than offset the discomfort. But knowledge for what ends? Do I want to know *how* to do sorcery, or does my real interest lie in what people believe about sorcery, and the *impact* of sorcery beliefs on life in the village? I worried about the effect that my learning sorcery would have on my neighbors, the people with whom I lived and worked. I mean, how would you feel if a man feared for his homicidal potential lived next door to you?

The next day decided things for me. Word travels fast in the village where gossip and information exchange provide a major form of entertainment for the two hundred fifty inhabitants. Besides, who can keep secrets through flimsy woven bamboo walls? I sneeze, and everyone within a twenty-five-meter radius catches a cold. Anyway, two people came separately to me that day to tell me the fate of fledgling sorcerers. "Marty," I heard twice that day, "do you know what happens to men who have just learned homicidal sorcery? All the established sorcerers get together, and they send powerful spells his way. It's a sort of test. If the new one commands true power, he can deflect those spells and survive. If not, if he has weak command, well . . . they plant what's left of him in the cemetary afterward."

I got my answer. The people of Ongaia didn't want another sorcerer, another man with power, living in their midst. Such a man can threaten community stability—an ever-present potential danger upsetting peoples' lives. The Ongaians don't want me hiking up the mountain to learn how to handle power. If I insist, if I discover how to "down" people, I'd cut myself off from the community. I'd become a pariah and blow my fieldwork. Building solid rapport with the people of Ongaia took a long time, and I'm not going to endanger those relationships and my academic future (and maybe even my chances of getting out of here in one piece) in search of esoteric knowledge. I'll stay here on the beach and be a good boy, the "white skin" providing occasional entertainment and valued goods to people.

I'm glad I read the signs and made my decision, because the villagers here sure want to keep me from Tangis. A couple of nights after the Tangis interview, Steamship came to the house to say that Tangis had wanted to see me during the day, to witness the final curing ceremony for Herman (similar, I understand, to the final ceremony I saw). Steamship said he had told Tangis we had important work and couldn't come. I could have strangled Steamship, because we spent that day in the village looking for something to do. Fathers can be so difficult at times.

After Herman's cure, life returned to normal and people showed no apparent concern about sorcery and sorcerers. Out of sight, out of mind. Then, about a week ago, Herman, still sick but a little more mobile, got embroiled in an incident involving a marauding pig. His big pig allegedly destroyed a garden, a major catastrophe for subsistence horticulturalists. Sorcery accusations bubbled to the surface again. Two days later, on November 10, Tangis showed up in the village, ostensibly to tell people about the provincial fair in Kimbe. Few, if any, believe that story. Tangis came over to our house that night. No sooner had he settled down with coffee and a smoke than our best friend and key informant, Paul, just happened to stop by. I felt chaperoned: Obviously, no one intended to leave us alone with Tangis. Tangis wanted to tell me some legends about the creator/trickster hero, Namor, but said he couldn't finish them in one night. He invited me to visit his village for a couple of days. If I would bring a jar of instant coffee, some rice, and some meat, we could "story" for hours on end. Paul promised him I would come and added that I would bring a load of nails for Tangis's new house. I thought Paul seemed rather generous with my possessions, but I guess he would promise anything to get Tangis away from me. We'll see what happens. I suspect I'll never get to Tangis's place.

The sorcery scare generated more positive fallout for my research. For months I'd tried getting Steamship to "story" about his career as a *tultul,* a government-appointed assistant village headman. I figured Steamship's tales would help me understand the colonial era here, the relationship between the villagers and the Australian administration. But Steamship would tell me *nothing.* His standard response: "Oh, I didn't have to do anything. The people were good, the government was good, everything was good, so I did nothing." To listen to Steamship, no one ever got upset or involved in disputes in the village. The government behaved benevolently, and people harkened to the *kiap*'s (patrol officer's) call. Harmony ruled. Sure! Then, some time after sorcery became an "approved" topic for our research, Steamship told me he owned a simple little spell, using a feather hidden under his tongue. This spell gave the user great oratorical abilities while simultaneously tongue-tying the opposition. Steamship said he used it often as *tultul,* when making peace in the village and for deceiving the *kiap.* I asked him about how he used it, and he began to answer the questions I'd asked months earlier. Once started, he didn't stop: Steamship spent the next three days relating his adventures during those halcyon years! I'd tried so hard for that information before, and then it all flew in through the backdoor.

So much of our information *does* come through the back door. Most often we get open and forthright answers to our questions, but occasionally we hit a topic that villagers don't want to discuss. Rather than push things, we just sit back and wait, keeping our ears open to what people say. Days, maybe weeks later we'll hear a stray remark on the topic and then jump on it. When villagers themselves mention the previously ignored topic, when they acknowledge its existence, they'll gladly discuss it and patiently answer our questions. Funny, Ongaians willingly answer specific questions, but often don't respond if they think we are "fishing." If we go into an inteview cold, with no prior information, we often end up no better off than when we started. But our slightest hint that we know something—anything—about the issue usually generates informative answers. The more we know, the more we can learn. That's where Jill's knowledge of Male'u comes in handy, and where patience, detailed notes, and a memory stuffed full of seeming trivia pays off. I've learned to slow down, to realize I can't do it all in one day. I play by Ongaia rules. Here, patience is the game. Wait long enough, don't push things, and we'll get most of the data we want. Before this simple fact dawned on us, we often felt frustrated with our lack of progress and suspicious of the way people responded to us. Frustration seldom bothers us now. If things don't come today, then maybe tomorrow—a true tropical attitude.

And speaking of tomorrow, it promises to be a busy day, so I'll end this here and get some rest in our tropical paradise. Right now the volcano groans and spits ash and smoke, and the sea breeze carries the promise of a storm. Real tranquility, eh? With luck I might get this letter onto a plane or a boat in a few days. Jill sends her regards. Take care, and write soon. Stuck here as we are beyond the edge of the world, mail is our main link with home.

Marty

SUGGESTED READINGS

Jill and I have, individually and collectively, written extensively on our Kilenge fieldwork. Our work covers the gamut from traditional ethnography to aspects of social change. Some examples are:

GRANT, J., H. SAITO, AND M. ZELENIETZ

1986   Where Development Never Comes: Business Activities in Kilenge, Papua New Guinea. Journal of the Polynesian Society 95(2):195–219.

ZELENIETZ, M.

1981   One Step Too Far: Sorcery and Social Change in Kilenge. In Sorcery and Social Change in Melanesia. M. Zelenietz and S. Lindenbaum, eds. Pp. 101–118. Social Analysis #8 (Special Issue).

ZELENIETZ, M., AND J. GRANT

1980   Kilenge Narogo: Ceremonies, Resources, and Prestige in a West New Britain Society. Oceania 51(2):98–117.

1986   The Problem with *Pisins:* An Alternate View of Social Organization in West New Britain (Parts 1 and 2). Oceania 56(3, 4):199–214, 264–274.

For a rather different view of the Kilenge, see:

DARK, P. J. C.

1974   Kilenge Art and Life: A Look at a New Guinea People. London: Academy Editions.

TWENTY-SIX

Turning Tears into Nothing

MILES RICHARDSON

You've been to Mexico before, haven't you? Anthropologists travel. It's part of their work, their work in the field, their work in the field of anthropology. It's their profession. But I wasn't certain, because at times they are so distant from their traveling, as if a part of them never travels, no matter how many miles, how many smells, how many sights, how many sounds, and how many hurts they may have walked, smelled, seen, heard, or bled from. It's the distant part that I am trying to contact. The distant part, you tell me, is that part of you that counts, groups, and orders. Constantly engaged and busy at work, it puts the uniques together, factors out the untidy, and bestows an elegant evenness to all. If it does that, it must be wise. Since it is wise, I want to ask it a question, a question about Mexico, about the people there, and especially about a little girl crying in the streets.

Now, don't be modest. You direct graduate students in their pursuits, you organize symposia at professional meetings, and you present ideas in learned journals. Having accomplished those things, you must know at least a little about a small girl with tears in her eyes.

Before I ask the question, I have to make certain that you are within the circle of my asking. I have to define the universe of discourse, as they say. The universe of discourse, the location of my asking and your responding, is not the country of Mexico, that ribbed land sucked dry by different peoples' struggles to be even before Cortés met Montezuma. The universe where we are to meet is the only one left as soon as you cross the border at Matamoros, Laredo, Juárez, Mexicali, and Tijuana. One step south of the border and the many Mexicos resolve into one, the city.

If you don't think that is true, and as an anthropologist you are prone to doubt—that's part of being wise—ask any driver of *Transportes del Norte*, "*¿En qué dirección está México?*" and he'll point south, where the city is.

Mexico City. How is its is? How would you characterize its being? Would you cite government statistics that more people live within its urbanized area than live in London, Paris, or even Tokyo? Would you point to the debate concerning the push-pull effect of rural to urban migration and then refer to the third-world phenomenon of urbanization without industrialization? Would you speak not only of unemployment but also quote estimates of underemployment? After presenting data on water quality, air pollution, and vehicular traffic, would you conclude with remarks about the explanatory inadequacies of both modernization and dependency theories? You would, and you would be correct, or as correct as your terms would allow you to be.

Were you to ask me, I would tell you to watch the sun struggle to shine through the filthy air, squint against the grit that comes up from the gray streets with each new swirl of chilling wind, hear the screech, the squeal, and the roar of traffic hurdling endlessly through the streets, smell the heavy sweat of the poor accented by the delicate perfume of the rich, and feel the small hurt of a tiny child fretting in his Pet Milk carton while nearby his mother offers a box of chewing gum to impassive pedestrians hurrying from here to there. If I were to say all of this, I too would be correct, or as correct as my words would let me.

And we both would be wrong. Even if you defined your terms with precision, they would err. Even if I chose the perfect word, it would mislead. This is true because Mexico changes. It doesn't stay constant. What was correct and firm yesterday at noon, the afternoon rains have washed away, and today there is a different city. Like the day I saw the little girl.

That day, the rains had done their job, and it was a new Mexico. The sun had risen with the vigor that it must have had on that first day the Aztec rekindled the world, and its rays came through the cleaned air to caress the city. A drop of moisture, left over from the rain, ran down the leaf of a plant springing up from a crack in a wall and then dangled in ecstasy as the sunlight gently touched it with a sparkle. With nature so transformed, the city was forced to follow. The traffic, which the day before was a snarling monster, became, under nature's spell, an exciting spectacle of courage and derring-do, and you wanted to applaud the skill of the individual drivers as they wove in and out, a gas pedal here, a gear shift there, and horn, a lot of horn everywhere—but with the magic of the morning the deafening honks become taunting calls that dare opponents to meet the challenger at the next red light. You admired the mother on the corner, her strong face, her black hair, her *rebozo* gracefully draped on sturdy shoulders, and you marveled at the way she lent her dignity to hawking gum on the streets. You had to smile at the baby sitting up in his cardboard carton, his enormous brown eyes exploring with trustful curiosity the world beyond the edge of his Pet Milk universe and his face constantly prepared to break into a big grin at the wonderful joy of it all.

I say "you" because the world that I was in had so changed that for a minute I thought that you were there, with me, as I walked down broad Juárez Avenue, passed the greenery of the Alameda, and approached the Hotel Prado. I wanted you there, to share the wonderful adventure of simply being, of being right then, at that point, together, in our lives.

Of course I was mistaken. You were off, somewhere, lost in a book by the anthropologist Claude Lévi-Strauss, enchanted by the elegant curvature of his logic as he orchestrated it through a symphony of binary contrasts. Foolish me. How could simply being there, on Juárez, passing the Alameda, and approaching the Prado, compare to such an exotic journey? Well, to each his own trip, and I was on mine, enchanted too, by all I could see, smell, touch, and even taste. Then it happened, the scream, the look, and the tears.

Only a few minutes before, she had been sitting against the wall of the theater next door to the Prado. In front of her, she had neatly unfolded a white square of cloth and on it arranged piles of pecans. She had placed the pecans equidistant from one another and from the edges and corners of the cloth. On top of each pile, she had with careful thumb and finger positioned a partially shelled nut in anticipation that the firm, yellow fruit thus exposed would entice a passerby to make a purchase. Unlike other street vendors, she did not harangue the crowds with calls to come and buy, but knelt quietly, her small body perfectly composed against the building's wall, and her livelihood positioned before her: yellow-topped, brown pyramids ordered into rows and columns on a square, white field. Rather than simply selling pecans, it was as if she had prepared an offering to the busy adult world that towered above her. At that moment, she screamed.

A van pulled up to the curb, and two men, the driver and his companion, got out, and without a glance or moment's hesitation, walked purposefully through the sidewalk crowd, passing just in front of me, and stopped before the little girl. She remained kneeling, her hands folded in her lap, her body pushed against the building, her head thrown back, and her mouth open, and from her mouth poured out a sound that rose above all other sounds in that world of sounds, dominating them, subduing them, and turning them into insignificant squeaks. If God, sitting on his throne in heaven, ever heard utter despair, he surely heard that girl's soul as it broke apart.

One man reached down and scooped up the cloth, made it into a bag, and handed it to his partner. The two turned back into the indifferent crowd, tossed the bag into the back of the van, and drove off.

A young attendant came out of the foyer of the theater and knelt beside the girl, careful to tuck the skirt of her uniform away from the dirt of the sidewalk. She put her hand, not unkindly, on the girl's shoulders. "*No llores, niña, no llores,*" she quietly pleaded and began picking up the few pecans left scattered about. She reached for the brown paper sack the girl had near her, and as she hurriedly threw in the pecans, she whispered again, "*No llores.*"

Two well-dressed, older ladies, their fat purses held safely against equally large bosoms, paused on their high heels to look down.

"*¿Qué pasa?*" one asked the attendant.

"*Nada*," came the reply, and to ensure they understood and would go on wherever they were going, the young lady replied again, "*Nada, nada. Nada pasa aquí.*"

The attendant, glancing back into the foyer and in answer to a querulous command coming from its darkness, got up, and pulled the child erect as she did so. She handed the girl the paper sack, and told her once again, this time her voice a hiss as she scurried back to her station, "*No llores.*"

A chauffeur, standing beside a Mercedes awaiting its passengers from the Prado, crossed over to the girl and gave her the change from his pocket. When he came back, I asked, "*¿Qué pasa?*" "*Nada*" was his first word, but he added, "*No tiene licencia.* "*¿Cómo?*" I asked. "*Licencia. Licencia. Los derechos. No paga. Ella,*" came the closed-mouth answer, the sounds barely escaping the drawn lips as if the chauffeur were afraid of his own words. "*Nada pasa*" was his final statement, the words punctuated by the firm shut of the Mercedes' door, the driver now finished with both me and the girl.

She was still there, against the building, holding the sack with both hands, the tears flowing, but soundless, not a sob or even a sniffle.

I reached into my pocket, took out my billfold, thumbed it open—the face of my own sixth-grade daughter staring at me in the precious rigidity of a school photograph—and took out several bills. The girl saw me, and her face hardened like the gray concrete behind her. She stuck out her hand, and when I reached out to give her the money, she snatched it away, curling it in her fist, stuffing it in her skirt pocket, and not giving it a glance—her eyes fixed on me, cased in tears which she was bringing, through a stubborn hardening, to a stop. Only little girls cry, and she was now knowledgeable in the ways of adults.

Don't cry, little girl. Don't cry. Nothing has happened. Nothing has happened here. The attendant, not much older than you and already in uniform, says so and has so informed the well-dressed curious. They, who have done so well in their lives, believe her, so shouldn't you?

No, nothing is happening here, little girl. The chauffeur says so, and he drives an expensive Mercedes carrying important people on their important trips from here to there and back again. He says it's nothing. You simply don't have permission to earn a living. To get permission, to have that right, you have to pay a fee. That's all. It is nothing.

Nothing is happening, so don't cry. Adults don't want you to cry. It makes them uneasy. It makes them think that something is not right, that something is happening. That's the reason they gave you the money, to keep anything from happening. They don't like things to happen, like little girls crying in public, on busy Juárez Avenue. That's the reason they always say that nothing is happening and give you money to make sure it doesn't.

Having finished accusing me of every sin I ever committed and some of yours too, the girl's eyes became completely dry except for one small and stubborn tear refusing to fall from its perch on an eyelash. Then it too dropped, a last rivulet of her childhood, and she brought up her hand to wipe it away in disgust. How could she have ever cried! She turned to join the other adults, busy with their business, and became one of the many figures moving away into their going, and so disappeared.

The sun, having spent itself in the procreation of the morning, now grew pale, and the afternoon promised in its small future to revert back to yesterday's stagnant past. With the sun so weak, the traffic beast rose again and curled its obnoxious body around the remains of the day, squeezing out the last ounce of its freshness. At the street corner, the little boy twisted his small body into a corner of the milk carton where he fought to preserve his tiny self even as a dark ooze spread between his legs. Her dignity burned away by desperation, the mother thrust out her hand at those moving past to become a pitiful demand in a city of such demands.

I too turned away, turned away and left, left Juárez, the Alameda, and the Prado. I turned away and left, and now I'm here, and I turn to you with my question.

You already know the question. You are smart as well as wise. But wait. Wait before you tell me that you don't know the answer because there isn't one, and turn away too. At least let me be certain that you see the question itself and that you recognize the way in which it asks itself, how it circles around us and includes all within its encompassing accusation: the attendant in her uniform, the well-dressed in their easily convinced high heels, the chauffeur back in his Mercedes with the door firmly shut, and the two men in the van, certainly them, in their officialdom of *licencia* and *derechos*, and more; the city in its absorbing enormity, the country in its dull poverty, and the Glorious Revolution in its studied corruption, and more yet; our country and its insatiability that bites off greater and greater chunks of the world's wealth, leaving less and less and eventually nothing at all; and finally, you and me and our profession, the terms you define and the words I choose, responding to the hand offering a package of gum, to the tiny body tossing in a cardboard carton, and to the tears now all dried under the harsh light of adulthood, responding to these happenings by calling them fieldwork and so making them into an everyday, workaday *nada*, a normal nothing; just so that is clear, I'll ask you once more, "Who's to blame?"

 # "Did You?"

WARD H. GOODENOUGH

When I was on Onotoa in Kiribati in the summer of 1951, I learned that, like most other Pacific Islanders, people there routinely greeted one another with "Where are you going?" or "Where are you coming from?" to which such replies as "North," "South," "Ocean side," or "Lagoon side" were customarily acceptable answers. The questions and answers were routine greeting exchanges among people who had lived their lives in the same community and already knew one another well.

The novice Westerner encountering Pacific ways may at first react to the opening question as an intrusion into his or her privacy, feeling called upon to explain where indeed he or she is actually going. Not so. When asked "How are you?" at home, we are not called upon to explain our actual state of health. "Fine, thanks!" ends the exchange. The same held in Onotoa.

More disconcerting to the Westerner learning to live with Onotoans was the routine exchange that took place when someone in a group rose to go out to relieve himself or herself. As one stood up to go, one heard the usual question, "Where are you going?" In this case the appropriate answer was "To the sea." Someone returning to a group after "going to the sea" was greeted with "Did you?" to which the appropriate reply was "I did."

Urination might take place almost anywhere that was a little out of the way, appropriately with one's back to anyone else nearby. The beach was the place people went to for more serious relief. Hence the expression "To the sea." There was no attempt at privacy. Indeed, a person squatting on the beach might be holding a conversation with someone at a house forty or fifty feet away without regard to gender. When finished, one completed the toileting by wading out into the water for a quick wash. It was all done very matter-of-factly.

Western colonial officials and missionaries had been unwilling to accommodate to this easy approach to defecation. For their convenience, each village had been required to construct an outhouse over the water in front of the village assembly hall. It was customary for visitors to beach their canoes there and to be housed in the "sitting place of strangers" in the assembly hall, a large, sacred public building whose use was

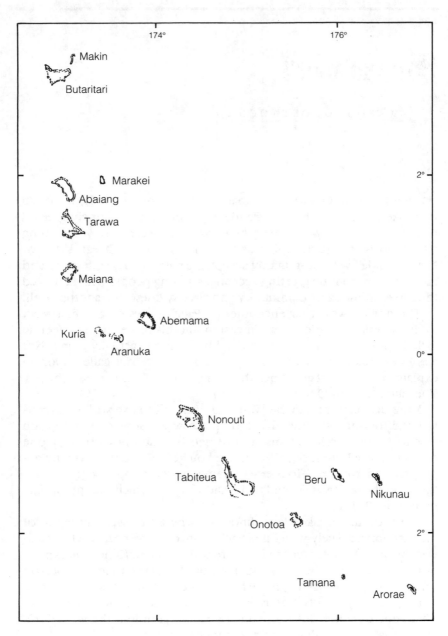

Kiribati (Gilbert Islands)

hedged by many formalities. Before there were outhouses, those approaching from all directions had an unimpeded view of this imposing building, which sat just above the beach. Now visitors were greeted by a small hut on piles out over the lagoon's shallows interposed between them and the assembly hall. It did not enhance the majesty of the approach. Even so, when visiting another village with Onotoans, I could sense a contagious, excited tension among my companions as we approached the beach before the assembly hall.

The outhouse itself made few concessions to privacy. Its square frame, resting on the piles, supported two parallel pieces of wood on which to place one's feet. There was a screen of coconut leaf thatch about two feet high, at the most, so that the user's body from midriff down was shielded from outside view in squatting position. About four feet of open space extended above the screen to the roof, providing the user with an excellent view of the beachfront and the various activities taking place along it. It also provided people on the beach with an excellent view of the occupant of the outhouse.

On Onotoa, to reach the outhouse in front of the assembly hall where I was housed, it was necessary to walk out on two long coconut logs, laid end to end. There was no handhold; it was a balancing act all the way. At the beach end of this walkway, the log was about two feet above the sand, requiring the user to clamber up on it, rise to a standing position, and then get into a state of balance before tightroping out the nearly fifty feet to the business end.

Except when the English lands commissioner came to work in the village, I was the only user of this convenience for toilet purposes. I found that, as a Westerner, I was expected to use it. The Onotoans had been required to build it to accommodate the modesty of people like me. My habits in such matters made me happy to use it, in any case.

The structure had other uses, however. It was a place much favored by children for fishing with hook and line when the tide was in. They would stand in the outhouse, hanging over the low thatch wall, or sit on the log walkway just in front of it with their handlines or improvised fishing poles. Their efforts were not signally rewarded, but occasionally they came up with a few small fish. Thus, when I had need to use the outhouse, it often happened that children were out there fishing. I would come to the end of the log, precious roll of paper in hand, and make throat-clearing noises. The young anglers would look up, see me standing there, and quickly scurry in to the beach, clearing my access to the outhouse and giving me such little privacy as it afforded.

Because I had expressed an interest in learning the then-popular form of dancing known as the "Multiplication Tables," which had been imported from Tavalu in postmissionary times, the Onotoans decided that the proper way to keep me entertained and, perhaps, out of possible mischief was to involve me in nightly informal dance sessions in the village assembly hall. Thus, I soon became well schooled in giving the answers "To the sea" and "I did."

There was an occasion when the schooling served me well. One afternoon I was seized with an urgent need to use the outhouse. As I rushed to the beach, clutching the toilet roll, I saw that someone fishing with a pole was sitting on the log about four feet in front of the entrance. It was one of the village's loveliest fifteen-year-old girls. My urgency did not permit the usual throat-clearing routine. I leapt onto the log and proceeded as quickly as possible up to the outhouse. As I approached the girl she reached behind her with one hand to keep from falling off the log while she leaned over to let me step around her. She then serenely resumed her fishing while I entered the outhouse, dropped my pants, and squatted. My performance must have announced itself a good hundred yards in either direction along the beach. The girl remained politely oblivious to it all, seemingly intent on her fishing. At length I finished, pulled up my pants, and emerged to return to the beach. Again, she grasped the log with one hand and leaned over to let me step around her. As I did so, she turned her head, looked up at me, and in a sweet, matter-of-fact voice asked, "Did you?"

Thanks to what I had learned, I managed to keep my balance and replied as offhandedly as I could, "I did."

SUGGESTED READINGS

GRIMBLE, SIR ARTHUR
1952   We Chose the Islands. New York: Morrow. (English Edition: A Pattern of Islands. London: John Murray, 1952).
1957   Return to the Islands. London: John Murray.

MAUD, H. E.
1963   The Evolution of the Gilbertese Boti: An Ethnohistorical Approach. Memoir No. 35. Aukland, New Zealand: The Polynesian Society.

 Munju

TRECIE MELNICK

The Hamats mean the most to me on the bad days. Those are the days of market ladies pointing to my purse and jacking up the prices, and small children tugging at my braids and running, yelling at me *"munju, munju,"* the young Central African men on the streets of Bangassou grabbing at my ass as I ride by on my bicycle. I try to look undisturbed and calm, but my front tire weaves in the sand, hands gripping handle bars, legs pumping, pumping. The vocal assaults slap my cheeks like locusts in the wind. Those faces blur in my sight. They become monstrous, exaggerated masks that follow me, moving in like spirits in an African novel. All bastards. I want to see the kinder side of Central Africa, to get away from the dueling hostility and the mutual racism. My own ethnocentrism has emerged again like a winged termite from its mound. I head toward the neighborhood where the Hamats live.

The dirt glares red in the early afternoon. From a distance, only a long image shows under the canopy shade. As I move closer, Mahamat's figure shifts, growing stronger as does his tall face with the bad right eye. He is the father of the Hamat household, tilting his chin up, straining to see through the harsh light. Stretched out on his side like a tired vine, one hand drips over the edge of the reclining chair—his chair—as he finishes a bowl of cassava sauce. He recognizes me and smiles with the good eye as I duck under the grass roof to shake his hand. *"Baramo"* ["How are you?"] I greet him.

"I'm fine. You haven't come to see Awa and Zeneba for days."

"I know. I've been busy with school. Are they here now?"

"Everyone's here. Go on in."

Awa's laugh leaps on the other side of the tall woven fence surrounding the Hamat compound. She calls in Sango, "Patrice? Finally, you've come." As I enter through the gap in the fence, she takes the bike and leans it against the house. She seems tall for a fourteen-year-old. Squeezing my hand she scolds, "We're very angry at you. You haven't come for a week. We thought you had forgotten us." She always says that. "Sit here," she commands, still squeezing. She arranges the triangle of cooking stones with her free hand, and finally she lets go of my fingers. Standing up, she pulls a handful of straw out of the roof of the cooking shelter.

I wonder how long it will last, a low grass roof just high enough to sit under while someone boils up a pot of peanut sauce. Some days, Awa and her sisters sit under the charcoaled roof, with friends, painting crimson lines of henna on each other's palms and feet. Year after year the underside of the grass cover grows blacker, as black as Awa's arms, and feathers of grass fall down in her hair. With each new fire the smoky scent becomes stronger, and the roof thins. Awa reaches over and yanks out another clump of roof. She crams the handful into the center of the smoking logs, and blows. The flames reach out and she places the beaten, blackened little teapot in the middle of the three stones.

It's a relief to be here with the Hamat women, who have become understanding and protective of me in the year and a half I've known them. It's here that Awa asks me, "What do white people eat?" and I ask, "Have you met the fiancé your father has chosen for you? Do you like him?" Here I can speak and gesture without checking myself because within the Hamat's grass encirclement we don't regret our differences but savor them.

Awa doesn't care one way or the other about her fiancé. She answers my questions with "I've met him. His name is Omar. I've met him twice." I prod her: "But what do you think of him?" She shrugs her shoulders. She knows she may not be married off for several years. She doesn't seem eager, unlike her sister Zeneba, who grins every time I ask her those questions.

Awa has two sisters, Zeneba and Dana. Today, both of them are up to their elbows in bright orange palm oil. Zeneba, who is the oldest of the three, dips her hands to the bottom of the pot pulling out the larger shucks of palm nuts while Dana strains the sediment with a basket. When I ask to help, Zeneba laughs, the contours of her broad face shining in the harsh light. Skinny Dana cocks her head to one side, orange running down her forearms as she pipes, "You don't need to help. You just rest and talk to us. Did you go to the market today?" Dana is just a couple of years younger than Awa. Her smiles don't burst out like Zeneba's. Her good-natured laughs are controlled, and the lips return easily to a serene pose. Mariam, Awa's mother, sweeps up discarded palm nuts, telling me, "You can't work yet. Have some tea first." Awa hands me the glass of tea, very sweet with cloves and a handful of sugar cubes. As I drink, Mariam puts her broom down and pulls a stool up next to me. She asks me how my week is going, how my classes are, and whether I've heard from my family. Then, scooting her stool closer to mine, she asks about each sister by name and also about my mother, father, and grandmother.

She questions me further, remembering what I'd told her about each family member. "Is Vikki still playing music?" "How is your sister who sells houses?" "Why isn't she married yet?" Changing the subject, I complain about being charged higher prices at the market. Zeneba snaps her orange-coated fingers once for emphasis and says, "They do that to

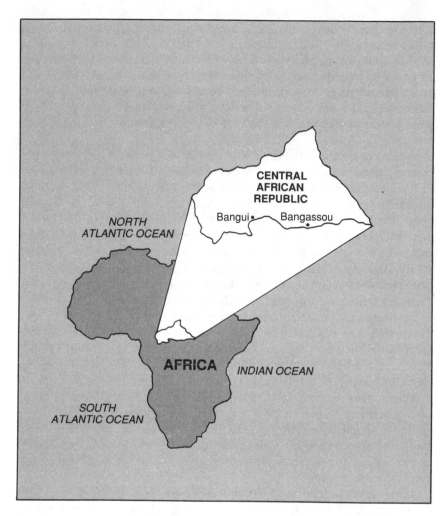

Bangassou, Central Africa

you because you're white. It's not fair. They raise the prices on us too. They say to me, 'You're Muslim. You have lots of money so you can afford to pay more—Muslim woman.' It makes me so mad." Mariam adds, "Next time you go to the market, go with Awa. She'll get you good prices."

I drink the tea down fast, eager to get my hands in the orange slime. This is the first time they've let me help make palm oil. Mariam first takes me aside and wraps an old piece of cloth around my skirt to protect it and pulls my stool over to the big pot. I swish my hands in warm oil, thick as honey. Then, following Zeneba's example, I reach to the bottom to pull out the palm shucks and set them aside in another pot.

With our hands deep in the oil, every now and then when Zeneba's eyes half close and she gazes down into the vat of orange, I snatch at her hand like a fish. Her eyes flash open as she chuckles and calls me a *"bandit"* (troublemaker). She snatches back at my hands. While we swim our hands in the oil, Mariam goes on about her brother, Isouf, whose second wife has just had a baby. It's a boy and the naming party will be next week. Will I come? Of course I'll come.

When I moved to Bangassou I knew that I couldn't expect popularity and that any kind of acceptance in the community would take a long time. But I had hoped to be able to find a few people I could count on. I first met Awa during my Saturday walks through Tokoy, the Muslim neighborhood. She brought me into her family's compound. There I met her sisters, her mother; eventually, Awa's father became less aloof and friendlier to me. I liked the Hamats from the start because they called me by name. And I made a point of writing down each of theirs to memorize them between the first meeting and the next. Zeneba's sounded the most unusual to me and was the hardest for me to learn.

Strangers call me "Melnique" if they know me as a teacher. The Central Africans use last names as Americans use first. If someone doesn't know my name and wants to get my attention, he may call out, *"Wali"* ("Woman"). When I first heard this I was insulted. I wasn't used to being called by a label. But this is also customary. If someone wants to get a stranger's attention, he calls them by what they are: Child. Woman. Man. Calling someone *"koli"* ("man") is like calling your waiter "sir." Frequently I'm called *"munju,"* which means "white person." Depending on the tone and context, *munju* has many connotations, sometimes neutral, often not: white person, foreigner, whitey, honky. I never get used to being a *munju*.

Munju used to refer only to French people. In colonial days, when the Central Africans heard the French saying "Bonjour" to each other all of the time, they came to call them that. The label "Bonjour" evolved into "Mungu" and came to refer to all whites. At its mildest, *munju* describes or identifies a white to distinguish her from a black person. "A *munju* who I have never seen before was downtown today."

From there the meanings become more derogatory. The implications go from "white person" to "white thing." For example, as I pass through a neighborhood, sometimes mothers hold their infants and say in Sango, "Look, look at the *munju*." But in another context a mother might say to her baby, "See the *munju*? If you're not good, that *munju* will eat you." In fact, there is a local legend of a white woman with long hair who lives in the river and at night pulls fishermen from their canoes to drown them. She is called the *"mamywhata,"* and for some children a *munju* and *mamywhata* are the same. No wonder when I walk through some parts of town, young children sometimes freeze, staring at my white skin and long braids, and then run off screeching for their mothers. After having four or five children flee in terror of my face in one afternoon, I become self-conscious. The adults usually just laugh and tease the child with, "Are you afraid of that *munju*? She's coming. She's going to eat you."

Children use the word *munju* a little differently than adults do. Some kids say "*munju*" innocently, trying it out as a word they have heard their parents use to refer to whites. Curious, they peek around their doors softly repeating "*munju, munju.*" If brave enough, they might come running out to shake my hand and stare at me.

It's cute at first, but soon the timid chiming of "*munju, munju*" becomes a clamoring like crows cawing from the trees. Bigger children with bones sticking out at all angles run after my bike, mouths opening like puppets, "*munju, munju.*" Skinny children with legs dry as firewood, come running out of their houses. Then the tall boys follow, with the long legs blotched with never-healing sores. The older ones don't run behind but stride beside me, hauling their houselike shoulders from side to side, hardening their consonants as they call out "*munju wali*" ("white woman"). Volume increases as I imagine the voices gathering behind me, closing in, jumping in front of my path and then away at the last minute. "*Munju*" seems to fall from the trees as I look to escape, glaring at the children. I am unable to distinguish between the innocent *munju* of little girls and the "honky-go-home" *munju*'s darting at my eyes. Those are the days when I walk, looking straight ahead rather than meandering. I clutch my market bag close to me and brush by the kids with their arms extended to shake hands. People recognize my mood and laugh. I can no longer differentiate between "*wali,* Melnique, *munju, munju wali, mamywhata, munjumunjumunjumunju*—Patrice!" Only people who know me well call me Patrice.

When I'm feeling defensive, Awa has to call out "Patrice" a couple of times to get my attention because I'm blocking everyone out. She assures me that she doesn't think I'm a *mamywhata* as we walk together through the Muslim section of the market and the name-calling dissipates. She tells me that when I was gone to Bangui, the capital, for two weeks her friends in the market would ask her, "Where's your *munju*?" Coming from Awa, the word means "white friend."

The Muslim community is less hostile to me because they know I'm friends with the Hamats. And the Hamats know what it's like to be in the minority. In the Central African Republic the Muslims are a small part of the population. Many of them are recent immigrants from Chad and Sudan. Mariam's parents came from Chad. As a Jew I am more comfortable with them. Our histories overlap. Unlike a few of my encounters with zealous first-generation Christians, the Muslims don't try to convert me. I've had Central African children conclude that if I wasn't Christian, I must be with the devil—a detail they'd learned in church. As a

Jew from Dallas, I'm often asked why I killed Jesus and why I killed Kennedy. The Muslims are as unfamiliar with Judaism as are other Central Africans. But like them, I'm not a Christian. This gives us something to talk about. I know a few Hebrew words, and sometimes we've compared Hebrew and Arabic to note the similarities. They are surprised to learn that Jewish law, like Islam, forbids the eating of pork. Although I don't practice, I discuss these details with the Hamats for a source of commonality.

When I was just getting to know the Hamats, they kept me at a polite distance. They expected me to sit in a straight-backed chair, at a little table inside the house, while family and friends sat outside together on mats and *barambo* [a type of wood] stools. They ate off the same plate digging their hands into the cassava mash and peanut sauce laughing and talking in rapid Sango while I sat inside, alone with my own plate. But eventually I was allowed to sit outside at a table fairly close to the others, though I was still given my own bowls of food. Sometimes Mariam gave me food different from what the others were eating. There is a stereotype that whites don't eat cassava root (*gozo*), so when I arrived Mariam would put some money into Dana's palm and send her off to the market to buy bread for me. I'd be given my own piece. I wanted to be down on the mats and *barambos* with the others, and eventually I was allowed to sit on the mat next to Mariam. But even then, I was given my own plates though I had graduated to being served *gozo*. And finally, I was allowed to share, eating off the same plates with the others. But Mariam kept a close eye on how much I ate, and when I didn't eat as much meat as she thought I should, she pushed some over to one side and designated it as mine. It was the end of Ramadan holiday, and they must have forgotten that I had ever been a "special guest." So there I sat, down on the mats with my hands in the same bowls, tugging at the same lumps of *gozo* and elephant meat.

Over time we developed a dialogue centered around photos and maps. I show Mariam my photo album, pointing out my high school friends, family, my house in Texas. "Where's Texas?" Mariam asks, staring keenly at a picture of my sister. She takes my map out of the back of the album and stretches it wide. "Texas is here."

"Where's Mecca?" she asks. I show her and she traces the path from Bangassou all the way to Mecca.

"Mmmecca," she sounds out. She taught herself to read. "We're going to Mecca someday."

"When?"

"When we have the money. That's the holy city. Here's Bangassou. Where's Dallas?"

"Here."

"Aiiiyyyooo! That's far."

The Hamats help me through the days when "*munju, munju*" stings my cheek, the days of curses under my breath. Safe inside the Hamat compound I forget the shouts of the young men on the streets. I forget as I help Zeneba dig shucks out of the palm oil, as I watch Awa and Dana paint crimson lines across our soles. Mariam takes her family pictures and mine, lays them across the map, and together we decide it isn't so far.

TWENTY-NINE

The Inseparability of Reason and Emotion in the Anthropological Perspective: Perceptions upon Leaving "The Field"[1]

KRIS HEGGENHOUGEN

Upon returning to New York City after a year with the Cakchiquel Indians in the mountains of Guatemala, it was most difficult for me to sit down directly and write in detail of my experiences in, and readings about, Guatemala. I was not quite the same person as before my field trip.

I glanced at the quotation pinned on my wall:

The anthropologist has been the disengaged man par excellence, dissatisfied at home and questing abroad.

And at other passages that had caught my attention:

The "professional" anthropologist is an alien. . . . He is estranged three times over: first in his own society, along with the generality of his fellow citizens; second, in the choice of his profession; and finally in relation to those whom he studies. . . . [but] . . . the authentic anthropologists will not make careers out of their alienation, but will understand it as a specific instance of a pathological condition, demanding political commitment and action; that is, they will reject the refined identity: "anthropologist." (Diamond 1974:94–95, 330–333)

In an effort to overcome this temporary sense of disequilibrium, I leafed through my notes in order to reflect on the total fieldwork experience and on the general purpose of anthropology. Before I could proceed I once again had to ask the questions: "What is fieldwork? Why do it?" in terms of the things I had just experienced. I felt a need to record my frustrations, hopes, and anxieties—almost as a type of confession.

I make *no apologies* for this *subjectivity*—this "presentation of self"—since I believe it is relevant for the reader to see the author

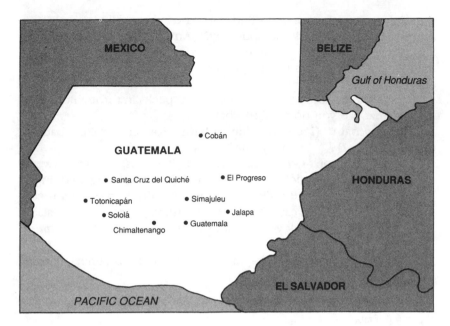

Guatemala Central Highlands

actually relating to people and situations. Through personal "intrusion" I hoped to achieve a complete, nonsterile, presentation of my experience as well as to increase the reader's ability to make an objective evaluation of what was being said. I wanted to present my feelings and my biases but deny that what was being said was therefore less "objective." In fact, I would argue the contrary.

The validity of the theory of knowledge that propounds the interdependence of reason and emotion, of subjectivity and objectivity, in the process of learning was particularly impressed upon me during my stay in Guatemala. In this essay I will attempt to discuss this realization. *The merger of the subjective and the objective is, in fact, one of the unique strengths of the anthropological approach.*

8 FEBRUARY 1974

Here I am in the village of Simajuleu. The radio is interminable next door. Here too! And the roosters, dogs, and pigs keep up a racket from four o'clock in the morning on. And I am tired. The altitude is only 6,000 feet, but combined with other things it's having an effect—and people wonder why I don't get out of my house before eight in the morning. But I'll get used to it, though life here is by no means all romantic. I keep having doubts about what I am doing. Am I wasting my time? Am

I getting at what I am here to find out? And what really is that? Who knows about "fieldwork methodology?" Am I doing the right things? Do I leave the village too often? Am I living in the right place? Am I reading and writing too much and not participating in the village life enough?

Serfarino, Francisco's twelve-year-old son, peeks in through the window. "What are you doing, Cristobalo?"

"Taking a bath." (I am not taking a bath. How can I take a bath in the dry season?) . . . "I am typing."

Arrogant me. Don't I know that is the way it is—just contact between people? "How do you do?" "How do you do?" "What are you doing?" "Walking." "Oh, you are walking." "What are you doing?" "I am cutting wheat." "Ja." "Take care then." "Yes, thank you. You take care also." "Oh, thank you." "Thank you." "*Tabana kwenta awi.*" "*Kwenta aka.*" "*Matiox.*" "*Matiox ok chawe.*"

Alejandra, Francisco's eleven-year-old niece, comes by, unexpectedly, with coffee.

13 FEBRUARY 1974

Cutting wheat. Cutting and binding, cutting and binding. On a yellow hillside among the brown and green of the pine trees with Inez and other men and boys. "Who taught you to cut wheat, Cristobalo? Let's cut your hair too, it's the same color." Talking, joking, working. Two boys rolling around goosing each other. Laughter. Far off on an opposite hill, one old man, all in white except for his red waist band, slowly, methodically, cuts his field. We, all in a group, spirited, cutting strips of cactus (*magay*) to tie the bundles of wheat. I carry more than a hundred pounds on my back for the first time with a tumpline across my forehead, up and down the *barrancas* (hillsides): aching neck muscles. The last few hundred yards, after about a two-kilometer walk, we make a race of it—and I keep up (Am I competitive? Am I into *machismo* things?)—falling down at the end, exhausted, gasping, sweating, and laughing. Lunch at Inez's house. Drinking *Kuxa* (homemade spirit). Oh yes, good *Kuxa* to make me feel mellow the whole afternoon. Tortillas and black beans.

8 APRIL 1974

What is all this "anthropology stuff"? Is what I learn worth anything? Would the people here want to buy it with a hundredweight of corn? Or, on a different scale, do we really have an influence over people in organizations that deal with human lives? Might it not be better to be a farmer, a carpenter, a physician, or even an artist—to make something concrete, to make a more definite contribution? It is impossible to keep from thinking this way when I live so close to these people who have, on the average, no more than five to ten *cuerdas* of land per family on which they might produce a total of fifty hundredweights of corn (at five dollars a hundredweight). One comes to think of the luxury of it all. In this juxtaposition, anthropology seems so parasitic. Who pays for the luxury? Do anthropologists return something? Not "anthropologists," but I—shall I be able to return anything? Will it matter?

13 APRIL 1974

Sitting on a bench against the adobe walls, I looked into Tata's eyes as he talked to me. The stench from his decaying mouth was overwhelming, but there was something in his face that held me. It was childlike yet old and mature—old and durable.

During a lull, I looked away and saw the gifts stored in the corner in anticipation of next week's wedding. In just one week, Christine, Tata's granddaughter, would leave and could no longer call this her home, though within her, in her thoughts and by inclination, it would continue as such for a long, long time. I played with the pine needles strewn fresh on the floor. The smell brought back Christmas in Norway, but it was also peculiarly tied to this place, it bound me here as well . . . to this place, to this room, where the mood was both festive and casual, pensive and lighthearted.

A long time must have gone by, much of it in silence. Then I realized Tata was sobbing. He was talking and mumbling and cried there next to me. Without thinking I hesitated slightly and then put my arm around him. I held this frail man next to me, felt the sharp shoulder blades of this so strangely strong man against me. It wasn't pity or even sympathy, and I wasn't being patronizing, the fear of which had caused my momentary hesitation. It was . . . well, I don't quite know what it was. I touched him, that is all. I felt him there beside me.

21 APRIL 1974

After the meals and the ceremonies, the *Kuxa* was again passed around, and handing me a glass, the host, Angel's stepfather, proclaimed: "Foreigners always come and always take things away but leave nothing behind. Teach me something! What can you teach me?" I wasn't quite sure if the emphasis had been on the "you," thus making it sarcastic, or on the "what," but the statement was clear. Outsiders exploit. Could I say that I was any different? I wondered what I could teach—what it was that I could give—and then I wondered about anthropology itself.[2]

28 APRIL 1974

At get-togethers, I am frequently asked to tell jokes. Everyone likes jokes and stories (me too), which are told and retold. A great number of them make use of the double entendre, and, of course, there are the off-color jokes. Yesterday, Ernesto told me that it is we students who can screw and "get it up" all the time but that he and the other *campesinos* (peasants) who work in the fields all day are too tired to do much of anything in the evenings.

6 MAY 1974

"Drink." Francisco spoke to me above the noise of the post–wedding party gathering. "If you are here observing us, that's the price you have to pay. Drink."

I finally stumbled my way home at one thirty in the morning; up and down the *barrancas*, following the sounds of those ahead. It was only four kilometers, but they were some of the worst I had ever walked. Having slept only three hours the night before, I was "out of it" and kept wondering what all of this had to do with "medical anthropology." I also kept thinking of Francisco's demand, which put me on the defensive, made me feel guilty. I saw it as an accusation. Do I use people? I don't see myself that way, but . . . don't I try to help with the water project? (But Kris, you can leave whenever you want to.) I don't make a pretense of being like the people here. I am different. But exploitative? I don't think so. But thinking of it always makes me uneasy. There was something to it.

The beautiful face of a ten-year-old girl looks in through the window at Cristobalo and his typewriter—playing with the petals of the roses Ernesto Colaj had bought from Aguas Calientes.

There I was: doing "anthropological fieldwork." Hoping, uncertainly, that I was there for reasons other than fulfililng requirements for a Ph.D.—convincing myself that there was more to it than gathering notes to write my thesis.

There I was: expectant, hopeful, and excited but also ill at ease, confused, anxious. Was I adequately prepared? Did my knapsack contain the tools to deal with it all? Would I find a method for gathering anything worthwhile? Finally, could I properly evaluate, focus, and verbalize my observations in a dissertation that might contribute to a better understanding of the concept of health programs in rural, peasant communities, particularly in Third World countries?

There I was: in Guatemala; in the highlands; in the Cakchiquel village of Simajuleu. Simajuleu literally means "The Edge of the World." I had come to the edge of the world to perform my rite of passage into anthropology. The classic mode of entry for all fledgling anthropologists,

I was coincidentally at the edge of the world at once, both literally and figuratively. I had come to the edge of my world to look at it from the Guatemalan mountains: to see, to learn, to try to understand that edge and through it, also to look from there at the center of my own world and at myself.

Of course, there were specifics to guide me. There was a health program. How did it work? Why did it work? How could others learn from it? Were there conflicts between "cosmopolitan" and "traditional" concepts of medicine? Was the health worker experiencing an identity crisis? These were the questions to be answered. There were notes to be taken about religion, social structue, and all of the socio-anthropological aspects one is supposed to examine during fieldwork. The goal was to put bits and pieces together in an ordered whole, to say something new, to say something possibly beneficial.

I was at "the edge of the world" then, to understand and make sense of the totality of this new reality. Francisco, Ernesto, Inez, and Nana . . . a whole group of unknown people. The fields. The sheep and the pigs. The handshakes. The eating and talking. The poverty. The working, walking, and incessant *mandados* (errands). The greetings, which seemed at first so repetitive. This culture in its entirety was my discrete anthropological province. My challenge was to comprehend this culture in order properly to evaluate the health program within its context.

By being there and by beginning to understand all of this I was in the process of becoming an anthropologist (I hesitate in using the term). But that did not answer all of it. Simply writing about a subject from a perspective not written about before—in my case an innovative health care program in a Guatemalan Indian peasant village—did not, somehow, satisfy the claim that one cannot become an anthropologist just in the classroom and the library.

What was so important about fieldwork? Was it really a rite of passage? If so, in addition to the intellectual observation, analysis, and recording, what was supposed to happen?

And that was it. Much later I realized it with my head also: *It was what happened. The anthropologist's feeling must lead his thoughts into the experience, if he is to fully comprehend the experience.* In short, his head must follow his heart if fieldwork is to be a rite of passage into anthropology. What happened was not just that I very slowly began to understand a new reality—a new culture. It wasn't just a study and an understanding of people different from myself, seeing their beliefs, ordering, and systems up close. I also had to go sensuously to the edge of the world. Without having been there, felt it, smelled it, touched it and been touched by it, I was not doing anthropology.

What a realization for a staid Norwegian: head and heart.

What fieldwork was really all about was being touched by a different reality. That is what I had to "learn." It included what happened to me as much as anything else—not just what I read and saw and "understood" but what I ate, smelled, and felt. What I heard and saw—what I experienced.

The pigs waking me at three, four, five in the morning . . . the hundred pounds of wheat on my back . . . the *Kuxa* . . . the mud . . . the wind, the hailstorm, and being soaked to the bone . . . the smoke in my eyes while eating beans with my fingers, the tortillas . . . the charcoal dust and no water to wash. Esteban playing his cracked guitar, smiling with eyes that had been blind three years, suddenly crying "Why? why?" The marriages, wakes, funerals, malnutrition, amputation of a finger . . . the pride, the humility, the persistence, the weakness. Tata's laugh and rotting teeth, his patched clothes, and his thin body walking every day stooped and rhythmical, as if dancing a half-walking, half-running gait, with dignity to hoe his fields.

I am not suggesting that I saw with their eyes or felt what they felt, but their world touched mine (and mine touched theirs). I felt it. It was the feeling of it all. That is how I suddenly saw the flesh and blood on Malinowski's skeleton (1961:17). All of this was important, important not so much because I began to make sense of it, ordering it, understanding it, but because it touched me profoundly—made me feel strong, happy, sad, frustrated, angry, tired, drunk, bored, overwhelmed. All of those things.

Realization of this extrarational dimension of fieldwork did not minimize my sense that it was a luxury, a holiday of sorts. Neither did it quell the uneasy thoughts that I was exploiting people.

The realization led, however, to an important conviction, tied to the dual nature of humans as thinking and feeling beings, that both elements are necessary and significant to the anthropological perspective, and in terms of which the "anthropological dialectic" might be understood. It seemed simplistically obvious that whatever an anthropologist had to offer, whatever was special about his or her contribution—as an "anthropologist"—had to be rooted *in feeling as well as thinking*.

Influenced by this duality, and joined through it with people quite different from me, I realized that the *rationale for anthropology made sense only in terms of justice and human rights*. This makes the anthropologist automatically responsible for action and subject to *an implicit mandate to convert theory into practice*. Understanding, derived from thought, and feeling, is the answer to "why anthropology?" and the effective communication of this understanding into practice is the essential rationale for the discipline of anthropology. The purpose is to give meaning to the kinds of changes that should take place in me, in the society where I live and, if possible, to make me understand how best to assist with changes among those with whom I did fieldwork. In other words, I identify with those anthropologists who see their task as one which ultimately, and consistently, returns to an analysis of "the salient structures of exploitation."

Camus's *Myth of Sisyphus* and Hemingway's *The Old Man and the Sea* powerfully present the persistence of human struggle which, prodded by hope and perceptions of Utopia,[3] strives for change and progress no matter how overwhelming the odds. "Man is destroyed but never defeated," states Hemingway, implying that the admission of defeat heralds the destruction of man: when he stops struggling, he is no longer man. Erich Fromm concurs by saying that "when we speak of man we speak of him not as a thing but as a process" (1971:viii).

Anthropology, together with other social sciences, must be in the forefront of this struggle—in the forefront of shaping this process. It must give direction to change away from exploitation. It must show us how to improve and how to progress. It must be employed to combat self-righteous proselytizing and conversion steeped in ethnocentrism, as well as the mindless and destructive "progress" of Icarus. It must fight actively against exploitation based on a greed that causes us to rob others while unwittingly bankrupting ourselves. Based on its special attempt to understand "the human condition" in all of its different facets, anthropology must actively help us understand change and progress in terms of the realistic, contemporary needs of human beings.

I counter those who argue that anthropology is basically a theoretical discipline—belonging within the realm of the academy and museum— by identifying myself with the arguments of Richard Volpe who (using Kant [1974] in his support) claims that "nothing is as practical as good theory and that the very soundness of any theory lies in its applicability. . . . The test of any theory is in its capacity to guide action" (1975:495).

Based on my reflections during fieldwork, I feel that thoughts and emotions that result from participation in the lives of fellow human beings during a "process of creation that moves back and forth between abstract concepts and concrete experiences" (Volpe 1975:495) are the only ultimate justification for what anthropologists do.

NOTES

1. This essay is a result of Ph.D. fieldwork experiences in Chimaltenango, Guatemala, where the author was associated with the Behrhorst Health Program and living in the Cakchiquel Indian village of Simajuleu. The paper constitutes the preface of the author's Ph.D. dissertation: "Health Care for the 'Edge of the World'" (Committee on Anthropology, New School for Social Research, submitted April, 1976). The views presented in this essay are those of the author and do not necessarily represent those of the institutions with which he is affiliated.

2. This is a dilemma no doubt shared by numerous anthropologists. Consider, for example, Robert Jay's comment: "Toward the end of my fieldwork in a Malay village in 1963, I was approached by a small delegation of villagers,

who said to me, 'You are a professor in an American university who has studied our village for a whole year. You must have learned a lot about us in that time and could you help us with our problems here. Will you please tell us some of what you know?" (Jay 1974).

3. ". . . life is impossible without something for which one can hope. Recognising ourselves as members of an emerging world community, we cannot escape assumptions, open or hidden, as to that for which they hope and as to what can be hoped for them. The general problem, then, is not simply empirical . . . it is also a moral problem, a problem of one's commitments in, and to, the world. Anthropologists have indeed commonly thought of themselves as belonging to the 'party of humanity' . . . and the world view of Gay ascribed to the Enlightenment as passionate rationalism and a tragic humanism, is not alien to anthropologists. It is, I would urge, the view best suited to them. . . . The tradition intended here requires a conception of the future, indeed a 'Utopian' conception (taking 'Utopian' in a positive sense of a projected ideal, not the negative sense of an unrealisable dream) and a theory of progress as well" (Hymes 1974).

REFERENCES

DIAMOND, S.
1974   In Search of the Primitive—a Critique of Civilisation. New Brunswick, NJ: Transaction Books.

FROMM, E.
1971   Introduction. *In* Celebration of Awareness, Ivan Illich, ed. Garden City, NY: Anchor Books.

HYMES, D.
1974   The Use of Anthropology. *In* Reinventing Anthropology. Dell Hymes, ed. New York: Vintage.

JAY, R.
1974   Personal and Extrapersonal Vision in Anthropology. *In* Reinventing Anthropology. Dell Hymes, ed. New York: Vintage Books.

KANT, I.
1974   On the Old Saw: That May Be Right in Theory But It Won't Work in Practice. Philadelphia: University of Pennsylvania Press.

MALINOWSKI, B.
1922   Argonauts of the Western Pacific. New York: E. P. Dutton. Reissued Prospect Heights, IL: Waveland Press, 1984.

VOLPE, R.
1975   Behavioral Science Theory in Medical Education. Social Science and Medicine 9:493–499.